12 Lenses I

Diversity
IN
SOUTH
AFRICA

First published in 2021.

ISBN: 978-1-86922-885-9 (Printed)
eISBN: 978-1-86922-886-6 (PDF ebook)

Published by KR Publishing
P O Box 3954
Randburg
2125
Republic of South Africa
Tel: (011) 706-6009
Fax: (011) 706-1127
E-mail: orders@knowres.co.za
Website: www.kr.co.za

Printed and bound: HartWood Digital Printing, 243 Alexandra Avenue, Halfway House, Midrand
Typesetting, layout and design: Cia Joubert, cia@knowres.co.za
Cover design: Marlene De Lorme, marlene@knowres.co.za
Editing and Proofreading: Jennifer Renton, jenniferrenton@live.co.za
Project management: Cia Joubert, cia@knowres.co.za

12 Lenses Into

Diversity
IN
SOUTH
AFRICA

Edited by

Dr. Preeya Daya and Professor Kurt April

publishing

2021

ACKNOWLEDGEMENTS

We are grateful that KR Publishing chose to take on this book project with us. We have been ably supported by their professional team, specifically Wilhelm Crous, Cia Joubert and Tina van der Westhuizen. Thank you Wilhelm for believing in the importance of this body of work, and its contribution to shaping organisational practice, HR practice, sociological practice, leadership practice and the positive outworking of its content in the broader South Africa. We would like to make a special mention of Cia Joubert who has been a tremendous partner for us during the writing and completion of the book. Thank you Cia. We are indeed grateful to all of our contributing authors, who are friends and all academic leaders in their own right, who overcame the challenges of busy schedules as well as challenging work and family responsibilities during the COVID-19 pandemic, while graciously responding to our multiple, demanding requests. We can all be proud of what we have produced together as a result of our passion for a more inclusive and justice-filled South Africa.

Preeya Daya

'We stand on the shoulders of giants'. I honour the contribution of my community in me; the darkest and brightest parts of society that came to be. The love of my parents, grandparents and more, and of course my beautiful children who I so adore. My sisters and friends challenge and nourish, together we create a world where people can flourish. My husband Shamlan is my greatest inspiration, there's never a dull day beside him in a life of exploration.

I dream of a world full of dignity, where respect and acceptance are the values of a community. A society where discrimination and disillusion, are replaced by the appreciation of individuality and Inclusion. Only then will our society be genuinely strong, when we have a place where we all belong.

Kurt April

My wife and life-long partner, Amanda and teenage son Jordan have, and still continue to teach me about the beauty and richness that diversity brings into one's life, when one chooses such an orientation. My only disappointment is that, after 27 years of democracy in South Africa, we are still having to publish and give insights into the challenges facing South Africa through the lenses of diversity and inclusion – specifically 'racism'. My hope in 1994, was that we would have had an eradication of most of its scourge by now, and that my son, his friends (from many backgrounds and countries), and his generation would be living in a much more progressive and inclusive society than we, the adults, have left for them to inherit. I commit to continuing to work at shifting the paradigm for them, and future generations, and thank Amanda and Jordan for continually partnering me on this journey.

Preeya and I, both associated with the Allan Gray Centre for Values-Based Leadership at the University of Cape Town, remain deeply thankful for the Gill Gray and the late Allan Gray's generous endowment so that we could, and can continue to, enjoy the privilege of being able to contribute to the body of knowledge within the discipline of diversity & inclusion, and remain committed to foster our work in some of the areas they, and we, consider important in society and organisations at large.

TABLE OF CONTENTS

ABOUT THE EDITORS

Dr. Preeya Daya

Dr. Preeya Daya is an Academic Director at the Achievement Awards Group and an Executive Director at the Leadership Dialogue. She has a PhD in Business from UCT, and Master's degree in Human Resource Management. Her consulting and research relates to Organisational Behaviour, including Diversity and Inclusion, Employee Engagement, Leadership and Personal Mastery. Preeya teaches on Executive Programmes for the University of Kwazulu Natal and the University of Stellenbosch and she co-convenes a PhD programme in Leadership, Systems Thinking and Complexity at the Durban University of Technology. She also serves as expert faculty for Master Leader, GetSmarter and MasterStart online learning programmes. Preeya was formerly a faculty member at the University of Cape Town's Graduate School of Business following a global career as a Human Resource practitioner.

Preeya is a research associate of the University of Cape Town's Allan Gray Centre for Values-Based Leadership and she serves on the Council for the Durban Chamber of Commerce, as Vice Chair on the Human Resource Forum. Email: preeya@daya.co.za

Prof. Kurt April

Prof. Kurt April is the Endowed Chair & Director of the Allan Gray Centre for Values-Based Leadership, specialising in Leadership, Diversity and Inclusion, at the Graduate School of Business, University of Cape Town. He is also an Orchestrator and Faculty member for Duke CE at Duke University, and Adjunct Faculty member of Saïd Business School, University of Oxford. Previously he was a Research Fellow at Ashridge-Hult Business School; Visiting Professor at London Metropolitan University; Visiting Professor at Rotterdam School of Management, Erasmus University; and Visiting Professor in the Faculty of Economics & Econometrics, University of Amsterdam.

Outside of academia, Kurt is the Managing Partner of LICM Consulting (South Africa); Managing Director: Leadership, Diversity & Inclusion Practice at Oxford Acuity (Singapore); shareholder and Executive Director of Achievement Awards Group (South Africa); as well as Ambassador of the global Unashamedly Ethical movement. He plays a range of roles and consults to many companies and organisations around the globe, having worked in 24 countries. Email: kurt.april@uct.ac.za

ABOUT THE CONTRIBUTORS

Prof. Melissa Steyn

Professor Melissa Steyn has been developing Diversity Studies as a field in Higher Education since she began studying Intercultural and Diversity Studies at UCT in 2001. She is the founding director of the Wits Centre for Diversity Studies (WiCDS), and has held the South African National Chair (SARChI) Chair in Critical Diversity Studies since 2014. She is best known for her publications on whiteness in post-apartheid South Africa. Her MA thesis, written while a Fulbright Scholar at Arizona State University, was published as *Whiteness just isn't what is used to be: White identity in a changing South Africa,* in a series edited by Henry Giroux. It won the 2002 Outstanding Scholarship Award in International and Intercultural Communication from the National Communication Association in the United States.

Melissa was also a recipient of UCT's Distinguished Teacher's Award (2009) and a CHE/HELTASA National Excellence in Teaching Award (2010), and was a Diamond Jubilee Fellow, University of Southampton (2014-2018). In 2013 she was featured as one of Routledge's Sociology Super Authors. Her forthcoming co-edited books include *Decolonizing the Human: Reflections from Africa on Difference and Oppression.* Email: melissa.steyn@wits.ac.za

Kudzaiishe Vanyoro

Kudzaiishe Vanyoro is a Media and Liaison Officer at the Wits Centre for Diversity Studies (WiCDS) and a Critical Diversity Studies (CDS) PhD candidate (WiCDS). His research focuses on resilience and homing strategies among rural queer people in a South African rural town, under the supervision of Professor Melissa Steyn. Kudzaiishe holds an Honour's Degree in Media and Society Studies, and a Master's Degree in Critical Diversity Studies. He was awarded the DST-NRF (The Department of Science and Technology (DST) and the National Research Foundation (NRF)), South African Research Chairs Initiative (SARChI) in Critical Diversity Studies (CDS) for his MA in 2018 and his PhD research in 2020. Kudzaiishe has previously published peer-reviewed articles on gender and sexuality representation online, using Critical Diversity Literacy (CDL) to analyse misogynistic language in two Southern African universities and the politics of nationality in the #ZimShutDown protests. Email: kudzaiishe.vanyoro@wits.ac.za

Prof. Stella Nkomo

Professor Stella Nkomo is a Professor in the Department of Human Resource Management at the University of Pretoria. She holds a PhD in Human Resource Management from the University of Massachusetts in the USA. Her research has focused on diversity, difference, and race and gender in organisations, particularly the exclusion of marginalised voices in management and organisation studies. She is the co-author of the critically acclaimed book, *Our Separate Ways: Black and white women and the struggle for professional identity* published by Harvard Business School Press, and *Courageous Conversations: A Collection of Interviews and Reflections on Responsible Leadership by South African Captains of Industry*, published by Van Schaik Publishers. Stella's research has been published in numerous management journals and edited volumes, and she is currently an Associate Editor for Equality, Diversity & Inclusion: An International Journal. Professor Nkomo has received numerous awards for her scholarly contributions, including the Sage Scholarly Contributions Award (Academy of Management) for her contributions to gender and diversity research in organisations; the Distinguished Woman Scholar in the Social Sciences Award from the Department of Science and Technology, and the International Leadership Association Lifetime Achievement Award. Professor Nkomo is an A-rated South African researcher. Email: stella.nkomo@up.ac.za

Prof. Nasima Carrim

Professor Nasima Carrim is a Professor at the University of Pretoria, a registered Industrial Psychologist, and the Chair for the Diversity and Inclusion interest group at the Society for Industrial and Organisational Psychology of South Africa (SIOPSA). She holds a Doctor of Philosophy degree in Industrial and Organisational Psychology, as well as a Master's degree in Human Resource Management and an Honour's degree in Industrial Psychology. In 2013, she won the Emerald African Management Research Fund Award for her research related to Indian male managers. In 2015 she received the Certificate of Merit for Teaching Excellence and Innovation, and in 2016 she won the Best Junior Researcher in Management Sciences at the University of Pretoria. Her research focuses on gender in management, culture, religion and minorities in the workplace from an intersectionality and identity perspective. Prof. Carrim has published in national and international journals and books, and has presented at various national and international conferences. E-mail: nasima.carrim@up.ac.za

Prof. Anita Bosch

Professor Anita Bosch has more than 20 years' experience in leadership positions, both in the private and higher education sectors. She attained a PhD from the School of Management at the University of Southampton, UK. Anita is a Professor at the University of Stellenbosch Business School, South Africa, and holds the USB Research Chair dedicated to the study of women at work. She is the editor of the annual *Women's Report*, which provides evidence-based insight into women's workplace realities with the aim of bridging the gap between academia and practice. More recently, Anita was twice invited to present on legislative direction regarding the gender pay gap in the South African Parliament. She is a Research Fellow at Vlerick Business School, Belgium, and regularly engages in public forums such as print, online and broadcast media. Email: anita.bosch@usb.ac.za

Dr. Claire Kelly

Dr. Claire Kelly is currently the Faculty Programme Manager: Transformation at Stellenbosch University. She holds a PhD in Psychology (which focused on racial identity and post-apartheid activism) and an MPhil in Diversity Studies (which focused on whiteness and masculinity) from the University of Cape Town (UCT). She has worked in higher education for 15 years in various capacities and has lectured at both undergraduate and postgraduate levels on intercultural communication, race, class, gender and critical diversity literacy. She has conducted research in the areas of transformation in South African organisations, whiteness, masculinity and activism, and has been an independent facilitator for a number of years. Email: clairekelly@sun.ac.za

Prof. Linda Ronnie

Professor Linda Ronnie holds a PhD in Education and Masters degrees in Education and Psychology. She is Professor in Organisational Behaviour and People Management at the School of Management Studies, University of Cape Town and is currently Dean of the Commerce faculty at UCT. Professor Ronnie is the proud recipient of the UCT Distinguished Teacher Award and the inaugural Emerald Case Writing Competition, and has won several best paper awards. Her research focuses on two key themes: organisational behaviour and people management and the pedagogical aspects of management education. Professor Ronnie has published on key topics such as the psychological contract, the intricacies of the employer-employee relationship, diversity, and change management. Email: linda.ronnie@uct.ac.za

Cal Volks

Cal Volks studied Psychology and Drama, graduating from Rhodes University, South Africa, with an MA in 1994. She is currently completing a PhD through La Trobe University in Melbourne. Cal previously worked as Director of the University of Cape Town's HIV and Inclusivity Unit, managing the university's response to sexual health as an issue of identity and inclusivity. Cal currently works as an infertility and reproductive health counsellor at the Victorian Assisted Treatment Authority in Melbourne. Cal has been awarded a La Trobe University scholarship made possible through an Australian Research Council grant. In 2016, she was awarded, together with her colleagues, a research grant by the SASH project run jointly by the respective departments of public health at Brown University, Rhode Island and The University of Cape Town. She was awarded an Erasmus Mundus award in 2012 to visit Freie University in Berlin to collaborate with staff and students undertaking research around HIV/AIDS prevention and support among young people in Southern Africa. Email: c.volks@latrobe.edu.au.

Gabriel Hoosain Khan

Gabriel Hoosain Khan is a queer activist, community development worker and facilitator who specialises in using creative interventions (using art, drama and creative writing) to build grassroots leadership, engage youth, and deal with intersecting social issues. Gabriel currently works as stream leader for inclusivity capacity building at the Office for Inclusivity and Change at the University of Cape Town. Prior to this Gabriel worked as a regional gender adviser at the United Nations World Food Programme, as well as with local and international NGOs. Gabriel has a Master of Arts in Education from the University of the Free State and served as a fellow on the Mandela Washington Fellowship and Facebook Community Leadership Programme. As an early career activist-scholar, Gabriel published a handful of book chapters, journal articles and activist content in the form of facilitation manuals and articles in the popular media. Email: gabriel.khan@uct.ac.za

Dr. Sianne Alves

Dr. Sianne Alves is a scholar-practitioner who has worked nationally in multisectoral partnerships that are dedicated towards preventing and responding to oppression and social justice. Previously, Dr Alves headed up the South African Chapter of an International NGO as a development consultant for government and community organisations. Dr Alves has formed part of the Ministerial Commission for Gender Based Violence in the higher education sector. She was a Senior Reviewer for The European Conference on Education for the International Academic Forum and presented at international conferences as well as many national conferences. Sianne has published seven peer-reviewed articles. Her research area is focusing on the conceptualisation of governance and management systems that amplify the voice and agency of previously marginalised and oppressed communities. Currently, Sianne is the Director of the Office for Inclusivity & Change (OIC) which is a unit that provides prevention and education on issues of race, disability, gender and anti-oppression. Email: sianne.alves@uct.ac.za

Prof. Gubela Mji

Professor Gubela Mji is the Director and a Professor at the Centre for Disability and Rehabilitation Studies at the Global Health Department in the Faculty of Medicine and Health Sciences at Stellenbosch University, South Africa. Originally a physiotherapist by profession, she has translated this into disability and rehabilitation studies. As the Director of the Centre, she leads a vibrant division which aim to improve the quality of life and level of community integration of people with disabilities. An NRF-rated researcher, Prof. Mji has published numerous articles in prestigious accredited journals and chapters in books. Her work focuses on disability, indigenous knowledge systems and rural health. She recently edited the book: *The walk without limbs: Searching for indigenous health knowledge in rural South Africa*. Email: gumji@sun.ac.za

Dr. Chioma Ohajunwa

Dr. Chioma Ohajunwa's professional training is in the field of special education. She has worked with children and youth with intellectual disabilities in communities within Nigeria and Liberia, gathering intimate knowledge about disability within the African context. Dr. Ohajunwa holds an MPhil in Disability Studies from the University of Cape Town, where she explored the inclusion of disability as a cross-cutting issue within the curriculum, and holds a PhD in Health Sciences Rehabilitation. Her current research is a critical analysis of the concept of inclusive education in three regions in Africa. Her research interests are in the areas of disability education; well-being and spirituality; inclusive policy development; indigenous knowledge systems; and transdisciplinarity. Dr. Ohajunwa convenes the Post-Graduate Diploma and Master's course on Disability Policy Analysis, and lectures on Human Rights and Indigenous Knowledge Systems in the MBChB Programme at the Faculty of Medicine and Health Sciences. She has also published articles and book chapters related to her areas of interest, and is involved in collaborative work with the Faculty of Theology and Faculty of Education at Stellenbosch University. Dr. Ohajunwa is a member of Advancing Disability Inclusive Research in Africa (ADIRA) and the African Network for Evidence-to-Action on Disability (AfriNEAD), which encourage disability-focused research within Africa. Email: chioma@sun.ac.za

Prof. Dion Forster

Professor Dion Forster is the Director of the Beyers Naudé Centre for Public Theology, an Associate Professor in Ethics, and the Chair of the Department of Systematic Theology and Ecclesiology in the Faculty of Theology at Stellenbosch University. His research is in Philosophical Ethics, with a primary focus on issues of human dignity in relation to political ethics and economic ethics in South Africa. Dion holds two PhD degrees, the first of which was in Systematic Theology and Science, which focused on notions of intersubjective identity in relation to African social identity ethics and cognitive neuroscience. His second PhD focused on the politics of forgiveness in South Africa. He has been a visiting professor at Duke Divinity School, the Humboldt University of Berlin, the University of Gothenburg, Sárostpataki Református Teológiai Akadémia, and Wesley House, University of Cambridge. He is an Associate of the Allan Gray Centre for Values-Based Leadership at the Graduate School of Business, University of Cape Town, and a Research Fellow of Wesley House, University of Cambridge. He is the author or editor of 13 books and numerous scholarly articles, and serves as an Editor for numerous international scholarly journals. Dion consults for numerous civil society organisations and companies on ethical issues, serves on the board of Unashamedly Ethical, and is a Member of the Expert Network for the World Economic Forum. Email: dionforster@sun.ac.za

Chapter 1

DIVERSITY IN SOUTH AFRICA: LOCATING THE DISCUSSION

Dr. Preeya Daya and Prof. Kurt April

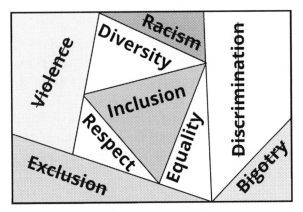

INTRODUCTION

South Africa, the land of opportunity. With glorious weather, geographically diverse topography, a vast array of flora and fauna; South Africa is unarguably one of the most beautiful places in the world to live. Moreover, it boasts a culturally rich society descendant from many countries and ethnicities around the globe.

The country's Achilles heel is the pervasive inequality that divides its 59 million inhabitants. Although Apartheid has formally been over for 27 years, its divisive nature still pervades daily life for most South Africans. Sadly, the country's Gini coefficient, which measures the financial difference between the rich and the poor, remains one of the highest in the world at 0.63[1], where 71% of the country's wealth is held by 10% of the richest South Africans.[2] The number of poor people continues to grow as the faltering economy fails to provide sufficient growth incentives, and unemployment fluctuates between 23% and 30%.[3] Education inequalities remain prevalent with a 50% school dropout rate, leaving large proportions of South Africans illiterate and innumerate.[4] About 3.6 million South Africans live in informal settlements, without proper housing, sanitation and water.[5]

---

1   The World Bank, 2020.
2   Ibid.
3   Stats SA, 2020.
4   Spaull, 2013.
5   Socio-Economic Rights Institute of South Africa, 2018.

Marches and strikes over unfair pay, unjust treatment, unequal pay and unfair discrimination haunt day-to-day life. South African society has become competent in navigating around these 'inconveniences', and is now skilled in dealing with these 'disruptions'. We dismiss our individual roles in the orchestra, blaming leadership and corruption, many of us no longer even hearing the screams of anger, frustration and sadness that pervade many disadvantaged groups and communities.

What does this have to do with diversity?

In South Africa, diversity is not seen as the valuing of unique individual difference, but rather as a proxy for dealing with past injustices. Apartheid divided the country by race, and legislation such as the Employment Equity Act, Broad-Based Black Economic Empowerment and other race-based quotas have drawn lines in our society to classify disadvantage as a means to rectify it. We use terms such as 'disadvantaged' and 'Black' interchangeably; equally, 'White' and 'entitled' are synonymous. This language is problematic because it limits discussions beyond assumptions, stereotypes, prejudice and discrimination. It keeps us locked in historically divided pockets; separate, but 'safe' from hurt, shame, blame and judgement.

What is diversity about, really?

Diversity is the recognition of difference. For individuals, these experiences are borne from visible or observable attributes such as race or ethnic background, age and gender *and* from less visible or underlying attributes such as education, technical abilities, functional background, tenure in an organisation, socioeconomic background, personality characteristics, values, belief systems and so much more.[6] These diverse traits 'intersect' differently for each of us and distinguish us as unique individuals. The concept of individuality is often lost as we are categorized by aspects or constructions of our identities and differences such as race, gender or age.[7]

While diversity relates to the rich intersectionality of our visible and underlying attributes, inclusion is an experience that relates to the respectful acceptance and valuing of one another's differences.[8] This experience allows us to show up authentically, as we are, without a façade required to 'fit in'. This builds confidence and allows us to thrive as individuals. In these contexts, individual differences are celebrated, and people are respected and treated with dignity. In group contexts such as schools or teams, inclusion manifests as 'belonging', where individual difference has currency and is respected and celebrated.[9]

---

6   Milliken, Martins, 1996.

7   April, Ephraim & Peters, 2012; Hearn & Louvrier, 2015.

8   P. Daya, 2014.

9   Wray, Hellenberg & Jansen, 2018.

The reward of authentic belonging manifests in a number of ways. Collectively, our diversity of thought contributes ideas and insights to problem-solving and decision-making, which increases the innovative capability of our teams.[10] It also goes without saying that spaces that value the unique contribution of every person are likely to benefit from high engagement and retention, which in turn leads to high commitment, participation, collaboration and performance.[11] In heterogenous spaces where diversity is present but not valued, diversity benefits are compromised by conflict caused by misaligned values, priorities, and communication styles.[12]

Is South Africa unique?

Discrimination, prejudice, bias and privilege are global constructs. Last year saw civil unrest in the USA with 'Black Lives Matter' campaigns. In India, caste discrimination is still prevalent, and in numerous countries, including 37 African countries[13], it is illegal to be in same-sex relationships. France's culture of religious irreverence has caused a global backlash in their relations and trade with Muslim countries.

South Africa's strength is the Bill of Rights enshrined the Constitution, which recognises the right of every person to be treated with respect and dignity, and protects their right to be treated equally. It prohibits discrimination on the grounds of race, gender, sex, marital status, ethnic or social origin, colour, sexual orientation, age, disability, religion, conscience, belief, culture, language and birth, among others. The legislation is further extended by anti-discrimination and equality laws, such as the Employment Equity Act and the Promotion of Equality and Prevention of Unfair Discrimination Act.

This legislation has created fertile soil for the principles of equality, but a gap remains between policy and practice.[14, 15] Although South Africa was the 5th country globally to legislate same-sex marriage in 2006, the LGBTQIA+ community continues to face violence and discrimination.[16] Similarly, while our parliament is one of few in the world to be constituted by 50% women, gender-based violence has never been more prevalent.[17] We are a country of polarity; progressive legislation that is hampered by weak implementation and even poorer enforcement. Once again, this is driven by a lack of access to quality education and pervasive poverty, which places issues such as fairness and equality second to safety and other survival needs.

---

10 Mangelsdorf, 2018.

11 Nair & Vohra, 2015.

12 Post, De Lia, DiTomaso, Tirpak & Borwankar, 2009.

13 Sutherland, Roberts & Gabriel, 2016.

14 Afrobarometer, 2019.

15 De Vos, 2013.

16 Sutherland, Roberts & Gabriel, 2016.

17 Afrobarometer, 2019.

The scale of the problem in South Africa is another key factor hampering progress on these key issues. Leading diversity in many countries involves bringing voice to minority concerns. At the close of Apartheid in South Africa (1994) 76% of the population were Black African, 11% were White, 9% were Coloured/Camissa, 3% were Indian/Asian, and 1% were unspecified.[18] If we consider historical disadvantage, this means that approximately 89% of the country were subjugated under White minority rule. Although many people have called for South Africans to leave Apartheid in the past, it is ignorant to pretend that the systemic consequences of this period are not pervasive. Deep psychological scars are prevalent, as are the social and financial injustices imbedded during this period, including the unequal ownership of land and the pervasive cycle of poverty brought about by lack of education.

Is equality a dream? Where do we start?

While is it important to recognise the systemic consequences of Apartheid as historic context, bias for action is based on the present and should not be clouded by historical baggage. While context provides a framing, baggage remains an excuse for inaction or a pardon for negative behaviour such as stereotypes and discrimination. Baggage manifests in the form of mental models, ideas and ideologies that are passed down over generations, which are often normalised in schools, organisations and communities. These are often left unchallenged due to the patriarchal nature of many South African cultures. The complexity is that these ideologies have become part of our identity, so the notion of challenging these constructs requires deep introspection.

The conversation about where we should start begins with identifying our individual agency, which is understanding that individual action enables or disables collective influence or change. To drive community and societal change, every person (including you and me) needs to take responsibility for their role in this journey. This means learning to pay attention to our own unconscious biases and blind spots, identifying our points of denial and resistance, and checking our willingness to change, or our curiosity to understand a different perspective.

What is this book about?

This book presents 12 thought-provoking chapters from academic leaders and is intended to promote thought and discussion on these topics. This book is not about blame and shame, and it is not a tool for humiliation; its intention is to facilitate constructive dialogue and open discussion on these important issues. It is evident that South Africa is becoming increasingly violent and aggressive in dealing with diversity-related issues. This violence is escalating because people are angry and there are few safe places where

---

18 StatsSA, 2000.

these discussions can be aired. As such, little progress is being made in dealing with the issues that cause hurt, anger, fear and all the other negative behaviours which ultimately manifest as violence. There is a need to bring voice to these issues, not only at a legislative level, but across every level and in all contexts.

Introducing the chapters in this book

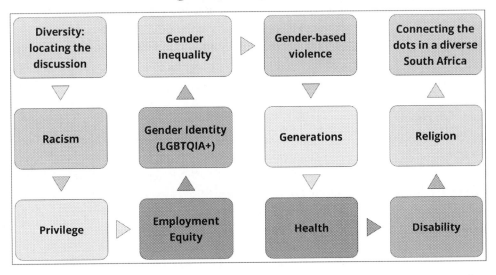

Chapter 2, The Narratives of Racism in South Africa, addresses the ongoing race narratives in South Africa – the ones that no longer have relevance, the ones that persist, the ones that continue to traumatise, the ones that died out and have been reignited, the ones that have changed and are still changing, and the ones that give us hope as a nation. Race and racism remain pertinent to all aspects of South African lives because there is no aspect of individual-, social- or organisational life in the country that is not political. The chapter initially differentiates 'race' from 'ethnicity', debunks genetic links to race, and contextualises its continued usage in South Africa. Thereafter, it describes the many ongoing race narratives in this country and unpacks a few of the contemporary and critical ones, while drawing from many of the broader narratives. Insights and discussions on *Race reconciliation and race reparations, Eurocentric knowledge production to decolonisation, Forms of aggression to microaggressions*, and *Atypicality and the psychology of racism* are enriched by the life history narratives and experiences of a number of research participants.

Chapter 3 is a critical reflection on privilege and complicity in South Africa. In times when formerly oppressed people speak of their oppression and oppressors, it is seldom that these individuals will come out and claim responsibility. Those who benefit from the exploitation of others may either claim ignorance or state that they are not directly responsible, even though they are beneficiaries of said exploitation. This chapter seeks to outline critical reflections on privilege and complicity in South Africa. In the end, the authors hope to contribute to existing knowledge that calls out privilege as a normalised phenomenon of modern societies. The chapter first contextualises privilege in South Africa through a brief account of how neoliberalism, ignorance and complicity maintain privilege and exacerbate poverty. It then proceeds to outline how intersectionality, kyriarchy and "the abyssal line" frameworks can be used to contextualise nuances of privilege in South Africa, before proposing a "proximity to privilege scale" as a tool to demonstrate the 'distance' between the privileged and the disadvantaged under specific power systems. In conclusion, the chapter shows how critical it is for privileged people to adopt both a responsible and empathetic consciousness to understanding that their positionality is maintained at the expense of others.

Chapter 4, reviews the progress of Employment Equity Legislation in organisations between 1999 and 2020. The Employment Equity legislation was introduced in 1998 to address racial imbalances and unfair discrimination in the South African workplace. When the Act was introduced in 1998, historically disadvantaged individuals made up 88% of our population, but collectively constituted just 13% of top management positions. Women constituted 45% of our working population but saw only 12% representation at top management.

The research found that there has been slow progress with respect to the progression of gender and particularly race representation since the legislation was introduced. In top management, White men and women remain the most prevalent at 66%, while Black Africans constitute 15% of positions, 5% less than in 2010. Senior management follows a similar pattern of representation, but at 43% representation, Black Africans now constitute the majority at the Professionally Qualified level. It is concerning that unfair discrimination, including issues of covert discrimination and unequal pay, remain prevalent. Inclusion remains evasive, suggesting that, for many, Employment Equity remains transactional for the purposes of legislative compliance instead of a systemic intervention aimed at driving transformation.

Chapter 5 focuses on gender identity and transformation in South Africa. Gender inequality was a major feature of Apartheid that resulted in the marginalisation of all women, but particularly African, Coloured and Indian women, who were also subjected to racial oppression. Hence, Apartheid was not just a system based on racism but also patriarchy, resulting in a gendered racial order. These two major systems of domination created different lived experiences for men and women, as well as particular meanings of femininity and masculinity in South Africa. At the same time, these systems stigmatised and oppressed other gender identities, including gays and lesbians. Because of this history, gender transformation is a difficult, complex undertaking which may help explain why progress has been slow.

Chapter 6, Gender inequality at work, introduces and debates commonly held assumptions about the inclusion of women at work in South Africa, and provides key definitions about gender concepts which are useful to researchers wishing to frame their studies. Gender in the binary is positioned against a backdrop of broader gender concepts, and definitions of equality, equity and intersectionality are provided in the context of gender equality. The rest of the chapter addresses complex topical questions that shape concerns about managing issues related to women in the workplace. An overview of the status of workplace gender equality in South Africa is provided, followed by a debunking of the myth that South Africa does not have enough qualified women to achieve parity in numbers. Other questions explore the gender pay gap, why employers have negative assumptions about care, whether women can be leaders in African culture, whether women should marry if they are serious about their careers, and what gender equality at work would be like, if it were attained. The chapter concludes with recommendations about future progress in attaining gender equality at work.

Chapter 7, explores the response *to gender-based violence in South Africa by higher education.* South Africa has one of the highest incidences of gender-based violence (GBV) in the world, costing the country almost R45 billion per year. Although significant policy and implementation gaps exist, one of the main reasons for this is South African society's (and institutions') continued investment in patriarchy and the pervasiveness of rape culture. However, the higher-education sector has seen relatively significant progress in addressing GBV in the last five years. This chapter asks what it is about the higher education sector that has enabled it to make this progress, and what we can learn from this. It suggests that the key to this relative success lies with recent feminist activism by students, which has provided important analytic proficiency, public pressure and methodologies for stakeholder engagement to advance the struggle against GBV in our institutions of higher learning.

Chapter 8 on generational diversity in the workplace explores the ways in which South African organisations across all sectors can address the challenges of a multi-generational workforce, accommodate the unique needs of employees of different ages, and embrace generational diversity overall. The shared experiences and values that define generational cohorts translate to different motivations, goals, and ways of working between generations in the workplace, which affect the people management practices of organisations. In South Africa, the historical events surrounding Apartheid, which shaped the experiences of our Baby Boomers, Generation X and Generation Y in unique ways, have also created additional challenges. The rise of Generation Z in the workforce; with their universally contrasting characteristics; places even greater pressure on organisations to create a culture of inclusion around all dimensions of diversity, including age. In order to remain competitive and secure highly sought-after talent, South African organisations must adopt strategies that create awareness of the unique characteristics of the different generations in organisations, and actively promote collaboration across generational divides.

The mental health of marginalised youth, which is affected by inequity, oppression and intergenerational trauma, is addressed in *Chapter 9*. This chapter focuses on two case studies that emerged from interventions with marginalised youth, which demonstrate that they are able to employ creative methods not typically offered in mainstream mental health services, such as art activism, to address mental health conditions. Critical questions remain about whether these innovations and moments of self-resilience are sustainable beyond the life of a research intervention without structural changes which enable relevant and inclusive health care, however. As facilitators, the authors acknowledge the suitability yet recognise the challenges of employing a Freirean methodology, particularly where mental health is a key focal point of the research enquiry. With the requirement for structural change necessary to sustain the mental health of marginalised young people comes the need for new facilitation skills, which will enable an understanding of what is required from young people as advocates for their own mental health.

Chapter 10, which reflects on disability through the lenses of Ubuntu and human rights, draws on the authors' experiences gained from observing the marginalisation of persons with disabilities (PWDs) in households of indigenous families. PWDs are often marginalised within society, however this chapter argues that PWDs and their families living within rural indigenous contexts are twice marginalised. This occurs on two fronts – marginalisation based on their disability and context, and marginalisation based on their knowledge systems and ways of being. This has the potential to alienate PWDs, impacting on their ability to access various resources and appropriate support for rehabilitation, particularly as related to the concepts of ethics and human rights. This research favours the recognition of Ubuntu as a moral ethic for rehabilitation practice when engaging with persons with disabilities and their families.

Chapter 11, which reflects on religious diversity and social cohesion, highlights the importance of religion for social identity and meaning making among South Africans. It also presents some of the opportunities and challenges that religious convictions, as well as the diversity of beliefs and practices among religious persons, can present in South African society. As with all forms of diversity and inclusion, there are certain strategies that can be considered, and carefully employed, to facilitate constructive and positive engagement among persons with differing beliefs, social practices, and expectations for the freedoms to exercise their beliefs. This chapter proposes two important theoretical frameworks that can serve to enhance the appreciation of religious diversity, deepen people's respect for differences, and encourage responsible engagement across the lines of religious differences. The chapter draws on the findings of a four-year empirical study on religious identity, social identity and social cohesion among South Africans.

Chapter 12 reiterates the call to personal, organisational and collective action to address the persistent discrimination which many people continuously face in their day-to-day interactions. We are reminded that, no matter who you are, every individual faces judgement by others when interacting-in-context, and that such judgement is premised on deep-seated beliefs, normative assumptions, mental models, power differentials, and generational fiction/stories. For the population majority, racism continues to be used as an economic tool, as it has done throughout the centuries, and serves to sustain a number of privileges for a minority of people in the country. Unfortunately, political rights and calls for economic representation in South Africa have not led to significant socio-economic gains for the majority in the country, due mainly to the indifference of those with power and privilege (who continue to act with either indifference, complicity or ignorance) and, as a result, threatens the continuance of our current democracy. Additionally, we learn that prejudice and inequality, even though evident and personally and systemically experienced on a daily basis by ordinary citizens, have been treated largely with indifference by many professions, disciplines and organisations – and that, in the future, this will no longer suffice as ordinary citizens will judge, and withdraw their purchasing power from, these professions and organisations based on their moral and human rights intentions and actions (inclusive of their non-action and lack of public voice on these fronts). The chapter concludes with a call for responsible inclusion from all – individually and organisationally, by ordinary citizens as well as those in positions of power – to draw from the best in our African heritage, the best in our Western heritage and the best in our Eastern heritage, in order to create a future that is desirable for all who live and work in South Africa.

Chapter 2

THE NARRATIVES OF RACISM IN SOUTH AFRICA

Prof. Kurt April

INTRODUCTION

The early promises of a unified South Africa as a rainbow nation after its first democratic election in 1994 and a breakaway from minority rule, has certainly in its delivery, in the main, been forgotten, side-lined, faded or adjusted, 27 years on. A major part of the country's centuries-old colonial history, Apartheid history and post-Apartheid/democratic history have always been intertwined with race. In 1994, the democratically-elected tripartite alliance – the African National Congress (ANC), the Congress of South African Trade Unions (COSATU) and the South African Communist Party (SACP) – introduced legislative measures to eradicate racism. One research participant for this book chapter (P4, Camissa, identifying as female) reflected on the promise:

> "I was so excited that I was finally going to be considered a full human... at work, in the shops, on the road, when travelling... without the accompanying filters through which other people viewed me. I believed that there would be no more racism... I could get any job, if I was qualified for it. I could live anywhere, if I could afford it. I could go to museums and restaurants with other people, if I paid for it. I could openly date and marry people from other races, if I was in love and inclined to do so. The stares would stop. The suspicion would stop. I could stop pretending... I could be me and be accepted for being me".

In addition to scrapping the Apartheid legislation, an extensive policy and legal framework was developed to promote affirmative action in education, employment, sport and other areas of life, including a far-reaching programme of Broad-Based Black Economic Empowerment (B-BBEE).[1] B-BBEE has attempted to move diversity from being

---

1   Durrheim, Mtose & Brown, 2011.

a political ideal to a practical business mandate. The belief in the end of racism in the nation, as well as the promise of a non-racial society, have endured in the minds of many citizens, however researchers and writers have, over the years, highlighted some of the enduring social, political and economic obstacles to the development of a mature, non-racial democracy in South Africa. These include low levels of industrialisation; poor public service delivery; ailing state-owned enterprises; widespread poverty; high levels of unemployment; violence; homelessness; weakened governance structures, particularly at municipality levels; considerable inequality in the distribution of wealth; skewed land ownership; low skills levels of the majority of the population; and a low educational level of large segments of the population.[2, 3, 4, 5, 6, 7] These latter issues are not the substantive focus of this chapter however, as they have been extensively explored and written about in relation to race, and are still being written about by researchers and journalists alike. Instead, this chapter will seek to shine a light on the less-mentioned aspects of racism in South Africa, specifically the changing narratives and therefore outworking of racism, and the resulting psychological and behavioural effects on those who reside in the country.

DEFINING RACE AND RACISM IN CONTEMPORARY SOUTH AFRICA

Du Bois[8] once commented that the widespread modern contempt for Black people is nothing more than a vicious habit of the mind. However, it is difficult to find one single definition of 'race' and 'racism', simply because race categorisation is a social construct and no definition sufficiently captures the pain and destruction it has caused for so many people and societies across the globe. In South Africa, 'Black' is a generic term that incorporates Black Africans, Coloureds/Camissa, Asians and Indians who are South African residents by birth or by descent (these groups are broadly referred to as people of colour in this chapter. Also, individuals who identify as male will be termed just 'male', while those who identify as female, will be termed just 'female'). Racial classification, a carry-over from our Apartheid legacy, is commonplace in South Africa even today – people, consciously and unconsciously, routinely and quite easily, catalogue each other as members of this race and that race, and assume that everyone can be catalogued (and it is right to do so, as it has always been done).

---

2   Statistics South Africa, 2019.

3   Bassier & Woolard, 2018.

4   Alvaredo, Chancel, Piketty, Saez & Zucman, 2018.

5   Geldenhuys, 2015.

6   Leibbrandt, Finn & Woolard, 2012.

7   Gibson & Gouws, 2003.

8   Foner, 1970.

The terms 'race', 'ethnicity' and 'indigeneity' were originally used to refer to marginalised and less powerful groups, linked to migration, colonisation and other kinds of subjugation.[9,10] 'Race' and 'ethnicity' are often used interchangeably.[11, 12] 'Race', however, is a contested scientific and sociological construct[13, 14, 15] – meaning that has been constructed from ideas, beliefs, assumptions and material practices. Many writers separate the terms 'race' and 'ethnicity' to designate 'race' as physical and biological variations such as skin colour, hair texture, body shape or certain facial features[16, 17, 18], and 'ethnicity' as cultural phenomena such as language, religious beliefs, values and dress code.[19] Montagu[20] emphatically claimed that 'race' is a meaningless construct based on unexamined facts and unjustifiable generalisations, and does not realistically define the continuous variations in biology between human beings. 'Ethnicity', as a defining category, was initially employed as a differential term to avoid 'race' and its implications of a discredited 'scientific' racism. Leech[21] asserted that 'ethnicity' is a conventionally used term to describe a group of people with some degree of coherence, common origins and shared experiences.

Prah[22] posited that genetics account for less than half a percent of the characteristics associated with 'race', thus no inferences can be made to cultural and behavioural practices. Notwithstanding this assertion, race is a construct which cannot be ignored in the discourse of South African identity formation and processes of socialisation, by virtue of the fact that the Population Registration Act of South Africa during Apartheid was premised on "racist and segregationist assumptions"[23], and prejudice and discrimination are customary and dominant categories of thought in society.[24]

---

9   Sharma & April, 2013.

10 Gunew, 1997.

11 April & Dharani, 2020.

12 Conley, 2003.

13 Prah, 2002.

14 Daya & April, 2014.

15 April & Josias, 2017.

16 Myeza & April, 2020.

17 Rose, 2004.

18 Valentine, Silver & Twigg, 1999.

19 Balcazar, Balcazar, Ritzler & Keys, 2010.

20 Montagu, 1974.

21 Leech, 1996.

22 Prah, 2002.

23 Adhikari, 2006.

24 Boxill, 2001.

If pushed for categorisation, the author's own preference is for the terms 'ethnicities' or 'racio-ethnic groups'[25], which highlight historico-social experiences and shared social identities. However, given that the formal classifications in the South African workplace are 'race-based' and national data are still captured based on 'race' (in order to address historical imbalances), this term has been used reluctantly in this chapter.

Racism is the enactment of the processes of racialisation. Tinsley-Jones[26] defined racism as: "a system of cultural, institutional, and personal values, beliefs, and actions in which individuals or groups are put at a disadvantage based on [assumed] ethnic or racial characteristics". Even though racism in South Africa started out being defined during colonialism (e.g., no Black person allowed to own arable land) and during Apartheid around more blatant acts (e.g., being forced off a Whites-only beach), modern racism in the country is a lot more covert (e.g., from individuals who endorse egalitarian values and behaviours, but who discriminate in subtle and rationalisable ways, such as supposed colour-blindness).[27, 28] Prejudice, coupled with a lack of trust, can ultimately evolve into racism. P5 (White, male) made the statement that:

> "Black people are just so aggressive... in the way they talk and use their big bodies, particularly when they really want to make a point. They are known to be dangerous... you know this from your research. Right? I don't know how much I can trust them at work, if they can't control their emotions. It's scary. I prefer not to have them on my team, if I had the choice. Things would just be easier."

P6 (White, male) similarly mentioned:

> "I don't see race when I am dealing with other people. I don't see skin colour. I am not like my parents... I did not grow up in that era. In fact, I am very tolerant of other people who are not like me... especially Black people."

Colour blindness denies the lived experiences of other people as it relies on the concept that race-based differences do not matter and ignores the realities of systemic racism. Tolerance, meanwhile, assumes a superiority, unlike true inclusion, i.e., that the person who is doing the tolerating is willing to 'embrace' the other only if they are closer (in look, behaviour and action) to the dominant individual, and do not make that individual feel too uncomfortable. Tolerance is most often the purvey and privilege of liberals, particularly White liberals. Racism is "discrimination by a group against another for the purposes of subjugation or maintaining subjugation. In other words, one cannot be

---

25   Cox & Nkomo, 1990.

26   Tinsley-Jones, 2001, p. 573.

27   Nyoka, 2016.

28   Dovidio, Gaertner & Bachman, 2001, p. 418.

racist unless [she or] he has the power to subjugate".[29] This is a point often missed in current narratives on racism in South Africa.[30] According to Mafeje, "The white liberals are implacably but insidiously opposed to any real change in power relations... While they are prepared to be ruled by somebody else, they reserve the right to reign, i.e., to enjoy general hegemony".[31]

Within the context of the dominant position of certain (mainly Western) ideas and people (White, heterosexual males who wield enormous social and economic power), race, race relations and racism have always been part of organisational life around the globe. These are most often experienced as struggles, strains, strife and conflict – across individual, organisational and systemic levels – with contestations over credibility, individual and group expectations, productivity, access to jobs and opportunities, and career pathways.[32, 33, 34, 35] Richard and Johnson[36], for instance, contended that "...group members who differ from the [dominant economic group] tend to have lower levels of psychological commitment, higher levels of turnover intent, and absenteeism than do [economically dominant] members". In South Africa, even though the majority of its citizens are people of colour, in the workplace – particularly at management and executive levels – people of colour are often a minority in number, but also in ideas and approaches within the dominant Western orientation of most South African businesses. Such dominance, underlined by hegemonic ideology that assumes cultural and biological inferiority, organises, regulates and determines the exploitation and dependence of less-dominant race groups.[37] Racism affects our intentions, emotions, minds, mental health, and even our bodies – it injures us all.

THE NARRATIVES OF RACISM IN SOUTH AFRICA

Why narratives? The concept of narratives is fundamental to the ordering of human psychological and social lives, laced with rich sets of interpretations and meanings, and provides potential meeting points between different stories and lives (self and the other).[38] Just as individuals construct stories of their lived experiences, so too do families, clans, communities, organisations and governments, particularly given the South African contemporary preoccupation with identity, African identity and the deconstruction

29 Biko, 1987, p. 25.
30 Nyoka, 2016, p. 905.
31 Mafeje, 1998, p. 45.
32 April & Syed, 2020.
33 Nkomo, 2009.
34 Byrd, 2007.
35 Takaki, 1979.
36 Richard & Johnson, 2001, p. 185.
37 Koopman, 1998.
38 Angus & McLeod, 2004.

and reconstruction of the modern South African identity, as people grapple with how they want to be known and accepted.[39, 40] The goal of the research underpinning this chapter was to understand how race groups position themselves in racial hierarchies, through the use of symbolic, narrated boundaries. In South Africa, it is interesting how the minority White group, through colonisation and Apartheid, constructed 'mainstream narratives' in order to assert superiority and power over other groups. The Apartheid narratives, with the accompanying actions of politicians, businesses and ordinary White citizens, were both purposeful and powerful in ensuring the subjugation of the majority population (people of colour). As modern day South African citizens come to terms with their ongoing oppression and inability to rise above the enduring colonial/Apartheid narratives, they are forced to turn to the uncritiqued discourses that shape their lives. Outside of academic halls, these appear to only ever be questioned and challenged by ordinary citizens during major crises or disasters in the country, such as publicly visible gender-based violence cases, Black Lives Matter protests, anti-White monopoly capital movements, calls for land appropriation without compensation, Rhodes Must Fall movements, Fees Must Fall movements, organisational blunders such as the use of only white mannequins at H&M, the recent hair advert debacle with Clicks-TREsemme and Dis-Chem's blackface mannequin, as well as the Covid-19 pandemic. It is during times like these that race and racism rightfully receive analytic attention, and important questions are asked: Who created the systems we take for granted? Should we continue with the systems as they are, or are they up for challenge and change? What narratives support the systems which we are subjected to daily? Who is deemed credible in the systems and their narratives? Why do they continue to be credible? What cultural and political discourses do they draw on? Who were the race narratives constructed for, and who benefits most from them? What were the original purposes of these narratives? Why have we been taking the narratives for granted? Should we continue to take them for granted? Which systems and narratives should we deconstruct? What context-specific narratives do we want to construct? What are the more aspirational narratives for us today? The narratives of race and racism in South Africa have been evolutionary in that sense, and have been continuously shifting, albeit slowly. I will shine a light on a few of the contemporary narratives in the country.

RACE RECONCILIATION AND RACE REPARATIONS

Just prior to, during, and shortly after the 1994 transition from a segregated country to a democratic republic, the dominant narrative was one of reconciliation between the races. All people of colour in the country, despite their pain and loss as a result of over 40 years of Apartheid and centuries-long colonial oppression and marginalisation, had to calm their feelings of anger toward the privileged White minority, and instead allow

---

39 Riessman & Speedy, 2007.
40 Holstein & Gubrium, 2000.

for some to come clean about their ill-gotten deeds, actions and gains during Apartheid (without any consequences). People of colour could only look on, sometimes unable to hold back their tears through structures like the Truth and Reconciliation Commission. Shortly after the 1994 elections, their voices and anger were further stilled among the euphoric changes and theoretical access by previously marginalised citizens; they seemed out of place during the numerous nation-building exercises and sporting events that took place, including the 1995 Rugby World Cup victory, the 1996 Africa Cup of Nations victory, the 2007 Rugby World Cup victory, the 2019 Rugby World Cup victory, the 2019 and 2020 women's COSAFA Cup victories, as well as hosting the Rugby World Cup, FIFA World Cup and Indian Premier League (IPL). Many White people would like racism and talk about racism to be over, without engaging in constructive, reparative acts and implementation. A necessary reorientation, it requires of them to act on the facts and ongoing marginalisation of the country's majority, and to become involved in things that they are not always comfortable or willing to do, i.e., there needs to be a 'willing giving up', particularly on the economic front.

To this day, there appears to be no, unconscious, or little awareness of the privileges which White people still enjoy[41], the lack of competition they enjoyed under Apartheid, as well as the seized land and homes that were taken from people of colour and handed to them (sometimes for a 'market price' and sometimes not) to ensure that they had full access to the country's opportunities and enormous resources and wealth. The toil and labour of underpaid and exploited people of colour in businesses (which were, and still are, largely White-owned) and in White homes (as domestic workers, gardeners, artisans and maintenance personnel) were considered to be 'normal' and as 'how things should be'; still today there is an enduring race confidence in the White population that such racist narratives, and outworking, will continue to be as they have been in the past, and that their lives should be unchanged (an adapted form of normalcy bias[42]).

P12 (African Black, female) recounted:

> "They don't even notice how they were and continue to be privileged... and I am required to just co-exist with their Whiteness. I will no longer provide evidence because they don't want to notice the facts. They have all the proof they need. It's a burden, it's tiring... I am drained from having to continue to be nice with them, and always accommodate them... even the ones who claim to be allies of Black people and appear to embrace progressive political stances."

The majority of White people, though, did not come clean about their actions and inaction during their favoured time in the country, as their gains were largely embroiled

---

41 Rosette & Tost, 2017.
42 Omer & Alon, 1994.

in an erroneous narrative of superior race intelligence and seeming harder work than the majority population. A lack of contact as a result of racial spatial planning and advantageous geographic spreading by the national Apartheid government ensured that the narratives among White people were largely homogenous and did not cater to nor entertain 'other narratives' or the lived experiences of people who were not White. As a result, they mostly felt like it was their 'hard work' and diligence that got them into the social and economic strata which they occupied and continue to occupy, and not skewed policies/laws that kept people of colour from competing with them, financial directives to ensure loans/higher school subsidies for them than for others, preferential jobs, White affirmative action (even for the unskilled Whites, in the railways, post office, police service, power generation, ports authority, telecommunications industries and others), social engineering, and the health/educational opportunities they enjoyed which the majority did not have any access to. P2 (Asian, female) spoke to the privileged assumptions which she encountered in South Africa:

> "Just because I look like them in skin tone, they find it easier to disclose their assumptions about their supposed hard work and justification for their privileges to me... they complain about how everything is focused on Blacks now. As a South Korean, I am very familiar with hard work... but so too is every Black person in this country."

P1 (African Black, male) stated:

> "Yes, they walk and protest with me during Fees Must Fall... and now even with the Black Lives Matter protests. However, their solidarity is insufficient. Some of them continue – strut around as if they have a right. They need to feel their guilt, shame... and they must display some decency. When will they make proper reparations... to uplifting poverty and to make a difference in the lives of people who still remain poor and oppressed? They need to contribute for their illegal, unjust and ill-gotten privileges. I really don't care whether it was their great grandparents that did it, their grandparents who did it, or their parents who did it... I don't care. They are the beneficiaries... still, today. I want them to feel uncomfortable and confronted. They should!"

Subsequently, in South Africa today, the overwhelming feeling by the majority population is that too much was sacrificed in appeasing White people in order to retain their skills and to avoid capital flight in the early days of the country's democracy. Some quarters even went as far as claiming that President Nelson Mandela, at the time the first democratically elected President of the country, and the national ruling executive, were not demanding enough from White businesses, White ownership and White people in general, in terms of reparations for their skewed access and decades-long, White affirmative action and privileges under Apartheid. Many are disgusted that, even though some White people have acted constructively on their guilt and shame from partaking in Apartheid gains and never standing up against one of the world's greatest atrocities, the majority have not – and do not even feel that they should do anything to materially atone for their shame and guilt. Instead they continue to make demands on the country, as if it has let them down because their usual lifestyles, privileges and benefits are no longer the same as before. The denial narrative and continued choice of wilful ignorance by many White people have become intolerable for the majority.

EUROCENTRIC KNOWLEDGE PRODUCTION TO DECOLONISATION

Africa is a continent with a history of colonialism (a tool used to enrich the European world), which ingrained Western forms of knowledge and organisational structures while suppressing African identities, cultures, values and epistemologies.[43] Colonialism and missionaries influenced the creation of new narratives, knowledge and ethnicities in Africa through their provision of community, which filled a void imposed by contextual factors. Such factors consisted of social upheaval and disorientating change, which occurred at various pivotal points in history. Therefore, "while missionaries succeeded in creating ethnicity through the creation of sense-making stories and written language, which forged and defined indigenous groups, colonialism acted as both the cause of, and cure for, cultural disillusionment, prompting people to unite in the quest for much-needed security, protection and economic prosperity".[44] Similarly, religious texts and knowledge were also used to enhance and uphold White narratives in South Africa; "The use of the bible during Apartheid included attempts to legitimise both Apartheid as 'Christian policy' and to condone the (often violent) measures used to enforce the policy."[45] During the struggle and anti-racism years in South Africa, religion continued to be part of South African politics – and it continues to play that role today in modern South Africa, as it has never really been separated from South Africa's identity.[46] Decolonisation is a much-discussed subject in South Africa currently, and we must critically and rigorously look at the instruments of colonisation and the use of Western soft power strategies. Decolonisation, according to Mellet[47], is "the replacing of a systemic plague of conditions, with a 370-year cumulative negative effect on people's lives, with systemic solutions that will continuously keep giving for generations to come… At its core there must be a fundamental paradigm shift in social redress that affects all lives in South Africa in order to achieve real independence and freedom".

---

43 Nkomo, 2015.
44 Sharma & April, 2013, p. 54.
45 Punt, 2009, p. 248.
46 April & Forster, 2020.
47 Mellet, 2020, p. 314.

Referring to the work of Fanon, Freire and Memmi, Pyke[48] wrote that "several anti-colonial writers concerned with the psychological effects of colonialism on the oppressed in North Africa and South America described a 'colonised mentality' marked by a sense of inferiority and a desire to be more like the colonisers". Fanon[49] also noted that "the juxtaposition of the black and white races has resulted in a massive psycho-existential complex". Biko[50] insisted that the continued comparison with Whiteness by people of colour, as well as the resulting loss of self-esteem and self-hate, are unhelpful, and cautioned that South Africans have to start the decoupling with the necessary decolonisation of their individual minds first.

Oelofsen[51] encouraged a deeper understanding of the relationship between the decolonisation of the mind and the decolonisation of the intellectual landscape – the intellectual landscape referring to schooling (primary and secondary schooling), colleges, universities and other institutions of knowledge production. Even though racial segregation in South Africa has been abolished for over two and a half decades now, schools which served predominantly White learners under Apartheid remain functional, constructively imparting cognitive skills, while the majority of those which served African Black learners remain dysfunctional – often unable to impart the necessary numeracy and literacy skills that school learners need to enter college and university to study STEM subjects (which the country desperately needs), and ultimately contribute meaningfully to the developmental economy. The constituencies of these two school systems also remain vastly different, with the historically African Black schools still being racially homogenous (i.e., African Black) and largely poor, while the historically White, Indian and Coloured schools serve a more racially diverse constituency.[52] Irrespective of race, learners who are from middle- and upper-class backgrounds have migrated to formerly Model C and private schools (which are expensive and still dominated by mainly White teachers and majority White learners), hoping to access quality education and the promise of better educational outcomes, in order to get into the better South African universities or to study overseas. P13 (White, female) was open about what she thought racial mixing would do to the quality of her own children's education:

> "Now that there are so many Blacks in my children's former school, I don't know if they are making it easier to pass... to accommodate them, you know. You know what it is like. I don't want my children's education compromised because the teacher must slow down, or not cover everything, because they don't have good educational backgrounds. That is why I moved my kids to a private school."

---

48 Pyke, 2010, p. 551.
49 Fanon, 2008, p. xvi.
50 Millard, 1984.
51 Oelofsen, 2015.
52 Spaull, 2013.

P6 (White, male) was a lot more positive:

> *"For me... I like everyone coming to my son's school now. It looks more like the real South Africa. They are also learning things now that we were not taught... even history has been rewritten. I just want my boy to be able to apply anywhere in the world for tertiary studies, if he wants... it's about opportunities and being able to knock on more doors."*

The role of the community and family are known important contributors to standards of education of learners, however enduring poverty, a lack of quality nutrition, unequal provincial services and the spatial segregation policies of Apartheid have had lasting impacts on the inequality of access to quality education. In order to sustain precarious livelihoods, parents of colour, and their neighbours, have to leave their homes very early in the morning because of the long distances to work and the unreliability of public transport systems, and often return home very late at night, leaving their children to fend for themselves during the day. The lack of infrastructure (e.g. electricity or consistent power, lighting, private study areas in the home, tutoring and libraries); the fact that learners of colour usually live far from good schools (which are situated in expensive neighbourhoods and are thus geographically inaccessible); and inadequate telecommunication facilities (no computers/tablets, no fibre or ADSL lines, patchy cell phone networks, expensive cell phone data costs) in neighbourhoods of colour further embed the inequality in the country.

Communities and their members are thus unable to play their traditional African role of raising the children and future citizens of our country, even though the popular saying that 'It takes a village to raise a child' persists. Even the term 'community' is not neutral because of deep ideological and historical connotations that derive from embedded Apartheid language and practices. Hence, in South Africa, community is often construed in terms of essentialist ideas of race differences in which the identified 'us' is differentiated from the othered 'them'. This may also conjure up illusory notions of homogeneous or unified communities at the expense of the concerns of marginalised groupings within such communities.

P14 (Indian, male) raised the following:

> *"I don't want to bring up my time when I was at school, even though it wasn't that great. My parents were working class people, who really struggled, but there is an assumption in the country that Indians were closer to White... you know, skin tone for some but mainly in privileges and access during Apartheid. Black people think that we had it good... so it is a sensitive issue."*

The South African higher education system remains a colonial outpost up to this day, reproducing hegemonic identities instead of eliminating them.[53] Transformation and epistemological redress cannot be achieved without a reformed tertiary education curriculum, which, in order for it to work effectively for decolonisation through education in specific contexts, will have to be reconstructed, re-examined, reinterpreted, reconsidered, and most importantly, acted on.[54, 55, 56, 57] Universities have a responsibility to orient the minds and lives of students to a richer and fuller understanding of the world, and not just draw on knowledge and perspectives from the West, which has traditionally been the case in South African universities. We need to insist that our students read more widely (through making it required reading in our courses); include literature, art and writers from the African continent and other emerging economies; invite African organisational and community storytellers into our lecture theatres as guest speakers – particularly those speaking to the unique regional and continental challenges we face; celebrate role model African managers and leaders and write/publish case studies on them; encourage our academics to collaborate and research with other African universities; and get our students to travel to other parts of the continent.

P9 (Camissa, male) reflected on his University experience:

"I want to see my challenges of duality and identity struggles reflected in what I am studying. We are not really mentioned in the books and the theory... maybe here and there, but not really. Even the talk among my fellow students is always about African Black and White... we are never mentioned or considered. I feel like I am caught in the middle, and not heard. Never heard."

P10 (Camissa, female) similarly stated:

"When I was studying at varsity, I wanted to see my community's challenges reflected in what I was studying. I was always forced to compare myself to some other standard which was not me. How do you think I must feel after years of doing that?"

In addition to the horrors of grouping and structured, socially-engineered racism, few realise the complicity of disciplines and industries during Apartheid, for instance, the praxis of psychology in establishing and preserving the White, racist, political hegemony

---

53 McKaiser, 2016.
54 Mashabela, 2017, p. 3.
55 Heleta, 2016.
56 Molefe, 2016.
57 Shay, 2016.

and social inequality of the post-colonial country.[58, 59] Stevens[60] stated that: "...psychology did not merely display a lack of commitment to critical reflexivity, but for the most part engaged directly in forms of knowledge production that invariably supported stereotypical notions of race and therefore, also oppressive social relations in South Africa". Over the last two decades, South African scholars of psychology have increasingly critiqued the complicitous relationship of their discipline with regard to race, racism and society's oppressive social conditions and behaviours. Psychology, however, has not been the only discipline or industry which has been quiet on the matter. Similarly, even Africa's knowledge about leadership is largely based on theories the West has provided, starting as far back as the colonial times until today.[61]

Decolonisation, which can be described as economic emancipation as well as liberation from Western knowledge domination, thus remains a priority for many countries in Africa.[62] The central theme of 'decolonising the mind' is to overthrow the stronghold, even the authority, that coloniser traditions and belief systems have over Africans.[63] This, in his view, demands a dismantling of the beliefs and assumptions we hold as 'truths' on an individual level, as families, as communities and in our organisations, and we are encouraged to critically interrogate and critique the systems which uphold them.

In organisational life, for instance, when we strategise ways forward, instead of exclusively drawing on the industrial-economic paradigms of Porter, BCG, McKinsey, Ansoff and the like, we also can turn to strategists and strategic thinking from Kenya, Ghana, Morocco, Nigeria, Tanzania, Egypt, and so forth, as well as locally-based strategists from southern Africa. There needs to be a pride and confidence in our own, contextually-based and relevant knowledge, in our Africanness, and in our local systems of knowledge production. There needs to be an embracing of our African modes of strategising via storytelling, myths, inter-subjectivity, community and communal ideas, engaging local insights from those on the ground, and engaging with communities and customers regularly (and not just C-suite members and executives) where appropriate, in order to enrich our so-called objective-based quantitative approaches. Decolonisation does not mean ignorance of colonising ideas, notions, traditions and structures of power – it simply means a denial of their authority over African thinking and ways of being; a moving away from blind allegiance to them and, in particular, our notions of what and which pathways determine competent leadership.[64]

---

58   Duncan, van Niekerk, de la Rey & Seedat, 2001.
59   Nicholas, 1993.
60   Stevens, 2003, p. 190.
61   Mendelek-Theimann, April & Blass, 2006.
62   Nkomo, 2009.
63   Ibekwe, 1987.
64   Ibekwe, 1987.

Decolonisation is about a state of self-reliance, living in tune with African sufficiency traditions, assertiveness, and self-advancement involving everybody.[65] Mellet[66] asserted that decolonisation cannot simply be about the illusion of power and making the circle bigger to expand the White middle class with a critical mass of Black middle class, marching in tune with the Western world's dominant civilisation and economic paradigms. Most South Africans tend to think of themselves in racial terms first before they think of other aspects of their identity.[67] What South Africa requires is a decolonised orientation, in which we embrace the useful knowledge and systems from our European and Asian heritages, and reorient ourselves to our home and continental heritages, knowledge and systems; we need to embrace a sufficiency and abundance philosophy through redistribution of our knowledge and psychological emancipation, rather than keep Africans hooked on the scarcity modality. People of colour in the country need to rethink and reorient their identities and narratives, and have to come to think about themselves differently in order to act differently and confidently take up more powerful roles in society and in business.

FORMS OF AGGRESSION TO MICROAGGRESSIONS

South Africa, its non-racial Constitution and laws, as well as its citizens, have, in the main, shifted away from being openly aggressive to others who are different to them and desisted from open displays of racism, sexism, ageism and homophobia. However, what currently prevails in South Africa is what Kelley[68] observed in another context: "Subtle and not-so-subtle traces of earlier, virulent racism remains buried in polite language and erudite discourse." Research participants P7 (Black, female), P8 (White, male) and P15 (Black, male) noted respectively:

> "I was told that I am not like the [other Black people], and that I was not lazy nor aggressive. In fact, I was told that I was special... very nice, in fact."

> "Even though I have spent my entire adult life fighting Apartheid, I was told that I don't belong, and that I should 'voetsek' out of the country. I was made to feel that I will never truly be African... even though I was born here, and I am not first generation at all. On one occasion, I was promptly asked to leave a work meeting, because only Africans were being consulted."

> "I couldn't sit around listening to jokes about Black women. As a Black man, it was not funny... and also not acceptable. Who do they think they are? There are no such thing as innocent jokes. It is hurtful and makes it okay for those horrible views to persist."

---

65 Biko, 1987.
66 Mellet, 2020, p. 314-315.
67 Fischer, 2007.
68 Kelley, 2000, p. 214.

Microaggressions and their harmful psychological and behavioural consequences are experienced by all in the South African workplace, however they are disproportionately experienced by people of colour and women (particularly in workplace settings), who suffer the brunt of bias, comments or actions that communicate negative messages about their less dominant group membership. Microaggressions are harder to detect than overt aggressions and discrimination, especially when enacted by the dominant White group (prototypical group), as they are often in positions of power, generally shape the narratives, and are unaware that they are causing harm. Sue[69] defined microaggressions as statements that repeat or affirm stereotypes and disapproval about people of colour, women, the LGBTQI++ community, and other less powerful groups, or subtly demean or express discomfort with their members. Such comments, she explained, also position White, male, heterosexual culture as normal (prototypical) and those who are not that as aberrant or pathological (atypical). She added that microaggressions assume that all less powerful group members are the same, minimise the existence of discrimination against the less powerful, and seek to deny the perpetrator's own bias or minimise real conflict between the dominant culture and less powerful cultures. Sue[70] identified three forms of microaggressions, the first of which is *microassaults*, which are more overt forms of discrimination in which individuals deliberately behave in discriminatory ways but do not intend to offend someone, or they may think that their actions are not noticed or harmful, e.g., a comment like "He throws like a girl" to suggest that someone does not throw well. The second, *microinsults*, are more subtle statements that unintentionally or unconsciously communicate discriminatory messages to members of target groups. P7 (African Black, female) recounted a microinsult she received:

> *"'You speak so well, so articulate', they said... I am always listening for these kind of jibes, and so I not always listening in work meetings... I am not 'present' all of the time. It distracts me from fully concentrating on my work."*

The third, *microinvalidations*, are a form of microaggressions that reject or undermine the lived experiences of a member of a non-dominant group, e.g., earlier in the chapter when P6 (White, male) unconsciously invalidated the daily effects of skin colour for people of colour, when he expressed that he did not see colour when dealing with other race groups. P17 (African Black, female) was told that she was being oversensitive when she brought up being uncomfortable with some of the statements being used at work in relation to her. Research has shown that our bodies are negatively affected by microaggressions, particularly long-term exposure to them, in relation to our motivation, memory and brain executive functioning. In addition, our mental wellbeing is negatively affected in the form of anxiety and depression. Ultimately, unchecked microaggressions in the South African workplace can lead to

---

69 Sue, 2010.
70 Ibid.

psychological withdrawal, damage to the self-esteem and confidence of individuals, workplace disengagement, conflict among colleagues, and workplace resignation.

ATYPICALITY – THE OUTWORKING OF THE PSYCHOLOGY OF RACISM

Oppression is described in psychology as states and processes that include psychological and political components of victimisation, agency and resistance, where power relations produce domination, subordination, and resistance.[71] Very little is known about the actual wellbeing, related to race, of refugees, immigrants and foreign-born nationals in South Africa. Nativism and narrow nationalism can be problematic in contemporary South Africa[72], particularly for those considered to be from 'other race groups'. In one of the most unequal societies in the world, South Africans debate who belongs in the South African narrative, where in the narrative they have a place, and how they may fit into/ not fit into the national narrative. We notice that foreigners are referred to differently in the main – a form of communicative discrimination: 'expats' is the term mostly used for foreigners from majority-White countries, e.g., from countries in Europe and from North America, and 'immigrant' is the term mostly used for foreigners from majority-Black or majority-Asian counties, e.g., from countries in the rest of Africa or from India, China or South-East Asia. Many foreigners remark about their increased race or ethnicity awareness when first coming to South Africa. P3 (Indian, female) and P11 (Black, female) remarked:

> "I literally didn't know that I was Indian until I arrived in South Africa. It was so weird for me ... an immigrant Indian, I was told. Race is an ingrained marker of identity for most South Africans. You cannot go to a party, a social event, a business function in South Africa without race or race issues coming up at some point. Sometimes it is masked by other words and insinuations... but race lurks in there somewhere."

> "I only became Black once I got here... before that I was just a human in my country of Kenya. And not only was my awareness raised that I was Black, I was also asked about what kind of Black I was... what clan or tribe. Apparently, this was important for others to know."

Also noticeable is how foreigners are seen and which narratives are used when they are spoken about by South Africans, i.e., they are seen through group lenses, without cognisance of the difference nuances. In addition to their race, the intersectional effects between subgroups are examined: How relatively older foreigners experience different kinds of racism to much younger individuals; how differing levels of formal educational

---

71 Prilleltensky, 2003.

72 Mbolo & Mabasa, 2019.

qualifications (and the named institution at which it was achieved) often lead to differing engagement with South African organisations and society at large; how social class affords some foreigners better experiences in the country and more respect/leeway from South Africans than those less resourced or from lower social classes; how conversant a foreigner is in English or one of the other official languages in South Africa and how it allows them to have better access and network a lot better than others (cultural racism); how those with below-average household incomes end up in informal neighbourhoods occupied by South Africans who see them as direct threats to their livelihoods, therefore inflicting the worst racist discriminatory behaviour; and how those with rural backgrounds/ rural worldviews experience much more substantive racist encounters than those who are more urbanised, amongst others. Black African and Asian immigrants typically suffer more and harsher forms of xenophobia and xenophobic violence than White foreign expats in modern day South Africa. In general, foreigners are treated as ethnic and racial strangers, and as disturbances and threats to the narratives indigenous South Africans are trying to create and implement for themselves. Yet racial nationalism and narrow nativism, often experienced as xenophobia by foreigners, are antithetical to our non-racialism ideals as a nation and to our Pan-African aspirations.

Notions of exclusion are deeply rooted and internalised in the psyche of people of colour in South Africa. Colonial and Apartheid racist notions have embedded beliefs in their psyches, such as not being fully human; not being sufficiently civilised; being intellectually challenged; being made for manual labour; not being capable of successfully holding managerial and leadership roles; being lazy; lacking the maturity and emotional control to properly engage with social vices such as alcohol; and White is right – White mannerisms, White accents, White complexions, White cultural orientations and social norms, to name a few. Myeza and April's[73] research revealed that some African Black professionals believe that their success is attributable to the fact that there were not enough Black people to compete for the roles they occupied, rather than the fact that they deserved their roles based on merit or because they were exceptional. Professionals of colour have internalised many of these beliefs and end up believing them to be true[74], as per P15 (African Black male):

> "There is almost no expectation. We are there to make up the numbers. We are there almost like kids. We are there to be seen and not heard. I know that White people have the experience, the professionalism, and they know what they are doing... over many generations, and maybe we will never catch up to them. I don't see many Black people competently doing what they can do right now."

---

73 Myeza & April, 2020.
74 Lowe, 2013.

The South African workplace is not inviting nor accepting of anyone who is not prototypical, particularly in management and leadership positions. Atypical individuals, such as people of colour, require immense mental and emotional fortitude to stay resilient throughout their atypical career journeys. P15 (African Black, male) lamented that:

> *"Every day I have to deal with people who don't want me in those spaces... so when I wake up each morning, I ready myself for battle... yes, battle, because I must be a fighter every day just to stay sane. Every day you have to have your guard up."*

P2 (Asian, female) spoke about the ridicule she endured at her workplace:

> *"I am never sure how seriously I am taken in my Boardroom presentations. I know that my content is good.... and they write that off to me being Asian, and therefore assume that I am naturally gifted with working with numbers. But I hear the sniggers and comments in Afrikaans about how small and cute I am when I walk in. It is never directly told to me ... but I feel like my credibility is undermined because I am Asian, small in frame, and not White and tall like them."*

Racism is still consumed and experienced in complex ways in South Africa within the hegemonic ideology of White power in the world – among people of colour, or even as reverse racism. People of colour report experiencing discrimination from people who look like them and are noted to be from the same racial group, e.g., being closer to the dominant White economic group in skin tone. People of colour who are lighter in skin pigmentation (known as 'yellow-boned') have been shown to get better access to jobs and, on average, rise to greater heights than those with darker pigmentation.[75] Even with its Apartheid history, colourism is still widely practiced in South Africa, in which people of colour enact prejudice against other individuals of colour, typically from the same ethnic or racial group, with darker skin tones. P7 (African Black female) noted that in a number of jobs (including her current one):

> *"I have been penalised for my Blackness... I still am."*

Racial isolation can contribute negatively to the emergence of leaders of colour, with professionals of colour choosing to turn down opportunities where they would be the only person of colour in a work environment. However, even when there are other people of colour in an organisation, some atypical people of colour may still feel isolated. P7 (African Black, female) commented on how she was treated, because she was perceived to be the same, but different:

> *"Other Blacks, my colleagues... they don't invite me to lunch, and also not when they go out at night, or on the weekends. Just because I went to a Model C school and speak*

---

75 Myeza & April, 2020.

English with a slightly different accent, they choose to shun me. They also don't gossip with me. I also want to feel like I belong... like I am part of the community of my own people at work."

P10 (Camissa, female) shared that:

"As a counselling psychologist, I encounter racism on a regular basis... mainly from White clients, and it surprises me every time. Being a person of colour, I have come to almost expect it... still causes a twinge in my stomach. But I have had an African Black client tell me recently that, since the time we have been working together, 18 months, she has been suspicious of me because of my lighter skin and because I am Coloured. While I appreciate her openness in telling me, I still feel a bit distressed. Not only do I have to prove myself to Whites, but I am also having to do that with other people of colour."

Concern amongst people for their own and their children's futures, as well as jealousy towards those seen to be newly enjoying privileges available to them, have been known to result in a victimisation mentality in previously advantaged and affirmed groups. Ironically, this is now expressed by pockets of the White community in South Africa.[76] A lack of trust towards another group of people, for example a different race of people, could develop into paranoia and evolve into claims of reverse racism. P5 (White, male), for example, asserted that:

"As White people, we are experiencing a lot of reverse racism in South Africa now. We are not sure of our futures with affirmative action and B-BBEE, and are unable to get career progression in jobs... mainly government jobs and at state-owned companies. I also feel like Black people can say anything to me, but I have to be very careful in what I say back in response, or even what I say in general."

P13 (White, female) attempted to justify her views on reverse racism:

"I just don't want unqualified opportunists to jump on the bandwagon and benefit from B-BBEE... when there are a lot of qualified and experienced White people who must now step out of the way. It's not right."

P4 (Camissa, female) had her own view to share on claims of reverse racism from White people:

"Our parents had to train the new White recruits during Apartheid... and then the White people became their managers and bosses, because only Whites could have those jobs.

---

76 April & Dharani, 2021t.

Now they don't have White affirmative action anymore, and so they moan about reverse racism. They must just get on with it, like our parents used to."

The apparent shift in *power from* what was previously taken for granted and from one group to another, *power over* resources, *power over* others, and the shift in *power to* affect other people's lives, goals and ideals, is what appears to be concerning for some in modern South Africa. White South Africans are faced with the need to reinterpret their old selves, their old identities, and their old narratives in the light of new knowledge and possibilities in the country. South Africans of colour have to find constructive and inclusive ways of responsibly dealing with their newfound power and create new narratives of hope for all in our diverse and non-racial democracy. This research has shown that power is a concept that is both fluid and dynamic, and has come to possess numerous meanings for different individuals and different groups.

CONCLUSION

Although the socio-political act of liberation began with the advent of our democracy in 1994, the true benefits of the promised non-racial democracy is not yet enjoyed by all. In fact, racism is alive and well in contemporary South Africa, igniting and reigniting its persistent narratives. It is important to understand the narratives in the country, as well as their history. More importantly, each and every one of us need to play our role in the social act of liberation – it is our responsibility to advocate and to raise the voices and consciousness of those who lack power and/or the capacity to do so themselves and, where they cannot, to be their voices. It is also our responsibility to raise the consciousness of those who oppress and disempower, and to continue to do so while respecting the dignity of all. We need to help enable the majority of the country to gain control over the knowledge and knowledge systems which structure their lives, decolonise and decouple knowledge rooted only in Eurocentric thinking, and interrogate the institutions which seek to undermine the lived experiences and local knowledge of all South Africans, and thereby protect the hard fought freedoms of all of our people. We need to call out colour blindness, colourism, stereotypes, sexism and reverse racism whenever we see and encounter it, and we need to help others critically construct new narratives for their lives and their ways of being.

Although organisations must be inclusive in their approaches, we must demand that they put more effort into eradicating the use of the oppressive, Apartheid-era microaggressions and narratives in boardrooms and in formal work engagements. This attack on the psyche and behaviour of people of colour must be swiftly eradicated, with sanctions, through the formulation of appropriate organisational policies and procedures. We must continue the fight to dismantle oppression of every kind, and create social and economic narratives that recognise the humanity of all people who work and reside in South Africa.

KEY TAKEAWAYS

1. Racism remains salient for indigenous South Africans, as well as for foreigners residing and working in South Africa. Racism remains a reality in all aspects of people's lives in modern day South Africa.

2. People of colour remain institutionally marginalised for a number of multi-faceted and multi-dimensional reasons; most are not easy to undo, but it is clearly possible.

3. Decoloniality is characterised by de-linking knowledge rooted solely in Western thinking and Western notions of credibility. South Africans need to wrestle back their pride and confidence in their own context-relevant knowledge and informal and formal systems, through community and wider stakeholder engagement and idiosyncratic ways of engaging others, and institute these in their schooling, colleges and universities, as well as in organisations.

4. Colour blindness and colourism are very different concepts, but both describe individual- and group-adapted strategies to survive within the hegemonic ideology of White patriarchy.

5. Power is tied to control over, and access to, information and resources. A broader distribution of power is essential for the sustainability of our fledgling democracy.

Chapter 3

CRITICAL REFLECTIONS ON PRIVILEGE AND COMPLICITY IN SOUTH AFRICA

Prof. Melissa Steyn and Kudzaiishe Vanyoro

INTRODUCTION

This chapter shows how neoliberalism maintains privilege and complicity and exacerbates poverty in South Africa. It argues that neoliberalism achieves this through its focus on policies that do not fully embrace redistribution, but emphasise individualism and merit as criteria for wealth acquisition. The chapter highlights how the African National Congress-led government has tried to deal with poverty through assistance funds without addressing fully the structural factors that led to the large poverty gap in the country. The chapter also describes how neoliberal individuality and ignorance played out during the Rwandan genocide and xenophobia in South Africa. The chapter goes on to show how complicity and privileged irresponsibility sustain power systems through an outline of how the ignorance contract is an important strategy for those who are implicated in oppression. From there, we grapple with the nuances of privilege by way of explaining the concepts of intersectionality, kyriarchy and the abyssal line. After proposing what is called the "proximity to privilege scale", the chapter concludes with five key takeaways for the reader.

How neoliberalism maintains privilege and exacerbates poverty

In South Africa today, privilege is concealed by neoliberal policies and institutions. While oppressive conditions exist in liberal, democratic societies, they are not explicitly stated as policy but as normal conditions of our major economic, political and cultural institutions.[1]

---

1   Hinson & Bradley, 2006.

Neo-liberalism shoulders property rights which protect White intergenerational wealth amassed through the exploitation of Black people, leading to the further entrenchment of their oppression. As Santos argued, neoliberalism is "Hostile to any kind of progressive social redistribution, that is to say, distribution in favour of the popular classes".[2] Neoliberalism's hostility towards redistribution justifies the accumulation of wealth and the exponential growth of inequality. The result is social fascism, an occurrence characterised by societies that are politically democratic, but at the same time very excluding.[3] While women and men, Whites and Blacks, heterosexuals and homosexuals alike can vote in these societies, the unequal structures of the past hold.

Neoliberalism was adopted by the African National Congress (ANC), with the first democratically elected government in 1994 following the neoliberal economic advice of the World Bank, the International Monetary Fund (IMF), and various Western governments.[4] "One of the most problematic policies implemented during this period was the South African government's abandoning of the principle of access to clean, inexpensive water as a human right, and their turn toward market provision of water."[5] Framed as progress, the burden of privatised basic resources such as water weighed heavily on the poor who could not afford it. The downside of neoliberalism in South Africa was that it seemed to "spread the market into the very life of the poor through the commodification of basic services, and [...] turning of the poor into micro-entrepreneurs relying on microcredit".[6] These micro-finance and other social entrepreneurship endeavours, which place the onus for poverty and underdevelopment on the individual while the state is excused[7], deepen poverty.

In this neoliberal and globalised world, instead of redistribution policies of the welfare state, risk management methods are being used by giving financial or material aid for urgent basic needs.[8] These assistance funds include South Africa's social protection scheme[9], which gives beneficiaries social grants to reduce poverty, improve consumption and welfare, and promote social transformation.[10] This scheme includes the State Old Age Pension, the Disability Grant, the Child Support Grant, the Foster Child Grant and the Care Dependency Grant.[11] "Social grants now reach a quarter of the population and are

2   Santos, 2017, p. 243.
3   Ibid.
4   Nega & Schneider, 2014.
5   Ibid, p. 492
6   Desai, Maharaj & Bond, 2011.
7   Nega & Schneider, 2014.
8   Diker & Türkün, 2013.
9   Patel, 2012.
10 Neves, Samson, van Niekerk, Hlatshwayo & Du Toit, 2009.
11 See Samson, MacQuene & Niekerk, 2005 and Neves, Samson, Niekerk, Hlatshwayo & du Toit, 2009

one of the country's most important poverty reduction instruments."[12] Although social grants successfully reduced the poverty gap between 1993 and 2008, South Africa still has poverty and inequality, which continue to be strongly associated with race, gender, education and space politics.[13]

Other problems, such as the 11% rise in urban poverty and an increase in the number of poor living in households with uneducated people, also occur alongside these developments. This is why differentiated social development strategies that take account of particular local conditions are appropriate in complementing large public assistance programmes of this kind.[14] This stems from the realisation that people's challenges are not singular, but multiple. Patel further reviewed the gendered 1998 Child Support grant which is largely accessed by women.[15] While it is important for addressing the challenges of single mothers, this particular grant reinforces the gender binary of care, further exacerbating the unemployment of women.[16] This is despite the fact that for the social protection scheme to be transformative it should be gender equality conscious.[17] Following Patel, "It cannot be assumed that if women and children are targeted in poverty reduction programs that it will automatically lead to greater gender justice".[18] Welfare provision also propagates new injustices by depriving dependent persons such as the elderly and disabled of their rights and freedom to exercise agency in the employment market.[19]

Failure to think holistically about varying needs leads to the further entrenchment of poverty among the poor. While cash transfers act as an instrument in overcoming income poverty, there is also a need to address the needs of beneficiaries holistically.[20] Further, in some cases, cash transfers are dehumanising. Reliance on them entails, "Being legitimately subject to the often arbitrary and invasive authority of social service providers and other public and private bureaucrats, who enforce rules with which the marginal must comply, and otherwise exercise power over the conditions of her or his life".[21]

By their vulnerability to abuse from both society and state agents, the impoverished person's struggles become multi-layered. Social grants in South Africa also give

---

12 Patel, 2012.

13 Ibid.

14 Ibid.

15 Ibid.

16 Ibid.

17 Sweetman, 2011.

18 Patel, 2012, p. 118.

19 Young, 1988.

20 Patel, 2012.

21 Young, 1988, p. 281.

beneficiaries limited choices on how they prefer to access them. For example, we have witnessed how in South Africa's 2020 COVID-19 state of emergency, social grants have become a health hazard for beneficiaries. While the social grant beneficiaries risk their lives by breaching social distance in the queues for grant collection, those who occupy affluent spaces are not exposed to such risks; their privilege insulates them from risking physical contact while queueing for social grants. In the same vein, a lot of South Africa's media reporting during COVID-19 has shown that social distancing is a luxury that the poor who reside in illegal settlements or rent small rooms for their families cannot afford. All these examples go to show the weaknesses of adopting a one-size-fits-all approach to addressing the impacts of poverty and COVID-19 in South Africa.

This is evidence of neoliberalism's dire consequences, which include the formation of "layers within layers" of disadvantage. For example, one can think of xenophobia in South Africa as a symbol of a crisis within a crisis, where Black people "turn against each other; victims against victims and the oppressed against the oppressed".[22] Xenophobia results from a spillover of citizen opposition to migration and is a by-product of political scapegoating.[23] Nkealah posited that inequality in access to proper housing explains the inevitability of the 2008 xenophobic attacks on immigrants starting in a place like Alexandra Township.[24] Yet privileges such as White privilege, which accounted for the majority of Black people's impoverishment in South Africa through the history of Apartheid, continued unmarked during and after the xenophobic attacks. Writing on xenophobia, Santos commented:

> "Poor South Africans are turning against the immigrants from Nigeria, Mozambique and Zimbabwe. These immigrants, although they have less than 1 per cent of the wealth in South Africa, are victims of racism and xenophobia. The white population makes up 8.4 percent of the population and they have 86 per cent of the wealth in South-Africa. Victims turning against victims."[25]

The table below summarises the number of xenophobic incidents that took place in South Africa between 1994 and 2008.

22 Santos, 2017.
23 Vanyoro, 2019.
24 Nkealah, 2011.
25 Santos, 2017.

Victimisation	Total (1994-2018)	2018 (Alone)
Total number of incidents	529	42
Deaths	309	12
Physical assaults	901	29
Displaced	100,000+	1,145
Shops looted	2,193	139
Threats to safety or property	257	23

Figure 3.1: Xenophobic violence incidents and types of victimisation (1994-2018)[26]

Most of these incidents took place in Black residential areas, between Black South Africans and Black migrants.[27] These dynamics symbolise the "dog eat dog" mentality that neoliberal policies inculcate in South Africans. During xenophobia, the rich are quiet and exist as abstract actors in the minds of impoverished xenophobes. This scenario ensures the preservation of White privilege, through what Steyn termed the "ignorance contract".[28] The ignorance contract is demonstrated in the standing joke about how since democracy one cannot find anyone who supported Apartheid in South Africa.[29] It "... shows how ignorance functions as social regulation through forming subjectivities that are appropriate performers of ignorance".[30] The management of ignorance is, therefore, a technique of control which produces and maintains unequal positionalities.[31] While Steyn coined the term "ignorance contract" in the context of how White hegemony is held in place in South Africa, we use it here more generally to describe how those in positions of race, gender, sexuality and class privilege choose to "unsee" oppression to maintain the status quo by protecting the(ir) centre from scrutiny. It is our "inevitable enmeshment in the social, with all its complex intersectional dynamics, [that] constantly creates, recreates and redraws centres and margins".[32] Through the language of ignorance, disadvantage becomes abstract; "a thing that exists 'somewhere', but never here among us."

The ignorance contract makes visible the fact that xenophobia in Alexandra appears to be an issue that has nothing to do with the rich and/or White people in Sandton, yet it is. Ignorance also shapes the framing of xenophobia in the media as an issue that "has nothing to do with us" but only those who reside in those areas. Ignorance of the

---

26 Mlilo & Misago, 2019, p. 3.
27 Ibid.
28 Steyn, 2012.
29 Ibid.
30 Ibid, p. 9.
31 Ibid.
32 Ibid, p. 387.

spatial disparities that facilitate the resurgence of xenophobia is functional. This can be likened to how in *Murambi, the Book of Bones*, novelist Boubacar Boris Diop hinted that while Rwanda was suffering a genocide, the world was mocking the "barbarism" of Black Rwandans, in between their preoccupation with the 1994 FIFA World Cup. One of Diop's characters in the novel, Michel Serumundo, stated that:

> In my heart of hearts I knew I was wrong. The World Cup was about to begin in the United States. The planet was interested in nothing else. And in any case, whatever happened in Rwanda, it would always be the same old story of blacks beating up on each other. Even Africans would say, during half-time of every match, "They're embarrassing us, they should stop killing each other like that." Then they'll go on to something else. "Did you see that acrobatic flip of Kluivert's?"[33]

The point Serumundo made here is that those in other countries conveniently forgot or ignored that Rwandans were in a time of war and genocide. This is why scholars[34] posit that it is common that when a group of people tastes the lovely fruits of wealth and success, it barely realises the gravity of the oppression of the other. In other words, the privileged groups become complicit.

Complicity and privileged irresponsibility as sustaining power systems

Complicity has become a very important subject in contemporary academic conversations on social justice.[35] A framework of complicity speaks to how individuals' lack of recognition of their privilege is morally inexcusable. Ignorance and complicity employ distancing strategies which allow privileged individuals to be comfortable with their disengagement with issues.[36] Complicit White people, for example, can maintain and reproduce racism while believing themselves to be morally good.[37] Powerful ideological systems assure White people that the suffering of Black people is not their fault or problem. Such views ignore the fact that it is not only individual actions that ensure the privilege of Whites, but organised systemic racist orders relegate racial others to the margins. As a result, White complicity is not reduced to "doing or not doing", but to just being.[38] By existing in a space or "zone of being"[39] where racial privilege exists, one is already complicit.

---

33 Diop, 2000.
34 See Biko, 1981 and Steyn, 2015.
35 See Applebaum, 2007 and Rothberg, 2019.
36 Applebaum, 2007.
37 Ibid.
38 Ibid.
39 Fanon & de Sousa Santos, 2018.

The complicit ones do not only occupy social locations of privilege, but may also occupy "epistemic locations" of privilege.[40] Epistemic locations are knowledge-based spaces that define what the "truth" is in the world. Stoudt, Fox and Fine argued that "privilege is an epistemological standpoint of empirical psychology that has been disguised as objectivity".[41] Such privilege allows individuals or groups to construct their own "objective" knowledge of themselves as innocent in shaping the status quo because that is just "the way things are". The "way things are" is structural injustice which is also collective harm.[42] Privilege points toward the non-voluntary, systematic and unconscious facets of domination[43], hence, Monahan argued that:

> You don't have to actively *do* anything, good or bad, deliberately or accidentally, to be privileged, you need only occupy the privileged category within a *system* of oppression. Likewise, a given privileged agent need not affirm, intend or even recognise his or her advantages to be privileged.[44]

The privileged need to assume some form of responsibility that acknowledges that their positionality results in collective harm. Collective harm is reproduced through cultural, economic and political institutions which exist with or without the intent of the individual who benefits from them. While meritocracy suggests that whatever is "earned" resides outside of privilege and that merit is a legitimate criterion for the rewarding of particular groups or individuals, collective harm speaks to how the space for one to even demonstrate their "excellence" is created through the exclusion of others. This discourse of privilege that results from merit is a part of our societies today.[45] The privileged ones therefore think, "I am what I am today because I earned it through hard work". This obfuscates the fact that their privilege is a result of membership and access to a certain group in society.

Meritocracy also neglects the fact that one's privilege interlocks with the exclusion of others. For example, male privilege, White privilege, class privilege, heterosexual privilege and ability privilege, are all understood in relation to some corresponding mechanism of marginalisation such as sexism, racism, heterosexism, ableism, ageism and so forth.[46] Privileged people are often unable to realise that they pursue their ends in the world because other people are there to serve their needs.[47] For Tronto this is "privileged

---

40 Grosfoguel, 2011.
41 Stoudt, Fox & Fine, 2012.
42 Applebaum, 2007.
43 See Applebaum, 2007 and Monahan, 2014.
44 Monahan, 2014, p. 75.
45 Ibid.
46 Ibid.
47 Bozalek, 2011.

irresponsibility", a term which "alerts us to the fact that those in a position of racial/gendered/generational privilege benefit from and make use of the services of the other, who meets their needs".[48] Those privileged by racial, generational and gendered markers may either not realise or take responsibility for their privilege or the lack of privilege of others.[49] "For example, domestic workers in South Africa service the needs of women and men who can pursue careers and have their houses cleaned and their children looked after."[50] For a lot of people who are served by domestic workers, there is a failure to acknowledge that the domestic worker is servicing the employer's privilege.

These women and men who benefit from the services of the other are the "implicated subjects".[51] Rothberg viewed complicity not as a binary of victim-perpetrator, but as a continuum in which the "implicated subject" experiences the convergences and contradictions of power.[52] This means that the "implicated subject" exercises agency in the positionality they occupy. In the US, for example, the implicated subject is implicated with slavery through economic, political and social advantage acquired through histories of perpetration.[53] "Implicated subjects are morally compromised and most definitely attached—often without their conscious knowledge and in the absence of evil intent—to consequential political and economic dynamics."[54] The implicated subject's complicity is tied to ignorance[55] and their existence involves "[s]ocially constituted ignorance and denial [which] are essential components of implication".[56] With or without knowing it, these dominant groups project their own experience as representative of humanity[57]; they produce unintentional stereotyping and cultural ignorance, which is easily dismissed as non-racist.[58] "Consequently, the difference of women from men, Native Americans or Africans from Europeans, Jews from Christians, homosexuals from heterosexuals, or workers from professionals thus becomes reconstructed as deviance and inferiority."[59] These distinctions form some of the binaries that "colour our political and social imagination".[60]

---

48 Tronto, quoted in Bolazek, 2011, p. 474.
49 Tronto, 1993.
50 Bolazek, 2011, p. 474
51 Rothberg, 2019
52 Ibid.
53 Ibid.
54 Ibid, p. 33.
55 Steyn, 2012.
56 Rothberg, 2019, p. 200.
57 Young, 1988.
58 Applebaum, 2007.
59 Young, 1988, p. 285.
60 Steyn, Tsekwa & McEwen, 2017.

The nuances of privilege: Intersectionality, kyriarchy and the abyssal line

Privilege is, however, not a simple thing to understand. For example, what happens if the "implicated subject" is a White woman who is governed by the rules of patriarchy? Theoretical frameworks such as intersectionality, kyriarchy and "the abyssal line" alert us to the fact that no identity is static or homogenous. Instead, there are always complexities in identities and positionalities; something which we refer to here as the "nuances of privilege". While complicity and ignorance frameworks can help us flesh out how domination is sustained in society, they do not fully account for the complexities of individual privileged identities and how they experience different systems of power. For example, some privileged people do not exist in fixed positions of conviviality with power. Rather, multiple factors impact identity and power, including race, class, gender, ethnicity and sexuality.[61] These need to be unpacked to enable a more critical understanding of privilege.

Privilege operates through the "boundary condition", which is the marking of distinctions between the privileged and others.[62] Boundaries are not only fixed and physical, but they can also be porous and symbolic.[63] "Borders are mechanisms for political projects of group building and consolidation that under certain circumstances can be crossed by some despite rigorous and selective policing."[64] In a study of interracial couples in South Africa, Steyn et al. found that interracial couples (between a Black woman and White man, for example) are a threat to the status quo because they transgress the actively-policed borders of privilege and disadvantage along racial lines.[65] "'Smudging' the lines, as racialized couples do, is a threat to the status quo".[66] We, therefore, need to briefly engage with various theories and experiences that complicate the fixed understandings of privilege and complicity as static.

The theory of intersectionality, coined by Crenshaw[67], acknowledges that people's experiences of life are not shaped by single, but by multiple, categories which make up their subjectivity. Instead of analysing gender, race, class and nation as distinctive social hierarchies, intersectionality analyses how they mutually construct and sustain one another.[68] Building on these insights, feminist theologian Elisabeth Fiorenza developed

---

61 Osborne, 2015.
62 Monahan, 2014
63 Lamont & Molnár, 2002.
64 Steyn, Tsekwa & McEwen, 2017, p. 274.
65 Ibid.
66 Ibid, p 274.
67 Crenshaw, 1990.
68 Collins, 1998.

the concept of *kyriarchy*, which adds understanding to how structural power operates. Fiorenza[69] referred to kyriarchy as a sophisticated pyramidal system in which social and religious structures of super-ordination and sub-ordination, privilege and disadvantage, interlock. Edstrom defined kyriarchy as "multiple systems of oppression interacting without the necessity of one being more fundamental than others".[70] For Osborne, kyriarchy, is "a theory of power that dovetails with intersectionality and describes the power structures intersectionality creates".[71] Kyriarchy also forms part of a critical feminist interpretation that realises the dehumanisation and the survival of women struggling against multiple oppressions.[72] By realising that oppressions are multiple, we are able to (re)imagine how intersecting identity markers influence whether one holds or loses their privilege across space and time.

These nuances are fully captured in Santos' concept of "the abyssal line".[73] In his analysis, Santos described a radical division between metropolitan and colonial social relations:

> The difference between the two sides is that on the metropolitan side we can claim rights, as we are fully human. Conversely, on the colonial side, the exclusion is abyssal, people are sub-human, and therefore have no rights.[74]

Santos' concept is essential for a micro-analysis of social relations in South Africa where extreme inequality means that destitution, hunger and overcrowding can exist right next to affluence.[75] In such a society there is an abyssal line separating the civil, metropolitan way of doing social relations from the violent, colonial way of social relations.[76] An example is when a woman is given a lower salary than her male colleague who does the same job; this is non-abyssal exclusion because it is a form of "exclusion with rights".[77] When this woman goes home and she is raped by her husband, she has crossed the abyssal line; she has lost all her rights and at that point she is no longer fully human.[78] The woman would have entered a space where gender is an important identity marker despite the rights that her class, for example, rewards her outside the home. Santos stated that:

> Women in our societies are often forced to live on the two sides of the line at the same time: they work in the formal sector of the economy as workers with rights

69 Fiorenza, 2013.
70 Edström, 2014.
71 Osborne, 2015.
72 Fiorenza, 1995.
73 Santos, 2017.
74 Ibid, p. 237.
75 Woolard, 2002.
76 Santos, 2017.
77 Ibid, p. 253.
78 Ibid.

(metropolitan sociability); but when they leave work and walk on the streets, ride public transportation or enter their homes they become targets of appropriation and violence (colonial sociability). Thus, these women cross the abyssal line every day.[79]

The concepts of metropolitan sociability and colonial sociability allow us to understand that despite one having their identity shaped by their race, rewards and punishments may shift if that person does not belong to the "right gender". Given a different gender marker, or a context where gender is differently valued, a White person's privilege would be revealed as context-specific. In other words, an alteration of one identity marker is enough to make a difference that makes a difference.[80]

Another example demonstrating the nuances of privilege is that of a rich male Pakistani who owns a spaza shop in a densely populated Black South African township. While this man has financial capital, he has little to no social capital. This means that he is likely to find himself powerless in the face of episodic xenophobic attacks and looting sprees. His financial privilege ceases to matter when the fundamentalisms of nationality are forged against his body and his business. His instances of power and powerlessness are therefore fluid. When he enters the bank he is afforded respectability by his banker, but once he leaves and enters his local community, he may be seen as an alien. Likewise, a Black man can also be powerful in his home but lack power in his workspace among his White male colleagues. Therefore, when people move between spaces, or "cross the abyssal line"[81], the affects, powers, punishments and rewards that they possess shift. Likewise, as Fiorenza's concept of "kyriarchy" shows, there is an interconnected social system in which one might be oppressed or subjugated in one context as a woman within patriarchy, yet could also be privileged within another as a woman of wealth.[82]

Proximity to privilege scale

While it is important to take note of these nuances, it can also be argued that other bodies have, since the beginning of colonialism, been systemically and discursively marked as indefinitely abyssal and without rights. These include women, Black people, people living with disabilities and queer people. These groups of people are no strangers to everyday experiences of dehumanisation and dismemberment. They represent a people who exist in a region of much further proximity from privilege. Gordon defined privilege as a grouping of norms that form an ideal subject who has access to a majority

79 Ibid, p. 253.
80 Steyn, 2015.
81 Santos, 2017.
82 Hanlon, 2014.

of rights.[83] Most of the "goods"[84] associated with human rights are more likely to be found amongst European heterosexual White men, and perhaps least likely to be found with non-European Black queer women. This example is not exhaustive because one can think about how people living with disabilities are also more likely to be dehumanised and excluded.

We therefore propose a "proximity to privilege scale" as a tool through which to abstractly demonstrate the "distance" between the privileged and the disadvantaged under specific power systems. This model considers questions around what 'being' and 'non-being' look like in certain moments. It also leaves room for readers to add other identity markers to the examples offered here. While this proximity to privilege scale is not exhaustive, it seeks to show how different contexts present different entanglements with privilege and complicity.

		Abyssal line	
Privilege ◄—— **Power System**	**Zone of being**	**Zone of non-being**	——► Disadvantage
(West) Eurocentric	European White	Non-European Black
Colonial	European White Educated	Non-educated Non-European Black
White supremacist	White	Indian, Colored, Black
Heteropatriarchal	Heterosexual Man	Homosexual Woman
Christonormative	Christian	Non-Christian
Capital(abl)ist	Capitalist Able-bodied	Non-Capitalist Disabled
Nationalist	Citizen Partisan	Non-citizen Non-partisan

Figure 3.2: Proximity to privilege scale

The scale demonstrates how within a (Western) Eurocentric power system, for example, the non-European and the Black person are further away from privilege. The European White person, on the other hand, is closer to privilege and is therefore complicit in the domination of the other. The space in between privilege (being) and disadvantage (non-being) is the abyssal line. It is a space which represents the porousness of bordering, and demonstrates how people can in some cases cross the abyssal line by acquiring the particular attributes needed to move closer to privilege. At the same time, it also shows fixed traits which cannot be acquired or shed through merit, effort or will, and these include Whiteness and (dis)ability. This means that while some people get to taste privilege in certain contexts, others will never get to experience it in a lifetime.

---

83 Gordon, 2004.
84 Monahan, 2014.

CONCLUSION

This chapter has shown how one mechanism through which privilege is preserved is neoliberalism, which entails complicity. While the tendency is to think of privilege and oppression as singular, these dynamics are multiple and interlocking. Through an exploration of the ignorance contract and a framework of complicity, we can see how privilege does not necessarily require the agency of the privileged to oppress. By "being" in a "zone of being" one is complicit in the entrenchment of privilege. We have also shown the nuances of this complicity by showing how alterations in particular parts of a person's identities can effect a change in their privilege or lack thereof.

The concepts of intersectionality, kyriarchy and the abyssal line have been used to demonstrate some nuances of privilege. At the same time, the chapter has stressed that despite these nuances, some people are systemically and discursively marked in ways that foreclose their possibilities of ever getting to taste what it feels like to have access to many psychological, social and economic rewards. It is critical for privileged people to adopt both responsibility and empathetic consciousness to understand that their positionality is maintained at the expense of others and with their implicit buy-in.

KEY TAKEAWAYS

This chapter proposes five takeaways for readers. The first is that privilege is the overarching determinant of oppression, i.e. privilege comes at the expense of a disadvantaged other. The second takeaway is that complicity and ignorance hold privilege together. This is because by claiming that they are unaware of other peoples' disadvantage, the privileged are essentially endorsing the status quo. This brings in the third takeaway, which is that privilege and disadvantage are interlocking systems. They are phenomena which are not static, but rather dynamic and subject to shift across time and space. As the chapter has shown, women find themselves feeling privileged in some spaces yet disadvantaged in others. Fourth, people living in the "margins of the margins" are endlessly disadvantaged, which means that they are more likely to always be disadvantaged across space and time. These may include people living with disabilities, the poor, black women and queer people, all of which are groups of people whose positionalities always mark out differences that limit access. In cases where a person has a multiplicity of these excluding identity markers, their lived reality is endless dehumanisation. The last takeaway is the need for us to acknowledge our privileged positionalities. This allows us to consider how our privilege thrives on the oppression of others by realising that occupying a dominant positionality leads to implicit buy-in.

Chapter 4

EMPLOYMENT EQUITY LEGISLATION: A REVIEW OF PROGRESS BETWEEN 1999 AND 2020

Dr. Preeya Daya

INTRODUCTION

In 1998 approximately 12% of the South African population were White, yet they constituted 87% of senior and top management positions.[1] Similarly, women constituted 45% of our working population but saw only 12% representation at top management. This imbalance is due primarily to South Africa's Apartheid history (1948-1994), which engineered inequality and large societal divides.

The Employment Equity Act of 1998[2] was enacted to enable the right to equality and human dignity, as outlined in the Bill of Rights enshrined in the 5th South African constitution (1997). Chapter III[3] on Affirmative Action in Employment Equity Act 55 of 1998 provides guidelines to 'equalise' the representation of people from designated groups (Black people, women, and people with disabilities), at all levels in the organisation. This is done through preferential recruitment of 'designated groups', a term used by the Act to describe historically disadvantaged people, including 'Black people', women and people with disabilities.[4] Black people[5] are described as Africans, Coloured and Indians. In this chapter, Black South Africans are referred to as Black Africans (BA), White South Africans as Whites (W), Coloured South Africans (Camissa) as Coloureds (C), and Indian South Africans as Indians (I).

---

1   Department of Labour, 2001.
2   South African Government, 1998.
3   Ibid.
4   Ibid.
5   Ibid.

To this end, the Employment Equity legislation requires that designated companies report annually on their five-year employment equity workforce plan, which is the projected composition of the workplace by race, gender and disability, at all occupational levels (top, senior, professionally qualified, skilled and semi-skilled). The intention is that the workforce represents the demographics of a region as a percentage within all occupational categories in the organisation. For example, if a province is constituted of 70% Black Africans, 10% Whites, 10% Coloureds, 10% Indians, and 45% women, companies operating in that region should represent these ratios across all occupational categories.

Chapter II[6] of the Act relates to the prohibition of unfair discrimination in the workplace on the basis of race, gender, sex, pregnancy, marital status, family responsibility, ethnic or social origin, colour, sexual orientation, age, disability, religion, HIV status, conscience, belief, political opinion, culture, language, a birth or any other arbitrary ground.[7] It refers to all discriminatory practices, including, but not limited to, equal pay, harassment and psychological testing. Updates to the Act were gazetted in January 2014[8] and September 2018[9], and a draft amendment relating to the addition of sector targets was released for discussion in July 2020.[10] While Chapter III on affirmative action relates to designated employers, Chapter II on unfair discrimination relates to 'all employers'.

Responsibility for the Act lies with the Commission for Employment Equity (CEE), a body that was commissioned by the Act, which resides within the structures of the Department of Labour (DOL). They are mandated to provide input to the DOL on codes of good practice, regulations and policies related to the Act. The CEE is appointed every five years and is largely constituted of industry representatives who contribute to the commission on a part-time basis. They release reports annually, which consolidate the information submitted by designated companies that are legally bound to comply with the Act.

The first part of this chapter uses these reports to provide an overview of the progress that companies have made over the last 21 years in transforming the middle, senior and top management of organisations. This is done through the analysis of the first[11], tenth[12] and twentieth[13] Employment Equity reports, which reviewed the 21-year period between 1999 and 2020. The second part of the chapter presents the challenges with employment equity as highlighted by experts in the field.

---

6   Ibid.
7   South African Government, 2018.
8   South African Government, 2013.
9   South African Government, 2018.
10 South African Government, 2020.
11 Department of Labour, 2001.
12 Department of Labour, 2010.
13 Department of Labour, 2020.

Understanding numerical progress (2001-2020)

Economically active population

The economically active population is comprised of people aged 15-65 who are considered to be the working population. Knowing the demographic information of this group is important, because it assists us to understand the scale of the misrepresentation, which helps us to identify our key areas of focus.

This table examines the EAP data reported in the Commission for Employment Equity's (CEE) 2001, 2010 and 2020 reports. The 2001 report reviewed data from 1999-2001, the 2010 report reviewed data from 2009-2010, and the 2020 report reviewed data from 2019-2020.

Table 4.1: Economically active population by race and gender group

	2001	2010			2020		
	Total	Men	Women	Total	Men	Women	Total
(Black) African	76%	39%	34%	73%	43%	36%	79%
Coloured	9%	6%	5%	11%	5.3%	4.4%	10%
Indian	3%	2%	1%	3%	2%	1%	3%
White	12%	7%	6%	13%	5%	4%	9%
TOTAL	100%	54%	46%	100%	55%	45%	100%

Source: Consolidated from Department of Labour[14]

Between 2001 and 2010 there was a 3% decline in the EAP of Black Africans, however this grew by 6% (to 79%) between 2010 and 2020. White EAP grew by 1% between 2001 and 2010, but declined by 4% between 2010 and 2020. The Coloured representation grew by 2% between 2001 and 2010, then declined by 1% between 2010 and 2020. The Indian representation remained stable between 2001 and 2020.

This means that over the 21-year period, the Black African and Coloured EAPs grew, the White EAP shrank, and the Indian EAP remained stable. While the gender balance appears to have been relatively unchanged between 2010 and 2020, the EAP of African females grew by 2%, White females declined by 2%, Coloured females declined by 1%, and Indian female data remained unchanged.

A notable limitation of the EAP as a benchmark measure is that it includes both employed and unemployed people. Unemployment amongst Black Africans is estimated to be about 47%, Coloureds 35%, Indians/Asians 27%, and Whites 13%.[15] These numbers are high,

---

14 Department of Labour, 2001, 2010 & 2020.

15 Statistics South Africa, 2020.

and this, coupled with historically unequal skill level, affects representation at the higher levels of organisations. In 2014, 62% of Whites were reported to be skilled compared to 51% of Indians, 23% of Coloureds and 18% of Black Africans. Further, it is reported that the skill level of Black Africans saw the smallest growth of all race groups between 1994 and 2014. Even more concerning is that the skill level of Black Africans between the ages of 25-34 was reportedly worse in 2014 than in 1994.[16] These statistics are worrying and relate to the concerns raised later in this chapter about the availability of suitably qualified Black African candidates.

Top management analysis

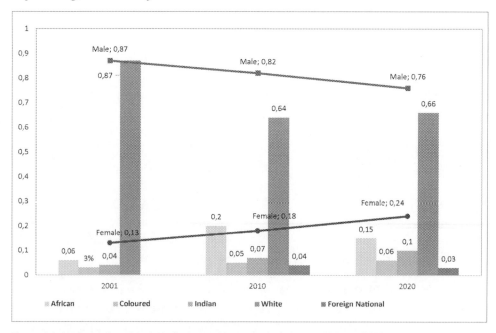

Figure 4.1: Analysis of race and gender in top Management between 2001 and 2020
Source: Consolidated from Department of Labour[17]

Between 2001 and 2020[18], White representation in top management (TM) decreased by 21% (to 66% of TM), Black African representation increased by 9% (to 15% of TM), Coloured representation grew by 3% (to 6% of TM), and Indian representation grew by 6% (to 10% of TM). In terms of gender, the representation of women increased by 11%, bringing the representation of women up to (24% of TM). The representation of foreign nationals was not reported on in 2001, but their representation declined by 1% (to 3% of TM) between 2010 and 2020. Progress on disability has been so negligible over the last 21 years that it is excluded from this analysis.

---

16 Ibid.

17 Department of Labour, 2001, 2010 & 2020.

18 CEE 2001 reviewed 1999-2001 and CEE 2020 reviewed 2019-2020.

The most notable concern in this occupational category relates to the representation of Black Africans, who saw a decline in representation in the ten years preceding 2020, despite a 4% growth in their EAP over the same period. Between 2001 and 2010, there was a 14% increase (to 20% of TM) in the representation of Black Africans. This gain was followed by a 5% decline between 2010 and 2020, which brought the growth over 21 years down by 9% (to 15% of TM). While both Black African males and females declined in the 'all employers' group, the decline was largely felt by Black African men, who saw a 4% decline (to 10% of TM) for 'all employers', and a 2% decline (to 8% of TM) in private industry. Black African females experienced a smaller decline of 1% for 'all employers' (to 5% of TM), and a small increase of 1% (to 4%) in private industry.

The workforce trend analysis (reviewing recruitment, promotion, skill spend and termination) supports these trends, but more research is required to understand the reasons for this deterioration. Black African male recruits declined by 2% to 17% of new recruits, promotions declined by 8% (from 21% of all promotions in 2010 to 13% of all promotions in 2020), and terminations remained high at 13% of the total. Although the terminations of Black African women grew by 2% (to 8% between 2010 and 2020), the recruitment and promotion of Black African females saw 4% growth to 13% and 11% between 2010 and 2020.

White males and females constitute 5% and 4% of our EAP, but constituted 66% of the top management positions for 'all employers' and 70% of the top management positions in 'private industry' in 2020. Between 2001 and 2010, White representation declined by 23% (to 64% of TM), then grew by 2% (to 66% of TM) between 2010 and 2020. White women constitute 13% of TM and White men hold 52% of TM positions. While the promotions and recruitment of White females grew to 14% and 11% in 2020, about 35% of all new recruits and promotions were White men. Although this number appears high, the recruitment and promotion of White men declined by approximately 6% between 2010 and 2020.

The Coloured population constituted 10% of our EAP in 2020, but made up only 6% of top management, and are thus underrepresented in relation to their EAP. Between 2010 and 2020, the representation of Coloured females improved slightly to 2% of TM, but the representation of Coloured men remained relatively stable at 3% of TM.

The Indian EAP remained constant at 3% from 2001 to 2020, but their representation in top management grew from 4% to 10% between 2001 and 2020, which took them to around 2.5 times their EAP. Indian men constitute 7% of TM, and Indian females make up 3% of TM positions.

White women saw a 6% increase (to 24% of TM) between 2010 and 2020. The trends show that the representation of BA females declined by 1% (to 5% of TM) between 2010 and 2020. In contrast, the representation of just White, Indian and Coloured females, grew by 4% (to 13% of TM), 2% (to 3% of TM) and 1% (to 2% of TM) between 2010 and 2020 respectively. White women are three times their EAP at 13% of TM, whilst African women remain grossly underrepresented with respect to their EAP at 5% of TM.

Senior management

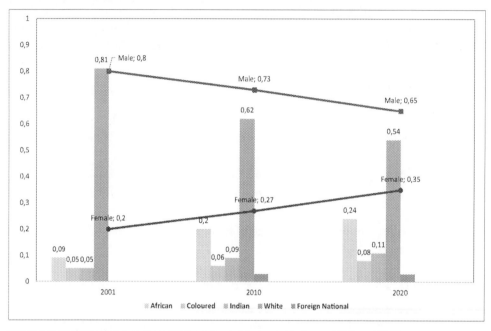

Figure 4.2: Analysis of race and gender in senior management between 2001 and 2020
Source: Consolidated from Department of Labour[19]

The gender balance at senior management (SM) saw a 15% improvement (to 35%) between 2001 and 2020.

Black African representation saw an increase of 15% (to 24% of SM) over the course of the 21 years, but 11% of this growth happened between 2001 and 2010, and 4% between 2010 and 2020 which demonstrates a declining trend amongst the representation of Black Africans. The representation of Black African females grew by 3% (to 6% of TM). Black African males increased by 1% (to 15%) in the 'all employers' category and 2% (to 11%) in 'private industry'. The workplace movement analysis indicates that 30% of new recruits in 2020 were Black African, compared to 47% Whites, 11% Indian, and 8% Coloureds. Promotion figures echo this trend, where 42% were White, 31% Black African, 10% Coloured and 13% Indian. Between 2010 and 2020, the recruitment and promotion of Black Africans, Coloureds and Indians improved slightly, and White numbers declined. For the representation of Black Africans to improve, we need to see a further increase

19 Department of Labour, 2001, 2010 & 2020.

in their recruitment and promotion, as well as gain a deeper understanding of why the termination rates of African males increased.

Coloured representation grew from 5% of SM in 2001 to 8% of SM in 2020. Their growth was steady over the 19-year period, but representation of this group at senior management is 2% short of their EAP at 10%. Between 2010 and 2020, Coloured females saw a 1% growth (to 3% of SM) and the representation of Coloured men increased by 0.4% (to 5% of SM).

Indians represented 11% of SM in 2020. Their representation grew by 4% (to 9% of SM) between 2001 and 2010, and by a further 2% between 2010 and 2020. Indian female representation grew by 2% (to 4% of SM), while the representation of Indian men grew by 1% (to 7% of SM).

White representation declined by 27% (to 54%) between 2001 and 2020. The representation of White men   declined by 10% between 2010 and 2020, to constitute 36% of SM in the 'all employers' category and 40% of 'private organisations'. The representation of White females grew by 3% (to 18% of SM) in the 'all employers' category and by 2% (to 19% of SM) in 'private industry' between 2010 and 2020.

Professionally qualified

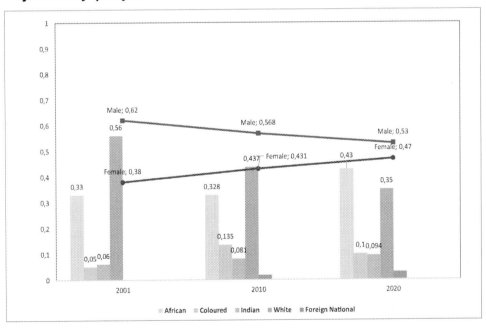

Figure 4.3: Analysis of race and gender in the professionally qualified category between 2001 and 2020
Source: Consolidated from Department of Labour[20]

---

20 Department of Labour, 2001, 2010 & 2020.

In the professionally qualified (PQ) occupational category, Black African representation remained unchanged between 2001 and 2010 (at 33% of PQ), then grew by 10% (to 43% of PQ) between 2010 and 2020. The growth in Black African female representation of 6% (to 22% of PQ) exceeded the 5% (to 21% of PQ) growth of Black African men. Between 2010 and 2020, Black Africans became the dominant population group in this occupational category, overtaking the population of White new recruits which declined to 35% (2020) from 40% (2010). Promotions of Africans increased to 46% (2020) from 40% (2010), while recruitment increased by 10% (to 41% of new recruits) in 2020.

In 'private industry', Coloured representation saw a 2% growth (to 11% of PQ) between 2010 and 2020 for Coloured individuals. In the 'all employers' category, Coloured representation increased by 9% (to 14% of PQ) between 2001 and 2010, then declined by 4% (to 10% of PQ) in 2020. This decline mirrored EAP population trends between 2010 and 2020, when the Coloured EAP dropped from 11% to 9%. In keeping with this pattern, the recruitment and promotion of Coloureds saw a significant decline in this period, and terminations increased.

Indian representation grew by 3% (to 8% of PQ) between 2001 and 2010, and by a further 1% (to 9.5%) in 2020. This growth is attributed to a 1% growth in Indian female representation (to 4% of PQ) for 'all employers' and to 5% in private industry. The Indian male representation declined by 3% (to 4% of PQ) between 2010 and 2020 in private industry, but remained unchanged in the 'all employers' category.

The White population of PQ declined by 21% (to 35%) between 2001 and 2020. Between 2001 and 2010, it declined from 56% to 43%, and dropped further to 35% by 2020. While the representation of both men and women fell in this category, White male representation declined by 10% (to 27% of PQ) in private industry and by 7% (to 20% of PQ) for all employers between 2010 and 2020. White women saw a 2% decline (to 18% of PQ) in private industry and a 1% decline (to 15% of PQ) for all employers between 2010 and 2020.

In terms of gender representativeness, women grew by 4% (to 47% of PQ) between 2010 and 2020.The representation of men declined by 4% (to 53% of PQ). This growth largely came from African and Indian females who grew by 6% (to 22% of PQ) and by 1% (to 4% of PQ) between 2010 and 2020. White female representation in this occupational category declined for both 'all employers' and private industry, and the 1% growth of Coloured females (to 5% of PQ) was limited to private industry.

Reflection on quantitative analysis

Table 4.2: Progress by race and gender (2001 to 2020 and 2010-2020)

	Africans		Coloureds		Indians		Whites		Women	
	2001-2020	2010-2020	2001-2020	2010-2020	2001-2020	2010-2020	2001-2020	2010-2020	2001-2020	2010-2020
Top management	6% (15%) **+9%**	20% (15%) **-5%**	3% (6%) **+3%**	5% (6%) **+1%**	4% (10%) **+6%**	7% (10%) **+3%**	87% (66%) **-21%**	64% (66%) **+2%**	13% (24%) **+11%**	18% (24%) **+6%**
Senior management	9% (24%) **+15%**	20% (24%) **+4%**	5% (8%) **+3%**	6% (8%) **+2%**	5% (11%) **+6%**	9% (11%) **+2%**	81% (54%) **-27%**	62% (54%) **-8%**	20% (35%) **+15%**	27% (35%) **+8%**
Professionally qualified	33% (43%) **+10%**	33% (43%) **+10%**	5% (14%) **+9%**	10% (14%) **-4%**	6% (10%) **+3%**	8% (10%) **+2%**	56% (35%) **-21%**	44% (35%) **-9%**	38% (47%) **+9%**	43% (47%) **+4%**
EAP	79%		10%		3%		9%		45%	

Source: Consolidated from Department of Labour[21]

Table 4.2 presents an overview of the progress by race, gender and occupational category between 2001 and 2020, and 2010 and 2020. The table shows growth over the 21-year period, including growth over the 10 years leading up to 2020. This comparison was made to understand the consistency of the progress over the last 20 years as a means to establish commitment to the aims of the legislation. The first two lines of every column relate to actual numbers in the respective year, and the number in bold reflects the growth/decline.

After 21 years of Employment Equity (2020), White men (53% of TM, 36% of SM) and women (13% of TM,18% of SM) continue to dominate Top Management (66%) and Senior Management (54%) despite declining numbers. While it is interesting to note positive growth at top and senior management over the 21 year period for Black African, Coloureds, Indians and Women, this growth tapers off over the last 10 years suggesting the diminishing of this enthusiastic start for top and senior management change. The representation of Black Africans remains the greatest concern because this representation has declined by 5% over the last 10 years at top management. While Black African representation at senior management has not declined, the growth slowed from 11% to 4% over the last 10 years (ending at 24%). Similar trends can be observed in the Coloured population. Representation is not on par with EAP and growth has slowed down since 2010.

---

21 Department of Labour, 2001, 2020.

Since Indians have reached parity with their EAP, their representation at Top and Senior levels is not concerning. At the Professionally qualified level, Black Africans are racially dominant at 43%, but it is interesting to note that this target was reached in 2010 and has not grown since then. It is also important to note that Black Africans are the only group at this level that has not achieved parity to EAP. The high unemployment in this category might compromise this goal for now. At 47% Women are the dominant group at the Professionally qualified level, signalling an important win for gender.

Table 4.3: Progress by gender (2010 to 2020)

	All men	**All women**	**BAF**	**CF**	**IF**	**WF**
	2010-*2020.*	2010-*2020*	2010-*2020*	2010-*2020*	2010-*2020*	2010-*2020*
Top management	82% *(76%)* **-6%**	18% *(24%)* **+6%**	6% *(5%)* **-1%**	1% *(2%)* **+1%**	1% *(3%)* **+2%**	9% *(13%)* **+4%**
Senior management	73% *(65%)* **-8%**	27% *(35%)* **+8%**	7% *(9%)* **+3%**	2% *(3%)* **+1%**	3% *(4%)* **+1%**	16% *(18%)* **+3%**
Professionally qualified	57% *(53%)* **-4%**	43% *(47%)* **+4%**	16% *(22%)* **+6%**	7% *(5%)* **-2%**	3% *(4%)* **+1%**	16% *(15%)* **-1%**
EAP	**55%**	**45%**	**36%**	**4%**	**1%**	**4%**

Source: Consolidated from Department of Labour[22]

Table 4.3 reflects progress by gender and race between 2010 and 2020. Since gender and population data were not reported in the 2001 CEE report, the 2001 to 2010 period is excluded from the analysis. Once again, the top rows of the cells reflect actual figures of the respective year, followed by the number in bold which reflects the increase/decline between 2010 and 2020. The analysis reveals that gender parity has been achieved at the professionally qualified occupational category, but more work is required at the senior, and particularly top, management levels. Based on misalignment with their EAP, the representation of Black African females needs attention across all management levels, and Coloured female representation needs more attention at the top and senior management levels. White and Indian females have exceeded EAP parity, and have therefore seen the greatest advantage from the Act. Whilst men continue to dominate top and senior management categories, the representation of women has seen more growth than the representation of men, in these categories, between 2010 and 2020. Although this is small progress, it indicates a movement in the right direction.

---

22 Department of Labour, 2001, 2020.

BARRIERS TO IMPROVEMENT

The next section of this chapter presents key concerns and insights regarding the barriers to employment equity in South African organisations. Qualitative interviews were conducted with senior leaders from the Commission for Employment Equity, the Department of Labour, and business, who were selected using purposive sampling.

Substantive equality

Substantive equality is said to "redress disadvantage; address stigma, stereotyping, prejudice, violence; enhance voice and participation; accommodate difference and achieve structural change".[23] Respondents raised concerns about substantive equality, which relates to the right to be treated equally, without discrimination or prejudice. It also refers to our ability to see one another as equal, regardless of whether they are men or women, Black Africans or White. The interviewees asserted that most organisations are not equitable, with one commenting that "people, especially African executives, are recruited into positions where we know they will fail because they don't have the right skillset... They are appointed to prove that they can't do the job. We often do not coach, mentor and support people to build the required competency and confidence, so they leave, depressed".

Further to unequal treatment, structural issues such as unequal pay[24] are still prevalent, and issues relating to workplace harassment are still occurring,[25] and unfair discrimination practices have escalated.[26] Respondents indicated that many organisations have unreasonable working hour requirements that exclude people with family or other demands, and do not create flexible workspaces where all individuals' needs are accommodated.

The inclusion illusion

"Diversity is a fact, inclusion is a choice."[27] Since substantive equality is still in question, workplace inclusion is a delusion. It is not possible to create belonging when staff feel that their dignity has been compromised, or when they feel that they are not valued, accepted and appreciated.

One respondent asserted that we need to make the time and space to have and grow from courageous conversations:

---

23 Fredman, 2016.
24 South African Government, 2013.
25 Department of Labour, 2020.
26 Ibid.
27 Frost, 2014.

"We need to interrogate what is going on in our organisations... the real issue is having those courageous conversations in our organisations. The deep talk about what irks us as people... being honest enough and willing enough to hear somebody say something that is totally unpalatable to me... and giving them the grace and the space to say it and work with it. I think that we are so concerned about spending time to make money and doing the work that we forget that it's in interrogating what and how we do things that can really unearth a lot about productivity... If a person feels excluded... they are not engaged, they only give you what they believe you ought to get for what you give them and the rest they keep to themselves – so they only bring a part of themselves to the work environment." Inclusion affects many things, including diversity of thought[28], which is said to improve the innovative capability of the teams or groups through enhanced creativity and improved problem-solving. Diversity of thought it is enabled by a diverse group with voice.[29] When a member of the group feels undermined, unequal, disrespected or unvalued, it is unlikely that they will make the effort (or have the space) to contribute their views and opinions, which would have enriched the collective insight of the group or team.[30]

Passive privilege and education

As per Steyn and Vanyoro's chapter in this book, the difficulty with privilege is that we are ignorant to our own advantage and take blind comfort in the abstract nature of it, in that it is somewhere out there, but not amongst us. We cannot deal with discrimination and disadvantage if we do not take ownership of our own behaviour.

One respondent mentioned that asking privileged individuals to support employment equity is like asking a turkey to vote for Christmas. She cited the challenge of asking a White business owner to hire an African candidate above their own children or family, who have been groomed for these roles.

> "Yes, I'm creating jobs, but I'm also positioning my daughter to take over. Now someone from a different race needs to take my business to the next level. I don't socialise with this person after work. Why would I trust a stranger to run my business, why would I want to feed someone else? We want to look after our own. This is a profound reality that we are not dealing with as government."

Respondents raised concerns regarding the shortage of suitably qualified African candidates, which they said justified recruitment within other race groups and foreign nationals. In a country where basic education is poor, skill and privilege are linked.[31]

---

28 Post, De Lia, DiTomaso, Tirpak & Borwankar, 2009.
29 Bell, Özbilgin, Beauregard & Sürgevil, 2011.
30 Ibid.
31 Statistics South Africa, 2014.

Compliance attitude

Respondents indicated that many companies pay lip service to employment equity and show low commitment to the genuine transformation of their workplace. They posited that the barrier analysis section within the company report submissions shows superficial analysis of the problems and lacks deep understanding of the challenges the organisations face.

A lack of commitment from executives is seen to be part of the problem. The respondents asserted that employment equity is "delegated" as a mechanism to absolve themselves of problems, and when problems do arise, labour lawyers are hired to intervene with solutions. This demonstrates their disinterest or poor commitment to transformation. To this end, a proposal to update Section 53 of the Act, which promulgates sector targets, has recently been released.[32] This will compel organisations to transform more rapidly, in alignment with these targets. Non-compliance with the Act will result in fines that are a percentage of turnover. A failure to meet targets will imply that the company is unable to meet the requirements for B-BBEE certificates, which will disqualify them from competing for government tenders.

Equal pay for work of equal value

Unequal pay is not a new concern[33], but progress on this issue is deemed to be slow despite the gazetted release of a Code of Good Practice on Equal Pay/Remuneration for Work of Equal Value in 2015[34] and updates to the Act in 2018.[35] Respondents posited that concerns of this matter consume a large proportion of the Commission for Conciliation, Mediation and Arbitration's (CCMA) workload but the employee is often unsuccessful because employers find technicalities to justify the difference in earnings, such as why a higher degree is required for one position but not another, and why therefore this situation warrants different pay. These technical issues are often difficult for employees to refute which means that the behaviour of unequal pay remains prevalent. This is made worse by delays at the Labour Court, or when companies drag out these payment disputes for years, making them difficult for employees with regards to financial and emotional pressure. Respondents indicate that many companies fail to value the importance of equal pay, and do not have frequent remuneration audits. Women are often paid less because they are not seen as primary providers and may be disadvantaged further when they do not receive performance bonuses or increases when on maternity leave.

---

32 South African Government, 2020.

33 Bowmaker-Falconer, Horwitz, Jain & Taggar, 1998.

34 Department of Labour, 2015.

35 South African Government, 2018.

Government structures

Interviewees asserted that the disjointedness within the Department of Labour structures was an important factor inhibiting the progress of Employment Equity in South Africa. The Commission for Employment Equity is an advisory body that was created to advise the Minister of Labour on policies and issues related to employment equity, but they reportedly have little influence on actual practice or policy because even though the structures exist, they are not consulted by the Labour Minister. The CEE oversee the creation of the yearly report, including the company barrier (to effective implementation) analysis. The Inspectorate, which also reports into the Minister, is a separate division to the Commission for Employment Equity, and are responsible for monitoring (and policing) the practice and implementation of all the Department of Labour legislation. Although they interface directly with organisations; mostly to inspect submissions, they don't provide policy input. This reporting structure means that although the Commission for Employment Equity collects and analyses employment equity reports, they do not have the mandate to shift or influence company practice through the inspectors.

Respondents indicated that this would not be a problem if the departments interfaced well, but they asserted that there is almost no communication between the departments, which is worsened by their differing philosophical stances on employment equity. A similar problem is encountered within the CCMA, which reconciles employment disputes. They have deep insight into operational problems such as unequal pay or workplace harassment, but have little input into the legislation. The respondents asserted that these structural and functional silos need to shift to aid robust and meaningful engagement that will guide legislation, policy and practice.

Reflection on qualitative input

This analysis reveals that Employment Equity is not lead by the sincere intention to create inclusive environments, where all difference is respected. This is evidenced by poor commitment to key issues.

The first issue appears to be the ownership of our own bias, prejudice, and privilege. Since bias and prejudice are usually unconscious, this requires ownership, intentionality, and vulnerability. Through this iterative journey of uncovering our blind spots, we create the space to genuinely level the 'playing field' around us, and deliberately work on making organisations equal for everyone. This equality means equal opportunity to be heard, to receive the right information to progress, to have supportive and encouraging management, the right tools and skillset, the right to equal pay and so many other variables that enable fair and just treatment.

Another key issue relates to leadership accountability. It is clear that Employment Equity is nothing more than a legislative mandate for most CEOs, despite the financial penalties that follow non-compliance. This is underpinned by the same ownership issues, but given the importance to the system, this needs to be addressed on a Macro level, beyond the mere signing off of Employment Equity reports. It is essential that we realise that we cannot continue to be consciously or unconsciously burdened by our individual and collective bias, prejudice, privilege, and stereotypes *and* create the equality that is required.

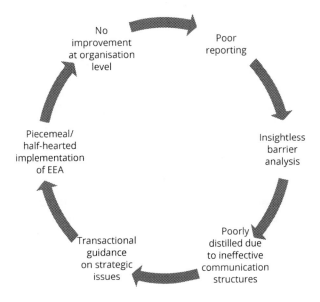

Figure 4.4: Systemic problems in the Employment Equity reporting process.

Figure 4.4 examines the procedural barriers to inclusion. Although many of the points raised above have already been highlighted in research[36], they have not been addressed in practice. This brings into question the commitment from all stakeholders, and/or suggests that we are 'stuck' in a repetitive cycle. Figure 4.4 demonstrates this 'stickiness' in the system, which appears to begin with poor reporting. The CEE reports the quantitative data in yearly reports which describes the trends in the data, but it fails to provide deep insight into the nature of the problems because the barrier analysis data provided by companies, is poor. This missing insight should provide granular information about the challenges organisations face, which should in turn inform the supportive action required by the Department of Labour, Commission for Employment Equity, Inspectorate, CCMA, Commission for Gender Equality, and other stakeholders. This performance gap is further entrenched when the CEE organisational roadshows present high-level trends to organisations; but fail to describe the issues that address fairness, and inclusion of all staff.[37]

---

36 Booysen & Nkomo, 2014.
37 Booysen & Nkomo, 2010.

While the CEE have made a number of revisions to the legislation such as new codes on equal pay and more recently violence in the workplace; slow numerical progress and numerous reports of unfair discrimination at the CCMA suggests that a different or revised approach is required to create equal and fair workplaces.

This revised approach should consider the holistic redesign of the yearly/five yearly Employment Equity reporting process. Part of the problem is that for many organisations this process is not seen as a strategy, it is a yearly admin process that involves 'tricking the books'. If the systems drives/supports a more coherent/ succession-based process, including a mandate for driving fair and inclusive change and the reporting of insightful qualitative/descriptive data, perhaps this trend could change.

This process should close the gap in relation to a supportive 'body' that will assist companies to implement the legislation by providing appropriate guidance on how to eliminate unfair discrimination and create inclusive work environments. Currently the Inspectorate plays the role of supporter and police, which confuses the messages sent to organisations and compromises the safety of a learning environment.

There is also a need to improve the format of feedback. While the CEE report continues to improve with every iteration, these trends fail to provide insight into the barrier analysis presented by organisations in their Employment Equity submissions. This barrier analysis should provide key insight and guide coherent and connected action for all parties. Once the CEE and all related bodies have reliable insights into the nature of the problem, they can use this insight to make recommendations for policy and practice.

CONCLUSION

There has been slow progress with respect to the progression of gender and race representation over the course of the last 21 years. Women have achieved gender parity at the professionally qualified level (47% in 2020) and Black Africans are now the dominant population group in this occupational category (43% in 2020). Despite declining numbers, White men remain the most prevalent at top and senior management followed by White women. Indians have achieved parity to EAP at top, senior and professionally qualified levels. The regression of Black Africans in top management and the slow growth at senior management is concerning due to the gross misalignment with the EAP and warrants further research. There is a need for further reflection on whether the skilled Black African population is able to meet industry skill requirements[38] in terms of the numbers and skillsets, preferably before sector targets are enforced. More research is also required to understand the slow growth in Coloured representation at top and senior management, and the decline at PQ level. The representation of women has seen

---

38 Statistics South Africa, 2014.

encouraging growth at top and senior management over the last 21 years, but this trend has slowed down over the last 10 years. Although disability is a focus in the legislation, progress at all occupational levels remains (embarrassingly) poor in this regard.

There is currently an assumption that non-compliance with the EEA legislation is borne from racism or sexism. Not discounting South Africa's prejudiced history, there is need for us to explore alternative narratives that are blocking the progression of Black Africans and Coloureds into senior and top levels of organisations. This discussion should include perspectives that reach beyond the legislation or challenge the current implementation of the legislation.

Of concern is the application of Section II of the Act, which relates to unfair discrimination. Although the legislation has been updated in this regard, poor implementation of this reflects a poor commitment to transformation. Substantive inequality, including issues of discrimination, privilege and stereotyping, is prevalent, as is unequal pay for work of equal value. Inclusion is an evasive construct given the prevalence of unequal and unfair working conditions in many organisations, and a legislative compliance-driven approach to employment equity continues to compromise sincere efforts to create belonging, high engagement, innovation and diversity of thought. Restrictive structures and inefficient flows of communication within the Department of Labour's organogram minimises the strategic input of the numerous stakeholders involved in the employment equity journey.

This chapter posits that there is value in employment equity legislation, because South African society is vastly unequal and our history suggests that waiting for organic change will not produce a transformed society. That said, the reporting process needs to be revised so that we can tackle issues of unfair discrimination, as it does not address covert but prevalent prejudice and privilege at work. It is suggested that a forum or structure be established to guide and support organisations to refine and improve their practice.

As we reflect on the next steps for employment equity, perhaps a contemporary perspective which considers today's injustice should shape a new version of the Act, recognising but not locating ourselves in past injustice. This might shift blame discussions and facilitate ownership of individual and organisational responses. Academics[39] argue that the designations of 'Black' and 'White' need to be made irrelevant if South Africans are to form a national identity. Some[40] argue that although non-racialism is a central tenant of the South African Constitution, divisive practice is prevalent and is perpetuated through affirmative action and the like. While race has been used as a proxy for past injustice, many of us, including mixed-race or members of the born free[41] generation

---

39 Mekoa, 2019.
40 Brassey, 2019.
41 Mbatha, 2018.

(Black Africans) struggle to locate ourselves in this discussion. Notions of non-binary gender have shifted our gender discussions onto a moving spectrum. Increasingly people are owning the richness of their intersectionality and younger generations do not appreciate limited boxes which confine their individuality. We need to move the conversation towards valuing unique individuals from all backgrounds and creating equality that extends to considering dignity and appreciating individuality. Although hard measures such as the EAP show us the scale of misrepresentation, they fail to guide the action that is required to shift these employment trends. The DOL continues to tighten the legislation with sector targets and the like, but until they tighten their reforms around unfair discrimination, increase leadership accountability of this process, and raise awareness about bias and embedded discrimination, 'Black people'[42] will remain outsiders, even from the inside.

KEY TAKEAWAYS

1. Despite a growing trend, more work needs to be done to increase the representation of Black Africans in top and senior levels. Part of this work relates to a deeper understanding of the individual and organisational issues that prevents their inclusion.

2. Despite declining numbers, White South Africans still constitute more than 50% of top and senior management and constitute the majority of new recruits and promotions at these levels.

3. Legislation is important in setting the agenda for transformation, but execution is currently poor and is not driving the intended results.

4. We need to have frank and honest discussions about the prevalence of unfair discrimination in our organisations, which includes stereotypes, discrimination and prejudice.

5. The representation of women has grown across all occupational categories, however more focus is required on the inclusion of African females.

ACKNOWLEDGEMENTS

I would like to recognise the contribution and valuable insight of senior officials within and related to the Commission for Employment Equity, the Department of Labour and business.

---

42 South African Government, 1998.

Chapter 5

GENDER IDENTITY AND TRANSFORMATION IN SOUTH AFRICA: PAST, PRESENT AND FUTURE

Prof. Stella M. Nkomo and Prof. Nasima M.H. Carrim

History doesn't change the past, but likely it changes the future.[1]

INTRODUCTION

Too often, efforts to transform institutions to achieve diversity and inclusion do not pay attention to the historical shaping of inequality and how it can inform the present. At the same time, the discourse of 'Apartheid fatigue' expresses a desire to not dwell on the past. This history may not be new for many of you reading this chapter, especially those who lived it, yet foregrounding this history may, as the opening quote suggests, inform the future of gender transformation. Gender inequality in South Africa has deep roots, which are shaped by its colonial, political, economic and social past. Because gender is a complex concept, the chapter begins with a discussion of its multi-dimensionality. The next sections provide an overview of the history of gender identity during Apartheid (recognising that a full exposition is beyond the space limitations of the chapter), followed by an assessment of the current status of gender transformation in post-Apartheid South Africa. It concludes with a discussion of future imperatives for achieving transformative inclusion for all genders in South Africa.

THE CONCEPT OF GENDER

When I was growing up as a young boy, I had this feeling of being a girl. I liked feminine things. My mother and father punished me when they caught me dressing like a girl and would remind me that I was a boy. I hated sports and that angered them. My childhood was miserable because I felt like I could live in my body. When I got older,

---

1   Attributed to Mohd Mustafa. Retrieved from: https://ownquotes.com/quote/149905

I realised there were other people like me. That's when I got the courage to make the transition to becoming a woman. Dintle (formerly Kananelo)

To fully understand the magnitude of the challenge of gender transformation in post-Apartheid South Africa, it is important to understand the complexity of the concept of gender identity. Gender identity is an important aspect of who we believe we are and how we think about, and express, our gender; it is self-defined. Gender identity also affects our lived experiences within society. Mistakenly, gender is often conflated with sex – it is assumed that one's biological sex matches one's gender. If a person's sex at birth is female, then gender will also be female. Further, the individual is assumed to have attributes regarded as characteristic of females (i.e. feminine). On the other hand, if an individual is born a male, he is assumed to have traits and behaviours regarded as characteristic of males (i.e. masculine).[2]

Contributions from feminist and queer theorists have brought much more complexity to the concept of gender.[3] First, scholars stress that sex refers to biological differences between men and women, while gender is the socially constructed and culturally determined roles of men and women in society. Second, the sex *assigned* to an individual at birth may or may not match their gender identity, as the vignette above indicates. Emphasis is placed on the word '*assigned*', which recognises that the labels society uses for different sexes are socially constructed. So, at birth, an individual's sex can be *assigned* as male, female or intersexed depending on anatomy. Third, gender is not a binary concept. Instead, it can best be described as an array of genders. This conceptualisation rejects thinking of gender and sex as comprised of two categories: male and female. There are instead many genders and sexes.[4] Another important theoretical development from Queer Theory[5] with respect to gender identity is the growing attention to sexuality, which refers to sexual orientation or sexual feelings, as well as the sexed body encompassing an individual's physicality and appearance.[6] Some theorists do, however, make a distinction between sexual attraction and romantic attraction.

In sum, it is appropriate to acknowledge that there are more than two sexes and two genders, thus we should speak of genders, sexes and sexualities. Gender and sexualities are performances and not biologically predetermined.[7] Although, feminist and queer theorists continue to debate the relationship among these concepts, they do agree that their meanings are dynamic, and historically, politically and socially determined (i.e. social

---

2   Morrell, 2006, p. 13
3   Butler, 1990; Reddy, 2004.
4   Ibid.
5   Rubin, 1993.
6   Swarr, 2012, p. 10.
7   van Zyl & Steyn, 2005, p. 20.

constructions). There is terminology to assist with understanding the spectrum of genders and sexualities, although it is important to recognise its incompleteness. Table 5.1 provides some of these basic terms and their definitions. As the table reflects, a person's gender identity may not match the sex they were assigned at birth, as sexualities are quite diverse. Additionally, distinctions can be made between the language for identities and those utilised from a medical perspective (i.e. transsexual), but this is not the end of the complexity of gender identity.

Table 5.1: A Basic Glossary of Genders and Sexualities

Cisgender	An individual whose gender identity matches the sex they were assigned at birth
Transgender	An individual whose gender identity differs from the biological sex they were assigned at birth.
Transsexual	Refers to an individual who pursues medical assistance (i.e. sex reassignment surgery) to physically transition to a different sex) to match their identity; some individual also prefer this term to transgender
Gender-nonconforming	An individual who expresses gender outside traditional norms associated with masculinity or femininity. Not all gender nonconforming people are transgender, and some transgender people express gender in conventionally masculine or feminine way
Nonbinary or gender queer	An individual who identifies as neither male nor female and sees themselves outside the gender binary. Such individuals may exhibit both traditionally masculine and feminine qualities or neither.
Gender fluid	An individual whose identity shifts or fluctuates. Sometimes these individuals may identify or express themselves as more masculine on some days, and more feminine on others
Intersex	A term for an individual born with biological sex characteristics that aren't traditionally associated with male or female bodies. Intersexuality does not refer to sexual orientation or gender identity.
Transvestite	A person who cross-dresses, or dresses in clothes typically associated with the gender opposite the one they were assigned at birth. The term **transvestite** is used as a synonym for the term cross-dresser, although cross-dresser is generally considered the preferred term
Gender-neutral	An individual who prefers not to be described by a specific gender, but prefers "they" as a singular pronoun.

Homosexual	Now viewed as pejorative (deviant) term that referred to individuals sex
Heterosexual	An individual attracted to someone of the opposite sex
Gay	An individual who sexually attracted to men
Lesbian	An individual who is sexually attracted to women
Bisexual	An individual who is attracted to people of their gender or other gender identities. It is not a way station from straight to gay, as it had once been described.
Pansexual	An individual who is attracted to people of all gender identities. Or someone who is attracted to a person's qualities regardless of their gender identity. (The prefix "pan" means "all," rejecting the gender binary that some argue is implied by "bisexual.")
Asexual	An individual who experiences little to no sexual attraction

Source: Adapted from Michael Gold[8]

There are two other important dimensions important to understanding the magnitude of the challenge of achieving gender transformation in South Africa. First, individuals do not have a single identity, but multiple identities at the same time. The idea of multiple identities and their importance have been captured in what is referred to as *intersectionality*.[9] Black feminist theorists originated this theoretical insight in response to exclusion of the lives and issues of 'women of colour' in both Western and non-Western societies in the work on gender in society and institutions. Intersectionality recognises the inseparability of gender identity from other categories of social difference, such as race, class, ethnicity, sexuality and nation.[10] African feminists stress the interconnections between identities, history and power.[11] The identity of any individual is not simply woman or man or gay or lesbian, but a conglomeration of other salient categories of social difference in a society that may, for example, include race, class and ethnicity. Race and ethnicity are particularly salient to gender identities and sexualities because the Apartheid state used its power to oppress its Black population while privileging Whites. For this reason it is important not to think of gender and sexuality as separate categories, but to recognise their simultaneity – gendered sexualities and sexualised genders – and racialisation.[12] We do try to convey these intersections throughout the chapter, perhaps not always successfully.

---

8   Gold, 2018.

9   Crenshaw, 1990.

10   Rodriquez et al., 2006, p. 201.

11   Mama, 2001.

12   Schefer & Ratele, 2011, p. 29. (We do try to convey these intersections throughout the chapter, perhaps not always successfully.)

Second, individuals with gender identities and sexualities that differ from everyday assumptions of two genders (i.e. males and females) and heterosexuality (i.e. sexual attraction to someone of the opposite gender) often face societal and workplace exclusion and oppression. Even though gender identity and sexuality are self-defined, in the sense of individual agency (making our own identities), external forces and actors impose their views on a person's or group's identity. These views can be manifested at the individual level as prejudice and bias, but also at the structural level through state policies and legislation, as well as the practices of organisations within a society. Queer theorists have developed the concept of *heteronormativity* as the suite of cultural, legal and institutional practices that maintain normative assumptions about gender. These assumptions are that there are only two genders (i.e. male and female), that gender reflects biological sex, and that only sexual attraction between males and females is natural and acceptable – *heterosexuality*.[13] The sister concept, *heteronormativity*, captures the linkage between patriarchal social systems that produce and maintain heterosexuality.[14] Thus, heteronormativity and gender inequality are intertwined. These last two dimensions of gender identity are important because people in a society may experience inequality, not simply due to gender but because of other marginalised human social differences (i.e. race, ethnicity, class, sexuality, physical ability, and other visible and invisible differences).

Achieving true gender transformation in South Africa means engaging with the complexity of gender in formulating policies and organisational practices to address inequality and oppression. Getting to the envisioned non-racial and non-sexist nation, which belongs to everyone who lives in it, requires briefly retracing the past to understand the present state of gender transformation, as well as future challenges.

Gender identity and sexuality during the Apartheid era

Gender identity and women

Gender and racial discrimination in South Africa were evident during colonial times, first by the Dutch colonisers and followed by the British. It continued throughout the early 20th century, however the election of the National Party in 1948 installed Apartheid as a formal system of political, economic and social separation of the races. Apartheid institutionalised the inferiority and oppression of its Black[15] majority population (Black African, Indian and Coloured/Mixed Heritage) in all spheres of South African society, and entrenched the superiority of White people based on the doctrine of White supremacy.[16] The Apartheid system accelerated the control of land and Black labour by Dutch and British settlers

---

13   Kitzinger, 2005, p. 478

14   Elder, 2003, p. 922.

15   The term Black refers to Black Africans, Coloureds and Indians.

16   Frederickson, 1982.

that had begun during colonial times.[17] Control of land and Black labour was central to maintaining the domination and economic prosperity of the White minority population.

Gender and race were the main identities supressed through legislation and repressive practices by the ruling Nationalist Party. These laws and practices illustrate that, although gender and sexual identities are subjectively defined, societal level structures and ideologies influence their formation as well as how inequality is experienced.[18] The Apartheid state focused largely on traditional understandings of gender as consisting of men and women. Women, in general, were treated as minors with limited legal rights to, for example, own property or enter into contracts. Common, statutory and customary laws gave husbands many rights over the bodies, properties and actions of their wives.[19] In the case of African women, the recognition by the Apartheid state of the 1927 Native Administration Act legitimatised the patriarchy within customary laws that gave African men control over women.[20] In reality, three types of masculinities subordinated women to men: (a) White masculinity represented in the political and economic dominance of the White Apartheid state; (b) rurally-based Black African masculinity perpetuated through indigenous institutions (i.e. chiefship, customary law and communal land); and (c) Black masculinity emerging from urbanisation and the development of separate and culturally distinct townships.[21] Bozzoli used the term 'patchwork of patriarchies'.[22] Common among these different forms of masculinity is the construction of men as dominant and authoritative, and women as passive and subservient.

Men dominated women and controlled the public sphere, while women were relegated to domestic roles. However, there were important differences in the effects of Apartheid laws and policies due to a *gendered racial order* emanating from a confluence of patriarchy and racism.[23] This order placed White women at the top, followed by Coloured and Indian women, with Black African women at the bottom.   It is important to remember that, under Apartheid, even the least privileged White women were members of the racially dominant class.[24] For example, the Women's Enfranchisement Act of 1930 gave White women the right to vote. Coloured and Indian women gained the right to vote in 1983 and Black African women only in 1994.[25]

---

17   Ibid.
18   Carrim & Nkomo, 2016.
19   Krikorian, 1995, p. 1.
20   Manicom, 1992.
21   Morrell et al., 2012, p. 12; Bozzoli, 1983, used the term patchwork of patriarchies.
22   Bozzoli, 1983.
23   Bozzoli, 1983.
24   Andrews, 1986.
25   Poinsette, 1985, p. 97.

Generally, in respect to employment, jobs held by women closely resembled domestic roles – nurses, teachers and domestic workers.[26] Even jobs obtained in the manufacturing sector were linked to domesticity (e.g. food processing, clothing and textiles).[27] But there were also significant racial differences in these limited opportunities. White women who worked had relatively greater access to better-paid and higher status jobs, such as clerical and administration positions. Indian, Coloured and Black African women, who were denied the same educational opportunities as White women, worked primarily in the lowest-paid, most unskilled jobs. As Table 5.2 shows, the types of jobs women could hold were clearly gendered and racialised, as reflected in data from Manpower Surveys in 1983.[28]

> *The South African movie* Poppy Nongena *released in 2020, captures the racial and gender oppression Black African women experienced during Apartheid. Poppy, a married Xhosa woman born in Langa Township, worked as a live-in domestic for a white family. From early morning till evening, Poppy did cooking, cleaning, washing, and childcare. She only saw her own family once a week and during the Christmas holidays. Although the Bantu Homelands Citizenship Act of 1970 forced the resettlement of Black Africans away from urban White areas to defined 'ethnic' homelands, Poppy was allowed to stay and work in Cape Town because of her husband's employment status. When her husband became ill and was unable to work, Poppy was deemed an illegal resident of South Africa and was required to move to her designated impoverished rural homeland. She dreaded the move because she knew there would be little prospects for employment. Poppy was very angry that she could be declared a non-citizen in the country in which she was born and bred. Now she understood what the young people in her township were protesting about.*

Beginning in the colonial era and cemented during Apartheid, Black African women who had historically held important roles in agriculture (i.e. cultivators of the fields) on their homesteads[29] were reduced to, what the Nationalist Party leadership referred to as, "superfluous appendages".[30] This designated identity for married Black African women (and their children) was commensurate with a migrant labour system that reduced Black African men to a source of cheap labour for work in the mines, farms and workplaces of an industrialising South Africa.[31] The Bantu Homelands Citizenship Act of 1970 forced the resettlement of Black Africans away from urban White areas to defined 'ethnic'

---

26   Pillay, 1985.
27   Ibid, p. 28.
28   Ibid, p. 27.
29   Walker, 1990.
30   Farah, 1974.
31   Kirkorian, 1995.

homelands.[32] Consequently, the wives and children of Black African migrant workers were confined to their respective impoverished homelands (although many resisted and illegally moved to cities).[33] Where a married Black African woman could live was tied to her husband's employment status. Black African women primarily worked in underpaid domestic jobs in households, and unskilled labour in some manufacturing industries in urban areas.[34] In general, Black African women were excluded from skilled professional and managerial careers, except teaching and nursing.[35] Manpower data for 1983 show that there were no Black African women engineers, architects and dentists, for example (see Table 5.2).[36]

Table 5.2: Occupational Distribution by Gender: Selected High Level Categories

Occupation	Male	White Female	Coloured Female	Asian[2]	African Female
Engineers	17 595	118	0	0	0
Chemists	1 738	295	16	4	3
Architects	1 910	64	0	0	0
Quantity Surveyors	3 521	78	0	0	0
Technicians	63 769	4 136	222	64	68
Dentists	1 967	52	2	1	0
Doctors	15 270	1 424	16	66	39
Pharmacists	3 778	1 216	26	7	17
Teachers	67 217	44 390	18 517	4 465	59 279

[1] Excludes the homelands of Transkei, Bophuthatswana, Venda and Ciskei.

[2] The category Asian at the time comprised Indians.

Source: Manpower Survey, No. 15, 1983 as reported in P. Pillay[37]

> *Elsabé Van der Merwe grew up on a struggling small farm in the Bushveld. At the age of 18, she left her family to seek employment in the growing manufacturing sector in Johannesburg. When she first asked permission to leave, her father was very opposed to his daughter living in what he called Sodom and Gomorrah. But eventually he allowed her to leave the farm in the hope that her earnings would supplement their*

32   Ibid.

33   Ibid.

34   Cock, 1980; Poinsette, 1985.

35   Poinsette, 1985, p. 117.

36   Pillay, 1985.

37   Pillay, 1985.

meagre income, despite being concerned about a young unmarried Afrikaner girl away from the authority of her father. Elsabé eventually got a job at a garment factory. Her father's fears were quelled when he learned Elsabé's respectability and moral integrity would be protected because she would live in a supervised hostel with other young women. Not to wanting to shatter her father's relief, Elsabé never told him about the verbal abuse and sexual harassment she had to endure from her male supervisors and colleagues.

While the migrant labour system disrupted the Black African family structure and prevented women from fulfilling their roles as wives and mothers, the ideal gender identity of White Afrikaner women – *volksmoeder* (mother of the nation) – was protected. Afrikaner women were literally viewed as the continuators of racial 'purity' (i.e. pure and decent).[38] There are two examples of how any perceived threats to this role were removed. First, in the 1930s, as Afrikaners left impoverished rural areas for urban cities, it was not uncommon for young single women to seek employment in the garment industry in cities like Johannesburg as a means to supplement the income of their families.[39] The state, church and broader Afrikaner society were worried about the moral decay of these women (pejoratively referred to as 'factory girls') and the potential erosion of the patriarchal control Afrikaner men exercised over their unmarried daughters.[40] Hostel accommodations were established not only to provide moral regulation, but also to save them for the *'volk'* (i.e. our people), win support for Afrikaner nationalism, and provide a docile labour force.[41] While these young women had some independence from the authority of their fathers, in the factories they were often subjected to the abusive authority of their male bosses. Second, the obsession with the regulation of White female sexuality (particularly of unmarried young women) is further evidenced by the passage of the Abortion and Sterilisation Act of 1975 that denied women access to abortions.[42] The independent, heroic identity attributed to White Afrikaner women veiled the reality that they were expected to be self-sacrificing and passive to male domination.

The gender identities and experiences of Indian and Coloured women were greatly shaped by the status of their racial groups. Whites were at the top of the racial order and Black Africans at the bottom, with Indians and Coloureds in-between. It is important to note that under Apartheid, all people of colour (Black Africans, Coloureds and Indians) were subjected to separate development and oppression. The lives and employment opportunities of Indian and Coloured women were severely restricted under the oppressive Apartheid system, as the next sections will demonstrate.

---

38   Hyslop, 1995.

39   Brink, 1987.

40   Hyslop, 1995.

41   Brink, 1987, p. 10

42   Klausen, 2010.

Indians migrated to South Africa in two groups: indentured servants (as a source of cheap labour for the sugar cane industry, and later for the railroad and municipalities in the province of Natal), and what are referred to as passenger Indians.[43] Passenger Indians were allowed to establish businesses and professional services, not only to Indians, but also eventually to Black Africans. These groupings created class divisions between the passenger Indians who were brought later to the country to meet the mercantile needs of the growing indentured servant population.[44]   However, in both cases, Indian women arrived in the country as appendages to their male counterparts.[45] Indentured women were oppressed by unequal and brutal working conditions inflicted by estate owners, as well as being responsible for their husbands and other indentured men. Both employers and Indian men treated women as property to be bought or given away for economic or domestic reasons.[46] Wives and daughters of middle-class passenger Indians generally did not work outside of the home and were subordinate to men. Indenture was terminated in 1911, and former indentured workers formed the largest part of the Indian working class, whose men worked as cultivators, craftsmen and petty producers. Often whole families (including women) were involved in small business commerce.[47]

> *Krisha, who is currently one of the first cohort of Indian women to occupy senior management roles in post-Apartheid South Africa, shared memories of growing up as a young Indian girl during Apartheid: "I think Apartheid was very rife in the era I was growing up in. I remember going to beaches and it would say blacks, whites and Indians. I remember in Durban those days that the buses and the toilets and certain restaurants were for Whites only. I remember those things and going to the beach front and you are a little kid and want to jump on the trampoline and the security guard would come to you and say 'it's for whites only' and you did not understand that but you grew up in that era. I grew up in an Indian township, and we were very close community. My father had raised my brothers not to do any household chores, as he believed that is a woman's domain and men should not be involved in doing housework. That is the Indian male mentality where they want the women to run a home, as it is their duty as females, but women should also assist them like men in their businesses. So my brother grew up in a house full of women – we were four sisters – and he never lifted a finger to assist in the house. My mother had no say in the matter, as my father would scold her if she even asked my brother to assist in keeping his room clean. My brother was therefore raised in a very patriarchal fashion where the men*

---

43   Radhakrishnan, 2005. (Passenger refers to the requirement that they could immigrate to South Africa if they paid their own transport costs. One of the most notable passengers was Mahatma Gandhi, who arrived in 1893.)

44   Carrim & Nkomo, 2016.

45   Seedat-Khan, 2013.

46   Desai & Vahed, 2013.

47   Freund, 1991, p. 421.

have their role and women have double roles – their traditional roles in the homes and to be career women."[48]

However, the legacy of how Indians came to South Africa had an indelible effect on Indian, social, cultural and familial life, as well as the gender identity of Indian women during the Apartheid era.[49] As migrants from India, both groups travelled with their homeland cultural practices, values, religions and castes, although they were modified for the new context in which they found themselves. Indian women played a key role in maintaining a sense of family and community.[50] Research suggests that the interaction between living in segregated Indian townships due to Apartheid policies and homeland cultural values entrenched the familial role of women as 'good' wives and mothers reflected in Krisha's story.[51] This historically dominant role fostered a construction of the ideal Indian woman's gender identity as one of docility and dependency – passive and submissive to men.[52] Yet the confinement of Indians to townships also had the effect of decreasing the incidence of extended families to more nuclear structures.[53] It was not unusual that working class women had to work out of necessity to contribute to the economic well-being of Indian families.[54] The 1950s saw a large movement of Indian women (married and single daughters) into waged work in manufacturing.[55] In 1970, 43% of employed Indian women worked in manufacturing, and the next highest percentage was in services.[56] Interestingly, Indian women gained access to factory jobs before Black African women, but were eventually replaced by them.[57] As Indians gained greater access to education (compared to Black Africans), more educated Indian women moved into office work and professional occupations.[58]

Coloured people were classified as 'mixed race' during Apartheid, yet more accurately they descended largely from Cape slaves, the indigenous Khoisan and other peoples of African and Asian origin who were part of the colonial Cape society in the late 19th century.[59] The reference to them as 'mixed race' erroneously suggested they originated primarily from miscegenation – sexual relations between European settlers and the indigenous

---

48   Carrim, 2012.
49   Freund, 1991.
50   Patel & Uys, 2013, p. 4; Maharaji, 1995.
51   Carrim & Nkomo, 2016.
52   Seedat-Khan, 2013; Hiralal, 2010.
53   Meer, 1990.
54   Freund, 1991.
55   Ibid.
56   Ibid.
57   Ibid.
58   Ibid.
59   Adhikari, 2005a, p. 1.

Cape population.[60] This belief evoked a negative stereotyping of Coloured identity that has been difficult to change. Perceived as racial hybrids, illegitimate and physically, intellectually and socially inferior, they have had to constantly resist this imposed identity even as the Apartheid government tried to exploit it (i.e. their hybridity meant being closer to the White race) to foster a wedge between Coloured and Black African people.[61] Their intermediate status in South Africa's racial hierarchy greatly influenced their identities.[62] For Coloured people this identity was a double-edged sword that bestowed more privileges relative to Black Africans, but also entrenched them as an inferior racial hybrids.[63] Some analyses describe the general characterisation of Coloureds as inferior, which led to them being viewed as children in need of the paternalistic guardianship of Whites.[64] Coloured women were pejoratively stereotyped as racially inferior and physically unattractive, but sexually available.[65] However, sexual relations with White men during colonial times had more to do with the power they exercised over Coloured women.[66]

Mavis Alexander was born in the multi-working class inner-city residential area known as District Six in the city of Cape Town. Her parents had managed to own their little home. Her mother worked in a fish canning factory where women were only allowed to perform two types of work: gutting or packing fish. These were also the lowest paid jobs in the factory. Her father worked in the custodial staff of the University of Cape Town. Before that both her parents and older brothers had worked on a wine farm in Stellenbosch. They left because it was impossible to earn enough to save for a different future for the family. With her very fair skin, long straight brown hair, and fluent Afrikaans, Mavis could have easily been identified as White. But Mavis soon became very aware of the oppressed status of Coloured people. She remembers the horror of the police going door-to-door chasing people from their homes. Mavis watched her parents scrambling to pack their belongings in 1976. Under the Group Areas Act of 1950 nearly 60,000 people were forcibly removed from their homes and sent to live in the Cape Flats. Her parents were only meagrely compensated for their home. Mavis attended Manenberg High School (for coloured children only), but dropped out at 16 to seek employment to assist her family. The best job she could get was at a zip factory but she did not earn as much as male workers. When the opportunity came she became a member of the Independent Garment Workers Union to fight for better wages and working conditions. Her parents were not happy with her decision as they had always believed it safer for Coloured people not to cause trouble.

---

60 Ibid, p. 6.
61 Adhikari, 2006.
62 Adhikari, 2005b, p. xii.
63 Adhikari, 2006, p. 156.
64 Ibid, p. 153.
65 Ibid, p. 152
66 Ibid.

Coloured people began losing their very limited civil rights in the early 19th century. Their remaining rights were stripped by the onslaught of Apartheid legislation, enacted by the ascendancy of the National Party.[67] In 1956, Coloured people were removed from the common voters roll. The Group Areas Act of 1950 forced the removal of over a half million Coloured people to the peripheries of cities and towns. A majority of Coloured people lived in the Western Cape during the Apartheid years, and this is where their primary job opportunities existed. Coloured women were a cheap source of seasonal labour on the fruit farms and wineries in the region. Entire families typically resided and worked on these properties (accommodation, food, alcohol and clothing were part of the 'wages' of the employed men).[68] Under this paternalistic system, Coloured men were designated as permanent workers, and their wives (or partners) worked only when their labour was needed.[69] Women (and children) were not paid for their labour. Further, the system fell outside of formal labour laws and was based on interdependent gendered and racialised power relations in which obedient and reliable workers were provided for by farmers, while non-conforming ones were often penalised and punished.[70] This created a layered form of subordination and oppression – women who had no employment rights were disempowered third parties to an arrangement between White farmers and exploited Coloured men.[71] Their fates were literally tied to those of their husbands (or partners), and it was only in the early 1990s that some reforms were legislated. Similar to Black African women, Coloured women also worked in low-paying manufacturing jobs, mainly in the food processing, textile and clothing factories, and as domestics.

Sexualities under Apartheid

As the previous section demonstrates, there is a bounty of historical research about gender that focuses on the status of women during Apartheid. However, there is much less history about LGBTQI+ (lesbian, gay, bisexual, transgender, queer or intersex) South Africans. This void does not mean that they had no presence in the National Party government's ideology or legislative agenda, nor does it mean that LGBTQI+ persons did not exist in Apartheid South Africa. Recent research, however, has examined their lived experiences and status during Apartheid to reveal how heteropatriarchy was core to maintaining a puritanical code of morality.[72] There are a number of projects resurrecting the history and experiences of gays and lesbians in South Africa. For example, Gay and Lesbian Archives (Gala) gives public access to an extensive collection of individual and organisational records that capture lesbian and gay social history and experiences in

---

67   Adhikari, 2005a.
68   Orton et al., 2001; Kritzinger & Voster, 1996.
69   Ibid, p. 470.
70   Ibid, p. 470.
71   Ibid, p. 472.
72   Elder, 2003.

South Africa and other parts of the continent.[73], [74] Heteropatriarchy is defined as "the social power structure that creates and maintains the heterosexist binary of masculinity and femininity and the associated social expectations (gender performances) determined according to biological sex".[75] Thus, the experiences of LGBTQI+ persons should be understood within a context where any sexual identity other than heterosexual was deemed deviant and abnormal. The legal power of the Apartheid state was used to stipulate acceptable sexuality.[76] Scholars have referred to this as Apartheid sexualisation.[77]

Heteropatriarchy was inflected with race in concert with the State's Apartheid policies and goal of White domination. In general, racial thinking (i.e. eugenics and racism) featured prominently in how the sexuality of Black people was constructed.[78] Racist thinking and academic scholarship vilified Black bodies as inferior and oversexed; African men were stereotyped as hypersexual, innately lascivious, sexually violent, and a threat to the purity of White women[79], while it was assumed that Black African women's bodies were available for White male pleasure.[80]

> On January 22, 1966, 19 year old John Bradley was very excited about attending what had been hyped as the queer party of the year. Invited guests included prominent socialites and entertainers. John had attended smaller gatherings as it was the only way to socialise with other gay men. He had kept his identity secret at university and from his parents. Little did John know that the South African Police raid in the early morning hours of the party would be the event that triggered the passage of legislation to criminalise homosexuality. When the national government instituted compulsory conscription for white males after the 1976 Soweto uprising, John found himself in the South African National Defence Force. When his homosexuality was discovered, he was taken to Voortrekkerhoogte Psychiatric Ward in Pretoria for treatment to 'cure' him of his homosexuality.[81]

The national government virulently controlled and policed the sexual activities and bodies of its citizens, particularly gay White men. There is a good deal of research about the efforts to control gay White men, but less on White lesbians and even less on the experiences of Black lesbians.[82] The 1957 Immorality and Sexual Offences Act (an updated version of

---

73   Manion & Morgan, 2006.
74   Potgieter, 2011, pp. 29-35; Potgieter, 2006.
75   Elder, 2003, p. 922.
76   Ratele, 2009, p. 300.
77   Shefer & Ratele, 2011, p. 30.
78   Dubow, 2015.
79   Schefer & Ratele, 2011.
80   Schefer, 2010.
81   Schaap, 2011.
82   Jones, 2008; Potgieter, 1997.

the 1927 Act) included, as immoral behaviour, sex between different races, prostitution, cruising, and immoral acts between a man older than 19 years of age with a man younger than 19.[83] In 1988, the law was extended to women and girls under 19 years of age, but lesbian sexual acts were not given the same attention (or level of criminalisation) as gay White males.[84] One can only speculate as to why less attention was paid to lesbian sexuality. Some research suggests that it may be reflective of the state's belief that women have an innate desire for men, and thus fewer were likely to be lesbians.[85] Interestingly, even though lesbians were not caught in the criminal net, the criminalisation of homosexuality had negative effects on their identities.[86]

Testimony during the Truth & Reconciliation Commission process (TRC) revealed that young White male conscripts in the South African National Defence Force were subjected to aversion therapy, consisting of hormone therapy, sex change operations and barbiturates to 'cure' them of homosexuality.[87] Homosexuality was viewed as a significant threat to Afrikaner masculinity, heterosexuality and procreation, and the morality of the Apartheid state. A special commission was set up to investigate homosexuality, and sex reassignment surgeries for transsexuals were funded by the State beginning in the 1960s. The Prohibition of Disguises Act of 1969 was passed to criminalise dressing in drag, and the police were known to raid parties of gay males.

At the same time, however, the government paid less attention to homosexuality amongst Black Africans, Coloureds and Indians.[88] Their approach centred on prohibiting interracial sex through legislation such as the Prohibition of Mixed Marriages Act 1949. This law was important to ensure the sustainability of a 'pure' White population and the political dominance of White people over Black people.[89] For example, the Apartheid State tolerated homosexuality within the Black male migrant labour system, particularly in mining.[90] The taking of 'boy wives' was not uncommon, and provided men living in hostels with sexual companionship as well as the domestic services denied to them because their wives were prohibited from living with them.[91] Researchers suggest that the state begrudgingly tolerated these same sex-relations because it assisted mining companies to confine workers to compounds, and dampened demands to bring their wives and families closer to their workplaces.[92]

---

83   Potgieter, 1997, p. 54.
84   Ibid, p. 54-55.
85   Ibid, p. 58.
86   Ibid, p. 62.
87   Jones, 2008, p. 397.
88   Ibid, p. 404.
89   Ibid, p. 398.
90   Swarr, 2009.
91   Murray & Roscoe, 2001.
92   Moodie (with Ndatshe & Sibuyi), 1988.

In summary, Apartheid legislation and its policies relegated women to subservience and subordination and, at the same time, criminalised LGBTQI+ people for deviating from the heterosexual ideal. Yet neither group were passive consumers of the identities imposed upon them. There are many stories of individual and collective resistance, and women asserted their rights through union organising and civil disobedience against Apartheid policies. Despite the differences in their lives and work experiences, South African women united to become a formidable anti-Apartheid force. The slogan arising from the historic Women's March of August 9, 1956, *wathint abafazi, wathint imbokodo* (you strike the women, you strike the rock), captures the persistence with which women pursued their desire for equality and social justice. Despite the criminalisation of homosexuality by the State and societal stigmatisation, research shows that gay life existed throughout the country, although it was racially divided.[93] This was also true for their organising efforts. It was only in the 1990s, after Nelson Mandela's release from prison, that the gay rights movement accelerated and was able to link to the broader anti-Apartheid struggle.[94]

Gender transformation in the post-Apartheid era

Women's organising galvanised after the 1956 march lost steam during the 1980s as the Apartheid government aggressively targeted anti-Apartheid groups and their leaders.[95] Additionally, debates about the place of feminism in the women's movement also contributed to their decline. However, in the 1990s with the unbanning of the ANC and other political organisations, women's organisations joined with the African National Congress Women's League (ANCWL) to advocate for the elevation of women's rights in the transition to democracy.[96] This move had both positive and negative effects for the equality of women. On the negative side, the oppression of women was considered within the context of nationalism and the priority placed on racial equality. On the positive side, women gained a voice in the national struggle for democracy. Using that voice, women were able to demand that women's rights be included as part of the struggle for justice, freedom and dignity.[97, 98]

Various meetings, seminars and conferences, comprised of several women's groups and the ANC Women's League, resulted in the National Policy for Women's Empowerment in 1990.[99] A broad coalition of women representing diverse ideological, political,

---

93 Geissiver, 1995.
94 Ibid.
95 Hassim, 2002.
96 Ibid.
97 Mvimbi, 2009.
98 Ibid, 2005.
99 Ibid, 2005.

economic, racial, cultural and religious perspectives were instrumental in shaping the gender agenda of the new democratic government.[100] Through the Women's National Coalition (WNC), they developed the Charter for Effective Equality in 1992.[101] The Charter contained prescriptions for how women's rights should be framed in the 1996 Constitution. Retrospectively, one of the biggest flaws of the Women's Charter was that it did not address the unequal power relations between women and men[102], yet the WNC was instrumental in opposing sexist principles in the Constitution and other policies. For example, the group ensured the inclusion of non-sexist principles in the Constitution when they opposed attempts by traditional leaders to exclude customary laws from being included in the Bill of Rights.[103] Their success is reflected in the extensive inclusion of women's rights in the legislative agenda of the new democratic government, which was elected in 1994.

The new government vigorously committed to gender equality and moved to dismantle the legislative underpinnings of Apartheid, with various progressive laws and policies being enacted to address gender inequality (see Table 5.3). The government also committed to the principles of gender equality in international protocols (e.g. the Beijing Fourth World Conference, the SADC Protocol on Gender Development, and the African Charter on Human & Peoples' Rights). No doubt these efforts and commitments have improved the status and rights of women to equality and social justice, yet persistent gaps remain between the envisioned equality for women and the everyday reality of so many women. The problem has a lot to do with how these laws and policies have been implemented by the government, society and organisations.[104] Feminist scholars and activists have been particularly vocal about discrepancies, contradictions and omissions.

Table 5.3: Legislation and policies targeting women and LGBTQI individuals

Policy	Year	Aim
National Policy for Women's Empowerment	1990	How the state should respond to empowering women
Women's Charter for Effective Equality	1992	Foregrounds vision of women's rights in South Africa and provides framework of rights which need to be translated into policies and programmes affecting women's quality of life
Reconstruction and Development Policy (RDP)	1994	Promote gender equality

100   Mkhize & Mgcotyelwa-Ntoni, 2019, p. 10.

101   Gouws & Galgut, 2016 p. 3

102   Albertyn & Hassim, 2004.

103   Hassim, 2005.

104   Albertyn, Goldblatt, Hassim, Mbatha, & Meintjies, 1999.

Policy	Year	Aim
Growth, Employment and Redistribution (GEAR)	1996	To stimulate economic growth of the country but could not address social needs to country especially needs of women.
Constitution of South Africa	1996	Rights and duties of citizens and structure of government
Bill of Rights (The South African Constitution) Chapter 2	1996	Guarantees and affirms right to equality for women, men as well as sexual orientation
Section 9 of the Constitution	1996	Prohibits discrimination based on sexual orientation
Commission on Gender Equality Act, No 39 of 1996	1996	Provides for the functions, powers, composition and functioning of the Commission on Gender Equality and provides for matters connected with it
White Paper on National Defence	1996	The South African National Defence Forces is not allowed to discriminate on grounds of sexual harassment
Employment Equity Act No. 55	1998	Redress employment discrimination faced by previously disadvantaged persons (one such group being women)
Immigration Rights for LGBTQI partners (changed to spouses in 2002)	1999/ 2002	LGBTQI immigrant partners'/spouses' rights to be protected
South African Gender Policy Framework for Women's Empowerment and Gender Equality (SAGPF) also known as National Gender Policy Framework (GPF)	2000	Provides a framework to guide the process of developing policies, laws, practices and procedures which would ensure equal rights and opportunities for women and men in all spheres and structures of government, the workplace, the community and family
Promotion of Equality and Prevention of Unfair Discrimination Act (PEPUDA)	2000	Special courts were established by this Act to address discrimination by private parties. The Act also prevents hate speech, harassment and homophobic attacks
Black Economic Empowerment (BEE)	2003	Addresses racial inequalities and negated gender inequalities
Broad-based Black Economic Empowerment Act No 53	2003	Promotion of Black economic empowerment, including women and disabled
Trans Access to Gender Marker Changes (Act 49)	2003	Trans people could alter their gender on formal identification documents

Policy	Year	Aim
Children's Act 38 (Adoption Rights)	2005	LGBTQI persons given the right to adopt children
Civil Union Act 17 (Marriage Rights)	2006	LGBTQI persons to be able to marry each other
UN Human Rights Council Resolution on Human Rights, Sexual Orientation and Gender Identity	2011	South Africa sponsors first UN resolution that affirms that LGBTQI rights are human rights
Prevention and Combating of Hate Crimes and Hate Speech Bill	2018	Reducing offensive speech and curbing hate crimes- to be revived

The first progressive piece of legislation was the Constitution of South Africa, No. 108 of 1996.[105] The Bill of Rights in the Constitution became the cornerstone of the State's approach to gender equality, as it addresses legislation and policies in different areas. The Commission on Gender Equality Act, No 39 of 1996 provided for the functions, powers and composition and functioning of the Commission on Gender Equality, and to provide for matters connected to it[106], but the Commission has encountered obstacles that hinder its efficacy. The 1994 Reconstruction and Development Programme (RDP) was designed to promote gender equality and included a lengthy empowerment strategy[107], however it was geared toward eliminating women's poverty and did not address other issues affecting their lives. The programme was subsequently replaced by the Growth, Employment and Redistribution Policy (GEAR) in 1996. With GEAR, the government shifted the provision of services to communities, which impacted poor, working class Black African women the most, inadvertently weakening the general promotion of women's rights.[108]

In 1998, the Employment Equity Act No. 55 (EEA) was promulgated.[109] While the intention of the EEA was to create equal opportunities for historically disadvantaged women and men in employment, there was no consideration of which women and men to target. Indeed, White women appear to have benefited more from the Act relative to Black women.[110] A race and gender analysis of firm-level data reported for 2016 indicate that Black African and Coloured women continue to be under-represented in high-skilled and management positions[111], however Black African and Coloured women do have relatively

---

105 South African Government, 1996b.
106 South African Government, 1996a.
107 Mvimbi, 2009.
108 Ibid.
109 South African Government, 1998.
110 Bosch, Nkomo, Carrim, Haq, Syed & Ali, 2015.
111 Espi, Francis & Valodia, 2019, p. 58.

higher representation in management positions in the public sector. The 2018-2019 Employment Equity Report sums up gender transformation as "steady but slow".[112] The Commission for Employment Equity has struggled to increase compliance, and it appears that organisations have not fully embraced the spirit of the law.[113] An important change to the Employment Equity Act in 2014 gave the CCMA the power to arbitrate unfair discrimination related to sexual harassment and equal pay for equal work.

In 2000, the government launched the National Gender Policy for Women's Empowerment (Gender Framework Policy – GFP) and enacted the Promotion of Equality and Prevention of Unfair Discrimination Act (PEPUDA). The GFP provided a formal framework for developing gender transformation in post-Apartheid South Africa and identified 13 challenges hindering the empowerment of women. There was much hope for this policy, especially in light of an Office on the Status of Women in the Presidency being created. Many female activists regard the development of the National Gender Policy Framework as a technical process which did not include the participation of women at the grassroots level. The policy was weakened by an absence of specific targets, objectives and plans, as well as being silent on political responsibility for gender mainstreaming.[114, 115] Although there were some initial efforts to inculcate gender mainstreaming within government structures, up until 2008 a gender mainstreaming policy had not been fully developed. The pillars of the GFP were to be reinforced through a National Gender Audit, but the audit was undermined as the recommendations were not implemented.[116] Critics argue that the policy treats women as a homogenous group and does not take into account the different categories of marginalised women in the country.

The Black Economic Empowerment (BEE) policy of 2003 also failed to address gender inequality, and in many cases, increased the marginalisation of South African women of colour.[117] BEE was replaced by the Broad-Based Black Economic Empowerment (B-BBEE) Act No 53. of 2003, which explicitly targets men of colour and women of colour as the beneficiaries. However, data indicate that the inclusion of women of colour in B-BBEE deals does not automatically translate into voting rights and management control.[118] Further, deals often benefit a narrow group of women of colour, as the majority continue to have limited access to business ownership.

Another important measure of the progress on equality for women is their overall participation in the national labour market. The *Quarterly Labour Force Survey* statistics for

---

112 Department of Labour, 2019.
113 Nkomo, 2011.
114 Holland-Muter, 2005.
115 Mvimbi, 2009.
116 Ibid.
117 Erlank, 2005.
118 B-BBEE Commission, 2019.

the unemployment rate from 2011-2019 reveal that the unemployment rate for women was higher than for men.[119] The 2019 Commission for Employment Equity (CEE) report indicates that the economically active population (EAP) consists of 54.7% male and 45.3% female. Female representation at top management levels is half their EAP (23.5%), while that of males is 76.5%.[120] Female representation in both public and private enterprises at top management levels is lower than their EAP. At the senior management level, female representation is less than their EAP (34.5%), while that of males is 65.5%. At the professional level, the percentage for women is more closely aligned to their EAP (44.9%).[121]

Philani Khumalo earned an MBA from Wits University with a speciality in marketing. She was hired as the first Black African women hired into brand management of a large advertising firm. There were only four other women of colour in the company, primarily in administrative positions. Although she worked hard to prove her capabilities, she found it increasingly difficult because of daily encounters with what she described as challenges to her abilities. One senior colleague queried her extensively about her education and background because she was, as he stated, "not a typical Zulu woman". She also noticed that she was never invited for after work drinks or the weekend parties that she would hear about on Monday mornings. The last straw was when she found out that her manager had asked another colleague to "keep an eye on her work" and that she was not assigned to prime customers. Shortly thereafter she left the company but wondered if she would be able to find a company that was truly transformed.

Rani, a senior Human Resources Executive shared a similar experience in post-Apartheid corporate South Africa: "In my last position I was the only female in Company B and from the time I walked into that company, I was like a dartboard. Three White men were aiming darts at me all the time. They were all my colleagues. I think you don't have to be quiet, you have to be active. Because what was happening is every decision I made I had to substantiate.

As the stories of Philani and Rani suggest, statistics tell only part of the story of the state of equality for women. There are a number of studies that continue to show that women within South Africa still encounter patriarchy, gender stereotyping and racism.[122] Traditional cultural gender norms that normalise male dominance still exist within society.[123] These norms spill over into the workplace, where women are marginalised due to the patriarchal values present in broader society. Recent research shows that women are often not perceived as management material, as they do not fit the male-manager

---

119 Stats SA, 2019.

120 Department of Labour, 2019.

121 Ibid.

122 For example, see Booysen & Nkomo, 2010; Carrim, 2012.

123 Martin & Barnard, 2013.

archetype.[124]   In some instances, women of colour from traditional backgrounds have to adjust their gender identities and cultural values to become more assertive and bold in order to fit into a male work environment.[125] Many South African organisations are still structured in ways that do not support women's career patterns, and married women are not perceived as management material.[126] Too many organisations give lip service to gender equality, and women continue to be marginalised through deeply gendered and racialised organisational structures and practices.[127] In sum, the improvement of representation of women in decision-making positions, and greater protection from discrimination and abuse, have not translated into full equality.

The progress on equality for LGBTQI+ persons also reflects a gap between legislative changes and actual practices. The new Constitution grants legal protection for sexual orientation, but it was subsequent court cases that gave more substance to the equality and rights of LGBTQI+ South Africans. It was only in 2006 that the Constitutional Court legalised same sex marriage, changing the definition of marriage from a heterosexual union between a man and woman to one between two persons (recognising there are many different genders who may wish to enter into matrimony).[128] Other court cases have clarified the meaning of 'family', which has been relevant to issues of access to employment benefits for partners, paternity benefits, immigration rights and child custody.[129] The Promotion of Equality and Prevention of Unfair Discrimination Act (PEPUDA) prohibits such forms of discrimination, including against lesbian, transgender, bisexual and queer women. The White Paper on National Defence (1996) further prohibits the South African Defence Force from discriminating on the grounds of sexual orientation.[130]

Taken together, these legal changes have opened up the space for the self-determination and expression of queer identities. The Prevention and Combating of Hate Crimes and Hate Speech Bill prohibited hate speech and hate crimes from being perpetrated on grounds of gender identity, sex (which includes intersex) and sexual orientation. The Bill lapsed when Parliament was dissolved on 7 May 2019. Yet legal rights are one thing – full acceptance by society remains a significant issue. The legal freedom for queer identities may have paradoxically opened them to homophobic attitudes and violent attacks.[131] Cultural and religious beliefs subject them to stereotyping, as well as subtle bias in the workplace and efforts to rescind their constitutional rights.[132] In May 2012, the National

---

124   Booysen & Nkomo, 2010.
125   Carrim, 2012.
126   Lumby & Azaola, 2014.
127   Hicks, 2012; Mathur-Helm, 2011.
128   Reddy, 2006.
129   Ibid.
130   South African Government, 1996b.
131   Swarr, 2012; Vincent & Howell, 2014.
132   Destanovic, 2016.

House of Traditional Leaders submitted a proposal to strip away the words 'sexual orientation' from the Constitution. This proposal was rejected by the State.[133] Lesbians in some Black African townships have been the target of violent attacks (including murder) and curative rape to 'restore' them to being women.[134] Physical violence has also been accompanied by claims that queer identities are unAfrican (and Western), despite research showing the contrary. (For example see *Tommy boys, lesbian men, and ancestral wives: Female same-sex practices in Africa*,[135] and *This has happened since ancient times... it's something that you are born with': ancestral wives among same-sex sangomas in South Africa*.[136] *Power and identity: An introduction to sexualities in Southern Africa*.[137] Take, for example, the international and national discourse around gold medallist runner, Caster Semenya. After Semenya, a South African track star, won the gold medal in the women's 800 metre event in the Olympics, the International Association of Athletics Federations (IAAF) ordered Semenya to undergo gender verification testing. The IAAF requested the tests because of what they described as Caster's muscular frame, deep voice and speed, i.e. they wanted to verify if she was truly a woman. Within South Africa, Black African prominent political leaders and others argued that homosexuality did not exist in African culture and fought against her exclusion from world competition by declaring that she is a 'woman'. There was even a national press conference where Caster was showcased in feminine dress to prove she was a woman. Although these expressions and acts of homophobia take a different form in contemporary South Africa, they suggest that heteronormativity remains a significant impediment to equality for all genders.

As the foregoing discussion indicates, the new democratic government can claim a number of liberal political gains towards gender equality. In addition to legislative and policy interventions to protect women and LGBTQI+ citizens from discrimination, there has been an increase in the political representation of women in political parties and the government.[138] Yet South Africa still lags behind in terms of achieving full gender equality for all genders, with many explanations being proffered for the slow pace of gender transformation. Changes to policies and legislation were brought about by intense lobbying by feminist and gay rights movements[139], yet the laws and policies enacted have not been accompanied by a fundamental change in unequal power and the removal of the racialised, gendered and heteronormative structures and everyday practices that impede gender transformation. In the case of women, feminists and NGOs argue that the Constitution gives the impression that gender equality is strongly enforced and

---

133 Lumby & Azaola, 2014.

134 Moffett, 2006.

135 Morgan & Wieringa, 2005; Nkabinde & Morgan, 2006.

136 Potgieter, 2011, pp. 9-19; Bhana, Morrell, Hearn & Moletsane, 2007.

137 Bhana, Morrell, Hearn & Moletsane, 2007, pp. 131-139.

138 Mvimbi, 2009,

139 Hassim, 2006,

pivotal to the political agenda, but the rights provided in the Constitution are abstract and focus on individual rights rather than achieving structural changes to the status of all genders. This focus on individual rights has led to an emphasis on a developmental approach to gender equality (i.e. the empowerment of women).[140] They also point to the initial prioritisation given to racial inequality that, at times, overshadowed the oppression of women and LGBTQI+ people.[141]

Instead, these activists argue, addressing gender equality requires understanding the heterogeneity of gender and the multiplicity of masculinities, that is, the intersection of gender, race, class, sexuality and masculinity.[142] Until this complex intersectionality is fully understood, gaps will remain in the development of policies, as well as in their full implementation.[143] This understanding is particularly urgent for governmental institutions. A recent study, based on interviews with 33 women in leadership positions in 46 national government structures, demonstrates the significance of a deeper understanding of the challenge of transforming institutions.[144] The interviews revealed the positive impact of women's movements and activism in engendering the recognition of women and promoting their representation within institutions. However, the data also revealed that a lack of political will on the part of male-stream patriarchal politics in the government, and the slow pace and effective development and implementation of gender policies at Ministerial level, are the main institutional barriers to gender transformation.[145] Participants in the study reported being stigmatised as "employment equity appointments", limiting their ability to influence change.[146] The authors concluded that, despite gender mainstreaming and employment equity policies, women leaders are still subjugated by interwoven male hegemony, racism, ethnicity, sexism, ageism and abusive practices in government departments.[147] Similar conclusions have been reached for research conducted on other institutions and studies of homophobia.[148] The exclusion of men, as agents for change, has also been cited as an additional impediment to transformation, particularly in terms of understanding and learning about masculinities.[149]

---

140 Mvimbi, 2009.

141 Mvimbi, 2009.

142 Ibid.

143 Ibid.

144 Mkhize & Mgcotyelwa-Ntoni, 2019, p. 13

145 Ibid.

146 Ibid, p. 15.

147 Ibid.

148 For example, see Daya, 2014; de Lange, Mitchell & Bhana, 2012; Destanovic, 2016; Dreyer, Blass & April, 2007; Jaga, Arabandi, Bagraim & Mdlongwa, 2002; Khan, 2010; Kiaye & Singh, 2013; Msibi, 2012; Senne, 2013; Ulicki, 2011; van Zyl, 2014.

149 Ratele, 2014.

CONCLUSION

Assessments of the progress towards transformation suggest that, despite good intentions, the new democratic South African government and the country continue to struggle with eradicating gender inequalities. There is no doubt there is still a long road to gender transformation, but there are some hopeful signals of the recognition to accelerate transformation.[150] On 17 May 2018, the CEE, together with the ILO and organised labour, organised business, government and community constituencies, held a meeting to discuss the end of gender violence and the harassment of women in the workplace.[151] The CEE also took part in the National Summit on Gender-based Violence in November 2018. On 20 August 2018, the CEE held a meeting in Parliament to review and amend the 1994 Women's Charter.[152] In addition to the identification of specific interventions, the most hopeful sign is the explicit linking of patriarchy and power to the inequality experienced by women.

Eradicating the deeply embedded patriarchy and heteronormativity in South Africa from colonial times to the present requires setting a vision for inclusive transformation that enables all genders to fully belong and contribute to South Africa – not simply tolerated or legalised – but unshackled from the strictures that limit the free expression of gender identity and access to social and economic well-being. Achieving this requires extraordinary leadership from all institutions, as well as every citizen, to move beyond thinking about gender identity as binary, reject patriarchal assumptions that value men over women, and abandon heternormativity that constructs LGBTQI+ people as deviants. These ideologies fuel gender inequalities, thus the unlearning and relearning tasks for everyone are changing both our minds and actions. This becomes possible if everyone understands that societies and the people within them are the ones who give meaning to ideas, labels to people, and create oppressive structures. The meaning of gender is socially constructed, and thus it can be reconstructed. The laws have paved the way, but now the goal must be realising their intent and becoming a non-racial, non-gendered, non-homophobic South Africa that belongs to everyone who lives in it. Ultimately, for South Africa to become the nation aspired to in the Constitution, it is the only choice that makes sense to denaturalise patriarchy and heteronormativity. Otherwise, as the opening quote implies, the past is not informing the future.

---

150 Ratele, 2014.
151 Author Commission for Employment Equity Annual Report 2018-2019, 2019.
152 Ibid, p. 7.

KEY TAKEAWAYS

1. Gender is not equal to biological sex (i.e. male or female). Instead, gender refers to the socially constructed and culturally determined roles of men and women in society.

2. Gender identity intersects with other categories of social difference such as race, class, ethnicity, and sexuality.

3. Contemporary gender inequalities in South Africa have deep roots shaped by its colonial, political, economic, and social past.

4. Despite good intentions and legislative reforms by the new democratic South African government, the country continues to struggle with eradicating gender inequalities.

5. Achieving true gender transformation in South Africa means engaging with the complexity of gender in formulating policies and organisational practices to address inequality and oppression.

Chapter 6

GENDER INEQUALITY AT WORK

Prof. Anita Bosch

*"Freedom cannot be achieved unless the women have been emancipated
from all forms of oppression." Nelson Mandela*

INTRODUCTION

This chapter provides an overview of gender inequality in the workplace in South Africa. The chapter is informed by more than a decade's interactions with business studies students about the differences between women and men, and why these are important for workplace outcomes. It draws on concepts contained in the chapter on gender of Nasima Carrim and Stella Nkomo, and focuses specifically on the status quo with regard to inequality in South African workplaces. This is followed by a discussion of complex questions that shape concerns about managing women in the workplace. The chapter commences with definitions of concepts as these relate to gender, and concludes with future directions to address workplace inequality for women.

Conceptual clarification

It is not precisely clear whether it was Aristotle, Voltaire or Socrates who insisted that we define our terms at the onset of debate. What is abundantly clear, however, is that many discussions have been unsuccessful in their aims precisely because narrators differed in their understanding of concepts, leading to miscommunication. As a starting point, it is therefore important to clarify the meaning of the term *gender*. The term is a much wider concept than the binary of woman and man, as gender relates to various hues of masculinity, femininity and androgyny[1], which are performed and expressed, and form part of, a person's identity beyond the initial classification of sex, which is assigned to

---

1   Geldenhuys, Bosch, Jeewa & Koutris, 2019.

us at birth. However, in this chapter, the term *gender* does indeed refer to the binary of woman and man, unless indicated otherwise. Using gender in the binary is appropriate for the topic of gender inequality at work, given that, in the South African workplace, two primary gender classifications are statistically recorded, namely male (or man) and female (or woman).

Gender inequality has been a hotly debated topic for as long as there has been an awareness about it and the courage to speak up against it. *Equality* refers to sameness in numbers, size, degree, rank, strength and value. Gender inequality at work is determined by searching for relatively stable patterns of differences between women and men in global, national, economic sector and organisational data. Once patterns of differences are found, determinations of the size, degree, value and rank are made, from which the strength of sameness or difference, i.e. equality or inequality, is determined. Whilst equality between the genders may seem like a lofty ideal, attempts at reaching precise sameness in numbers and treatment may have extreme consequences. For instance, requiring women and men workers to exert equal bodily strength, have the same international experience before assuming certain leadership roles, or having the same outputs by a certain age, may all carry inherent unfairness, as will be explored later on. Although gender equality can be more effectively measured, workplace policy should always include considerations for *equity*, i.e. meeting employees where they are with what they need. Irrational application of this principle is not the intention, such as remunerating employees according to their personal debt levels. Equity judgements should be made on historical injustices or social norms that entrenched unfairness against a specific grouping over time. Equity may therefore imply different treatment for women and men at work, with the view to reaching greater gender equality, in recognition of the social assumptions, roles and responsibilities that are differently placed on women than on men, and the effect thereof on women's access to, and successful participation in, paid work.

A further important distinction is also necessary within women as a grouping. It seems obvious to state that women are indeed different from each other. Already in the 1990s, Elisabeth Spellman stated that "...though all women are women, no woman is only a woman"[2], a sentiment about women's identities that was echoed by Judith Butler.[3] Yet these differences are often unrecognised and sometimes even ignored in the reductionist nature of organisations and business. *Intersectionality*[4] refers specifically to the identities that women have, and relates to social and political differences between women's identities, which create multiple overlapping distinctions in the hurdles that women need to overcome, as well as the status, privilege and recognition that are differently afforded

---

2   Spelman, 1990.
3   Butler, 1990.
4   Crenshaw, 1989.

them in the workplace or before entering formal work. Intersectional differences include race[5], sexual-orientation and socio-economic background, and, specifically, when collecting data about employed women, should acknowledge variations such as the presence and ages of children, whether the woman is a primary caregiver or not, if children reside with her, whether she is married, if she is in a long-standing romantic relationship or single, her age in relation to child-bearing and -rearing, and also beliefs about her, and her own beliefs, related to religion and culture.

Such specific descriptors provide important distinctions about the needs, behaviours and assumptions about women at work. Of importance when using these descriptors for comparative research is that researchers should statistically ensure that the measures they use are interpreted in the same way by different comparison groups, thereby eliminating biased results based on flawed scale construction.[6] These indicators and categories of differences between women are not static, but instead constitute multi-layered identities relative to historical power structures that adapt from context to context, resulting in constant movement up, sideways and down a gender-power hierarchy. In addition, the categories of difference change over time from generation to generation, and also over a woman's life course, for example childbearing years have now been comfortably extended to her mid-40s.[7] In conclusion, the intent of equality and equity is expressed by the following statements: *Equal but different*[8], and not *equal through sameness*.[9]

What is the status of workplace gender equality in South Africa?

It is a well-known fact that there remains a disparity in the representation of women and men in paid employment and leadership, as well as a gap in pay.[10] Statistics SA made a pronouncement in 2018 that "the South African labour market is more favourable to men than it is to women, and men are more likely to be in paid employment than women, regardless of race".[11] There have been pockets of advancement however, albeit small, such as the increase in employment numbers of women who are professionally qualified. In addition, 8% more women are employed in the public sector than men, and 40.4% of professionally employed people in the private sector are women.[12] The Commission for Employment Equity (CEE) report of 2019 noted a 1.7% growth in the number of women

---

5   Daya, 2012.
6   Steyn & De Bruin, 2020.
7   Jacobson, 2014.
8   Dlamini, 2016.
9   Evans, 1995.
10 Bosch, 2020.
11 Statistics South Africa, 2018.
12 Department of Labour, 2019.

at professional level since 2017, as well as growth in the 'skilled technical' category of women, which now stands at 48%.

Women remain underemployed in the semi-skilled and unskilled categories, yet national figures for 2019 from Stats SA[13] indicate that the category that employs the most women in the formal sector is elementary workers. The next employment categories that show high numbers are clerks, sales and services, and then domestic work. The only category of employment where more women than men are employed is clerks. The jobs that women predominantly occupy often require unskilled or semi-skilled individuals, or it may be that women do have skills, but that the economy does not offer them sufficient opportunity to access skilled work. In South Africa, the complex and disjointed geospatial layout of housing relative to industrial or commercial sites may also contribute to both women's and men's lack of access to employment that matches their skills. This may be exacerbated for women who take physical care of their families, making the relocation of family units to access better employment difficult and often impossible for most South African women.

Instead of disturbing family units, South African women often travel long distances to access work, sometimes being absent from home for periods of time. They also often take economic care of many extended family members, such as grandmothers[14] and other family members, who look after their children whilst the women are at work. It is estimated that women are 25%[15] more likely to look after extended family members than men, while the official unemployment rate for women in 2019 was 31%. In addition to formal-sector employment, women make up 38% of the informal sector. Women are underrepresented to a great extent in industries such as mining, utilities, agriculture, transport and construction.[16]

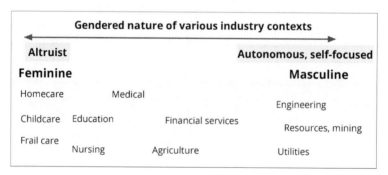

Figure 6.1: The gendered nature of industries

---

13 Stats SA, 2019.
14 Hatch & Posel, 2018.
15 Stats SA, 2015.
16 Stats SA, 2019.

Figure 6.1 portrays how gender influences the culture and assumptions of specific industries on a continuum, with feminine and masculine attributes as anchor points. Industries that are more feminine usually involve a high degree of caregiving as a salient feature. These industries usually employ a high concentration of women.

The main work done in feminine industries can be regarded as altruistic in nature, with a focus on humane, people-oriented and supportive intent towards the building of society. The culture with regard to pay for individuals in feminine industries is also premised on selfless service towards the greater good, and therefore the remuneration is usually lower than in masculine industries. Typical masculine industries have characteristics of autonomy and of being self-focused and 'rational'.

Pay in masculine industries is premised on individual contribution, and is usually higher than pay in feminine industries. Masculine industries' work builds society in a structural and things-oriented manner. Specific jobs within a feminine or masculine industry may have quite a masculine or feminine slant, such as being a training facilitator (a job that is feminine in nature) within the mining industry (a masculine industry). Industry type shows a marked correlation with a gender pay gap[17], as well as with the success that women as leaders may have[18], due to the perception of their suitability to the industry that followers may hold.

The number of women in top management remains problematic at only 23.5%, which signals that women are not included in the top decision-making roles of companies; there are 33% women in senior management in the private sector and 39% in government. Of importance is that top management only constitutes 0.8% of the total number of employees reported in the CEE report.[19] Furthermore, companies with fewer than 50 employees are not mandated to submit employment equity reports, and would therefore not be included in the CEE figures. The CEE report indicates that many women are employed by government – at both the national and provincial levels – and also in educational institutions, which could relate to more favourable conditions of work given the care role that women fulfil.

From a racial redress point of view, the proportion of women in the South African population is made up of 80.8% African, 8.8% Coloured, 7.9% White and 2.4% Indian/ Asian.[20] Women comprise 45.3% of the economically active population of South Africa, which is made up of 36% African, 4.4% Coloured, 3.9% White and 1% Indian.[21] "Compared

---

17 Blau & Khan, 2017.
18 Powell, 2011.
19 Department of Labour, 2019.
20 Stats SA, 2019.
21 Stats SA, 2018.

to the 2017 statistics, representation of the White Population Group (men and women) has shown a decline of 3.6% at Senior, and 4.3% at Skilled levels, respectively"[22], which is significant as only 2% of the total employed population in the CEE report are at senior management level and 26.7% are at skilled level. Furthermore, "the representation of designated groups (men and women) is at 60% for the Professionally qualified level and at 80% for the Skilled level".[23] The uptick in the number of women achieving post-school qualifications points towards a positive trajectory in the availability of talent from the designated racial groups.

Do we have enough qualified women to achieve parity in numbers?

The simple answer is yes. The increase in employment for women in the 'professionally qualified' and 'skilled technical' categories corresponds with the increase in the number of women graduating at universities. As reported by the Council on Higher Education in 2016[24], more women than men graduated in all the higher education fields, namely education, business and commerce, science, engineering and technology, and humanities. In addition, South African women and men between the ages of 15 and 64 are, on average, equally schooled at the pre-school, primary and secondary school levels, but in 2016 more women reported to have no schooling, at 55.3%, than men.[25] One could argue that women graduating in 2016 may not have gained sufficient experience to fulfil roles, but there were already a great number of women who had graduated in previous years, as can be seen in Table 6.1. These women would, by now, have gained the relevant level of experience to hold jobs that would support and stimulate the economy.

Table 6.1: Snapshot of qualified women in South Africa[26]

• In 2017, there were 867 female professors and 1,040 female associate professors at South African public universities and universities of technology.
• In 2012, 24,071 women studied towards Master's degrees, and 6,113 towards PhDs. In 2017, the figures increased to 31,127 Master's degrees and 10,159 PhDs.
• In July 2019, 38% (17,149) of all SAICA-affiliated chartered accountants (CA) were women. This is 38% of all CAs in South Africa.[27]

---

22 Department of Labour, 2019.
23 Ibid.
24 Council on Higher Education, 2018.
25 Stats SA, 2016.
26 Bosch, van der Linde & Barit, 2020.
27 SAICA, 2021.

To provide a more nuanced picture with regard to racial diversity, 60.8% of the CAs are white women, therefore there is still an under-representation of African and Coloured female CAs. Furthermore, many of the CAs have less than 10 years' post-article experience, and are mostly below age 40. While there are more white women CAs in absolute numbers than African (10,496 vs. 3,337), the growth rate of women CAs from the various racial groupings differs. Over the past 18 years (since 2002, when SAICA made comparable statistics available), the number of African female CAs increased by 97%, and white female CAs by 69%. Number increases have declined over time for the white population group overall – in the past 10 years, the number of African female CAs increased by 82%, and Indian/Asian women had a 63% growth rate compared to a 39% growth for white female CAs. White male CAs showed no growth percentage in 2019. At present there are more black African women CAs than males (3,337 vs. 3,001) and more Coloured women CAs than men (954 vs. 870). SAICA does not provide age statistics on their website, which limits reporting on the age distribution of female CAs. Information about women's post-article experience is also not publically available for analysis.

- From 2010 to 2017, there have consistently been more women candidate attorneys registered than male ones.

Access to, and the completion of, education is therefore a proven way for women to access formal employment, and women are taking this route very seriously.

Is there really a pay gap between women and men?

The mere thought of women being paid less than men, and that this difference in pay is baseless, seems inconceivable, and is therefore often dismissed without further thought. However, numerous studies point towards a gender pay gap globally[28], as well as in South Africa.[29] These studies relate to econometric analyses of national panel data that do not account for job-type differences, but, instead, use nationally aggregated data. An immediate response could be that national data may be too wide to make a determination about pay, however what these datasets point out is that women are consistently, over time, paid less than men.

Explanations for such differences are usually that women may work shorter hours or hold lower qualifications than men. The latter point has already been discredited in the previous section of this chapter. With regard to shorter hours, during analyses, the issue of differences between hours at work is overcome using hourly pay and controlling for hours worked in datasets. A study by Mosomi did control for these variables, and a gap of between 10% and 35% was still evident, depending on where the women were located in the wage distribution.

---

28 Blau & Khan, 2017.
29 Mosomi, 2018.

In South Africa, some of the pay gap can be explained by the type of work that women and men are employed to perform, in that women are often called to do paid care work and men heavy manual work. The mere fact that women's weaker muscle force makes it difficult to compete with men in manual labour, where lifting and carrying is required, has made a clear distinction between the sexes. However, women's bodies continue to outstrip those of men in endurance strength, as illustrated through modern-day African women's duties of tilling the land, fetching and carrying water from precarious collection points, and bearing children and tending to their care without respite.

While differences between women's and men's bodies are historically at the heart of perceived pay inequality, bodily differences do not explain inequality. Instead, one needs to look towards the value and worth that are ascribed to women and men, together with the assumptions that are inferred about their capabilities in contemporary society, to fully understand the forces that shape pay inequality. For work that involves manual labour, men are paid higher rates for substantively the same work as women. Practically speaking, this can be seen in households when male domestic workers are paid more than their female counterparts.

Reasons for the pay gap between women and men also point to the industries in which women predominantly work, as illustrated in Figure 6.1. Industry gender characteristics show a strong correlation with pay.[30] In layman's terms, feminine industries usually have lower pay than masculine industries. It is unclear whether the type of work conducted in feminine industries or the fact that feminine industries predominantly employ women is the driver of lower pay in those industries. An overview of key concepts about the gender pay gap and its mechanisms was provided by Bosch[31], who also called for greater pay transparency[32] and policy change to ensure equitable pay for women and men.

Why is care negatively regarded by some employers?

Caregiving is considered a woman's domain, irrespective of whether she has children. Women are often overlooked during job application processes and for promotion, based on the assumption that they will have children at some stage and then have a primary focus at home, resulting in them not being dedicated to their work. Even though there may, in fact, be no difference in the time and attention that a woman and a man devote to their work, employers may be more inclined to consider the employee who is visible at work, usually the man, as dedicated and competent. Many employers therefore regard the employment of women as having a low investment return, and that managing women is fraught with complications.

---

30 Blau & Khan, 2017.
31 Bosch, 2020.
32 Bosch & Barit, 2020.

Since women are biologically able to bear children, and the practice of taking leave after birth remains allotted predominantly to mothers[33], fathers may not feel comfortable taking the 10 days parental leave in South Africa, also referred to as paternity leave. Bonding with children may therefore occur differently for the parent who is at work. If the parents do not deliberately make equal parenting arrangements, the one who took leave during the birth or adoption of a child is likely to remain the primary caregiver of the child. Such an arrangement may work well within family units, but the implications are far reaching for women's careers, as, within organisations, it creates unequal conditions between caregivers (usually mothers) and employees without children.

Caregivers' availability to do work or to be fully present for work may be compromised. These circumstances do not preclude women from fully participating in work, but indicate the need for structures to support and enable them to engage with work on an equal footing with men. Without the availability of such structures, e.g. childcare, women may operate from a deficit in comparison to those men who are not primary caregivers. Whilst an argument could be made that men are increasingly playing a role in childcare, more so than previous generations, Ratele[34] cautioned that gender democracy is not practiced in South African homes, and that men remain ambivalent about gender equality. These assertions were confirmed in a German study analysing 20 years of national panel data for dual-income households. The study found that men were not taking up more housework duties, but that these duties continued to either be predominantly performed by women or outsourced, especially when women earn the greater income in a household.[35]

The gender deficit relates to mostly personal costs to women, such as a lack of sleep, which may lead to burnout and work-family conflict, which could lead to lowered performance outcomes at work. In addition, childbearing, which may occur more than once for a woman, introduces life events that are cyclical in nature to the workplace, such as starting again with feeding a new baby as you complete the cycle of weaning another child. This cyclical experience of time[36] may be part of the reason for the lack of understanding of women's needs, as it stands in stark contrast to the linear framing of time and progression, signalled through a conclusion-and-dispatch attitude towards tasks, which is often left unquestioned in the workplace. Pregnancy is therefore mostly undesirable at work.[37] Under these circumstances, women are metaphorically playing a match with one hand tied behind their back. Unfortunately, employers are not easily convinced that they should pay attention to these differences. Instead, they favour the equality approach of treating all employees in the same manner, as this is often

---

33 Pienaar & Kok, 2017.

34 Ratele, 2014.

35 Procher, Ritter & Vance, 2018.

36 Hughes, 2002.

37 Bosch, 2016.

the easiest way of ensuring that men are appeased. Through these sameness actions, employers entrench gender inequality.

Can women be leaders in African culture?

Gender relations have been in flux over the centuries, with power predominantly vesting in men, even though there have been notable examples of women holding great power. In Africa, there have historically been a number of women rulers, but their legacies were not textually recorded and were instead narrated between generations, resulting in limited information about their reign. Of those that were most prominent, four are mentioned here: Queen Njinga of Angola (1582–1663), who ruled over two kingdoms and was described as a great warrior, politician and diplomat[38]; the well-known Queen of Sheba, who donated materials, indicative of her wealth, to build the Temple of King Solomon[39]; Hatshepsut, the first female pharaoh of Egypt, who chose to invest her kingdom's wealth in building imposing structures and also in the arts[40]; and a most interesting individual, Queen Amina of Zaria in West Africa, who built a vast empire in approximately 1,576 AD through crafty military action[41], and believed that she should never marry, but, "instead, it is said, she took a different husband each night as she led her army in its campaigns. Then in the morning, she had him beheaded...".[42] Upon reflection on historical texts on the manner in which these women led, it is evident that leadership can be found in any individual, woman or man, if a person is given the opportunity to lead and has the traits and skills relevant to the context and era. Yet somehow, being classified as a woman or a man has, over the centuries, been essentialised to carry implicit meanings about ability – or more precisely, assumed ability or inability – in all spheres of life. This misdirection is further amplified or softened by the culture to which these individuals belong or happen to find themselves in.

Ratele[43] stated that African culture should not be conflated with "...patriarchal hetero-masculinist traditionalism...", as though men and women who are sexually attracted to people of the same sex were not present in Africa and do not represent one of the many forms of masculinity (or femininity) that always existed in Africa. Yet the predominant view is that African culture is deeply patriarchal, heterosexual and masculine out of tradition, thereby implying that tradition trumps any change and is generally static and morally good. Under such circumstances, resistance to "conscientizing men about gender equality... including but not limited to daily caring of children, participating in household

---

38 Heywood, 2017.
39 Adam & Eghubare, 2010.
40 McCollum, 2004.
41 Adam & Eghubare, 2010.
42 McCollum, 2004.
43 Ratele, 2013.

work, supporting affirmative action for women..., and doing work against domestic violence...[44]" is to be expected, as compliance with normative cultural behaviour would be expected of both women and men. Furthermore, globally, including in African countries, men may construe gender equality as a personal loss.[45]

Jewkes et al. urged us to work with the vulnerability that men might feel, so that they do not feel "blamed and judged"[46], however they also cautioned against letting men off the hook in exploring their complicity in gender inequality, predominantly through the lens of men's rights. African men, irrespective of race, are therefore not victims of gender reform, but rather partners in such change. When men are conscientised to being complicit in gender inequality, the quest for equality becomes less oppositional for women. Such awareness creates an opportunity for women to display their leadership traits and capabilities, and to be taken seriously in Africa.

Should a woman marry if she is serious about her career?

Declining civil marriage rates over a number of years and increasing customary and civil union marriages between 2017 and 2018 in South Africa[47] point to an interaction between socio-cultural, gender and economic factors that drive women's choices regarding marriage. Cultural practices such as men's payment of *ilobolo* remain deeply entrenched, and often serve as an impediment to customary marriages due to a lack of economic resources with which to conclude such agreements.[48] Furthermore, "customary law grants the power to control property to a husband, and views a wife as a perpetual minor under the guardianship of the husband".[49] In addition, polygamy remains a fundamental part of indigenous culture on the African continent, even though it is viewed as a practice that undermines women's rights.[50] In South Africa, marriage in Indian culture is often laden with expectations about compliance with pronouncements about wifeliness by the extended family.[51] Similarly, Afrikaner women are raised to be "dutiful daughters and passive martyrs"[52], whose role it is to be supportive of their husband as the undisputed head of the household.

44 Ratele, 2014.
45 Ibid.
46 Jewkes, Morrell, Hearn, Lundqvist, Blackbeard, Lindegger, Quayle, Sikweyiya & Gottén, 2015.
47 Stats SA, 2018.
48 Rudwick & Posel, 2015.
49 Mwambene, 2017.
50 Ibid.
51 Ahmed & Carrim, 2016.
52 Griessel & Kotze, 2010.

Taken together, these patterns and customs, as well as the need for economic independence, have led to many households in South Africa being headed by women.[53] Female-headed households are not a new phenomenon, and were, as a result of labour migration, already documented in the 1970s.[54] However, as women become economically independent, new dynamics are emerging in marriages, disturbing social expectations that women should primarily be home-makers, subsistence farmers and caregivers, and that they should expend a lot of energy on maintaining household relationships, including that of marriage. Similar to women from India, African women were found to commit fewer personal resources to marriage, with declining commitment to the marital role the older they became.[55] The median age for women who divorced in South Africa in 2018 was 41 years, which may coincide with increasing mid-career workplace demands placing strain on them to also fulfil social expectations of care and relationship maintenance. Gloria Steinem's statement that "men should think twice before making widowhood women's only path to power" uses wit to reinforce the idea that husbands' support of their wives' careers, not only as a spectator or beneficiary of their economic activity, but specifically by being a helping hand, including sharing responsibility for caregiving as well as emotional support, is essential in answering the question whether women who are serious about their careers should get married.

How will we know if we've achieved gender equality at work?

In order to fully appreciate the need for gender equality, the following statement illustrates a stark contrast in the views that society holds of women and men:

> "An observer not raised with our cultural assumptions would be struck by the fact that one half of the population was assigned by birth to activities which, whatever their private gratifications and social importance, carried no economic reward, little public status and very limited access to public power."[56]

In light of the above statement, it is said that we do not focus on improvements if we do not measure them. South Africa should comply with the stipulations in the Bill of Rights in the Constitution that guarantee equality of sex, gender, birth and pregnancy, amongst a number of other provisions. The *Gender Gap Report* is an annual publication of the World Economic Forum (WEF) that "benchmarks national gender gaps in economic, education, health and political participation criteria".[57] Although the report does measure gender-

---

53 Hall & Posel, 2019.
54 Rogan, 2016.
55 Bosch, De Bruin, Kgaladi & De Bruin, 2012.
56 Herrett, 2010.
57 WEF, 2020.

related improvements for nations across the globe, it is often erroneously quoted as measuring and reporting on the gender pay gap. Whilst South Africa is ranked 17th out of 153 countries in the WEF report, the lived experience of gender equality is clearly not fully measured and reported in the report, as, for example, gender-based violence in South Africa is disturbingly high.[58] It may be the case that South Africa is still promising equality to its women and not yet delivering on it.[59]

Workplace equality cannot exist without gender equality in the home and public spheres. To this end, Elizabeth Broderick[60] stated that gender equality can become a reality when women and men combine forces. Workplaces cannot be just in their dealings if women are favoured over men – the so-called 'crisis of masculinity'[61] – except where an organisation has identified and is trying to deal with a pattern of inequality that has persisted over time. Under these conditions, the specific issue to be rectified is attached to a timeline to ensure that there is remedial action with a definite goal, with achievement of the goal signalling an end-state to the unfair practice.

Farré stated that "gender equality does not mean that women rule over men; rather, it guarantees a level playing field that lacks all forms of discrimination against women".[62] One way of viewing such equality is encapsulated in the words of Sheryl Sandberg: "A truly equal world would be one where women ran half our countries and companies and men ran half our homes."[63] An organisation that makes an assertion about gender equality should follow it up with measurement of gender equality, however gender equity, which is more difficult to measure and structurally embedded[64], should be vigorously pursued with thoughtful intent.

CONCLUSION

Future directions

In conclusion to this chapter there are two aspects that may draw us into a different future. The first relies on men and women to conduct self-examination about their complicity in a larger workplace system from which men benefit. Such self-reflection is often uncomfortable and does not come naturally. Yet, even during self-reflection, we may err in how we frame and think about gender inequality. Here we should pay special

---

58 Gouws, 2017.
59 Sandberg, 2013.
60 Broderick, 2010.
61 Broderick, 2010.
62 Farré, 2013.
63 Sandberg, 2013.
64 Nkomo & Rodriguez, 2018.

attention to the impact that decisions, such as framing policy along the lines of sameness or difference, bring to women's work lives.

This brings us to the second aspect. Driving equality solely as a numbers game is missing the point. Women are increasingly able to push themselves to over-work in order to over-perform, similar to their male counterparts, so that they take up an increasing number of jobs. However, organisations remain structured according to principles that favour an 'ideal worker'[65]; i.e. workers are disembodied, available 24/7, and have no care obligations. It seems evident that ideal workers are fictitious, a myth even for men, yet the ideal worker is the benchmark against which performance and contribution is measured at work. A re-examination of this benchmark is urgently required as most women, especially those with care obligations, can by definition never be 'ideal workers'. In addition, the ideal worker myth is fuelling hyper competition and poor work-life balance for both women and men. Working towards gender equality is therefore as much about thinking as what it is about doing. Thoughtful action should enable progress that signals a change in the value that we attribute to women and the differences that they bring to work.

KEY TAKEAWAYS

1. Differences between women as a grouping are presented, as these provide important information about the needs and behaviours of, as well as the assumptions about, women at work, which informs research design and organisational policy.

2. A diagram of the gendered nature of industries illustrates the combination of masculine and feminine attributes and how these influence pay inequality.

3. There are sufficiently qualified numbers of women in all major disciplines of study such that a parity in numbers of women equal to that of men can be achieved.

4. As women become more economically independent, new dynamics are emerging in marriages, disturbing social expectations that women should primarily be homemakers, subsistence farmers and caregivers, and that they should expend a lot of energy on maintaining household relationships, including their marriages.

5. Equality in numbers only is missing the point – greater attention should be paid to organisational decisions that are taken along the lines of sameness or difference.

6. An organisation that makes an assertion about gender equality should follow it up with a measurement of gender equality, however gender equity, which is more difficult to measure and structurally embedded, should be vigorously pursued with thoughtful intent.

---

65 Brumley, 2014.

Chapter 7

RESPONDING TO GENDER-BASED VIOLENCE IN SOUTH AFRICA: LESSONS FROM HIGHER EDUCATION

Dr. Claire Kelly

INTRODUCTION

Over the last five years, there has significant progress in the higher-education sector in South Africa in addressing gender-based violence (GBV). This progress has occurred against the backdrop of some of the highest incidence of GBV in the world, as well as the upheaval of the largest student protests since Apartheid. This chapter asks the questions: *What is it about higher education in South Africa that has enabled it to make this progress under these seemingly impossible circumstances?* and *What can we learn about advancing meaningful responses to GBV in our institutions?*

This chapter starts with a picture of the socio-economic context of GBV in South Africa, including an overview of the prevalence of GBV and the legislative landscape. It will provide some theoretical and historical framing of GBV, in answer to the question of why, in spite of our robust legislative machinery, South Africa remains one of the most dangerous countries in the world to be a woman and/or LGBTQIA++. It will then go on to examine the response to GBV in higher education over the last five years, extracting three key lessons from this response that may provide clues for how we address GBV in other sectors.

GBV IN SOUTH AFRICA

South Africa has one of the highest incidences of gender-based violence in the world. According to the World Health Organisation in 2000, South Africa's murder rate of women was five times higher than the global average. This gap had closed somewhat between 2000 and 2015, but South Africa still remains just over double the global average.[1]

According to StatsSA's *Victims of Crime Report 2017/2018*, 250 out of every 100,000 women are survivors of sexual offences, compared to 120 out of every 100,000 men, and an estimated 68.5% of sexual offence survivors are women.[2] Alarmingly, the report also indicates that there are still men and women (albeit a minority) who believe that it is acceptable to hit a woman, a percentage that increases when that woman is married and the assailant is her husband. The report also indicates that, although both men and women's freedom of movement are curtailed due to fear of crime, women's movement is more so.

It is important to note, however, that statistics are notoriously difficult indicators to determine the extent of GBV accurately. There is, in fact, no single indicator that describes the full extent of GBV in South Africa. Crime statistics, although useful, only provide part of the picture. First of all, they report only sexual offences as a single category, yet there are more than 30 forms of sexual offences and sexual offenses are only one form of GBV. Secondly, they rely on reported crimes. It is well-known that survivors of sexual offences do not always report their assaults, due to, amongst other things, stigma, fear of the assailant, and the unhelpful attitude of the police.[3] The Centre for the Study of Violence and Reconciliation (CSVR) made this point in a 2016 report, going on to cite a number of small-scale community-focused studies that provide more detailed insights than provided by the national crime statistics.[4] Although they make the point that these studies also have their limitations (i.e. under reporting and non-generalisability), they argue that the insights they provide are helpful in better understanding the prevalence and nature of GBV as it plays out in South African society.

Cited in the CSVR report, a 2012 survey found that an average of 52% women (across Limpopo, Gauteng, Western Cape and KwaZulu-Natal) had experienced some form of GBV, the highest being Limpopo with 77%.[5] The same survey reported that, on average, 55% of men (in Gauteng, Limpopo and KwaZulu-Natal) admitted to perpetrating GBV, the highest being Gauteng with 76%. These figures are much higher than those reported by

---

1   WHO, 2016.
2   StatsSA, 2018.
3   Vetten, 2005.
4   The Centre for the Study of Violence and Reconciliation, 2016.
5   Gender Links, 2012.

StatsSA. The main reason is that the researchers used a more comprehensive definition of GBV that included more than 'sexual assault'. It is likely also that the women surveyed felt more comfortable speaking to the researchers about their experiences than reporting them to the police.

A study by the Institute of Security Studies roughly echoes the Gauteng figures cited above, indicating that 50% of women in Gauteng have experienced intimate partner violence (IPV). Alarmingly, 80% of men admitted to having committed GBV against their intimate partners.[6] Interestingly, this study also showed that married women experienced marginally more violence (53%) than unmarried women.

The CSVR report (2016) noted that IPV is a particularly lethal form of GBV for women in South Africa, with around 50% of all femicide being committed in intimate relationships.[7] It notes that in 1999, 8.8 per 100,000 of the female South African population aged 14 years and older were murdered by their intimate partners, which is significantly higher than international measures.[8] In fact, according to one study, the murder rate for women in South Africa was 24.7 per 100 000[9], with, on average, seven women murdered every day between March 2010 and March 2011.[10] This is staggeringly high compared to a global average of four per 100,000[11], and the highest rate ever reported in the world.

Beyond the obvious social justice and moral toll on our society, GBV also has an economic toll. GBV costs South Africa between R28.4 billion and R42.4 billion per year – or between 0.9% and 1.3% of GDP respectively – annually.[12] The study goes to great lengths to calculate the costs to individual survivors, the government, NGOs, as well as businesses. The table below represents a breakdown of those calculations.

Table 7.1: Estimated cost by affected group, based on GBV prevalence rate of 30%[13]

Affected group	Cost	Percentage contribution
Victims	R37,803,850,561	89.2%
Government	R513,551,244.39	1.21%
Civil society	R1,328,378,748	3.13%

6   Institute for Security Studies, 2011.
7   Abrahams, Mathews, Martin, Lombard & Jewkes, 2013.
8   Mathews, et al., 2004.
9   Abrahams, et al., 2009.
10 Abrahams, et al., 2013.
11 Dahlberg & Krug, 2002.
12 Muller, Gahan, & Brooks, 2014.
13 Muller, Gahan, & Brooks, 2014.

Affected group	Cost	Percentage contribution
Businesses	R2,734,855,038	6.45%
Total	**R42,380,635,591**	**100%**
As measure of GDP		**1.3%**

What is particularly interesting about these calculations is that survivors clearly bear the largest part of the financial burden. This is significant, as GBV, which is more than a human rights violation in and of itself, also puts women at further risk for economic exclusion.

However, the authors of the study[14] make it clear that there are a number of limitations to these calculations and that, as a result, they are woefully underestimated. They name the lack of unreliable data as a real limitation, for example, the government budgets to implement anti-GBV programmes are not always ring-fenced and, as such, are unidentifiable. The government expenditure also happens across many different domains, such as public health, education, justice and others. Businesses do not monitor absenteeism or underperformance that results from GBV. Furthermore there are certain costs which are just not factored in, for example costs of pain and suffering do not feature in the calculation of survivor costs.[15]

Table 7.2: Costs not accounted for in the current estimate[16]

Affected group	Costs not included	Significance
Victim	Pain and suffering	Pain, suffering and mortality amounted to 44% of the total cost of GBV in Australia in 2004.
Government	Lost tax revenues	Loss of income to individuals and loss of revenue to businesses both result in multiplier effects which negatively impact tax revenues to government.
Government	Transfer costs	Transfer costs, i.e. welfare payments to individuals, made up 2% of the total cost of GBV in Australia in 2004.
Business	Costs of hiring and training replacement staff	The inclusion of these costs would increase the overall cost of GBV to business.
Private health	Cost of private healthcare	The cost of public and private healthcare combined made up 32% of the cost of GBV in Australia in 2004.

14 Walby, 2009.

15 Ibid.

16 Ibid.

Affected group	Costs not included	Significance
Civil society	Cost of volunteers' time	The amount of time that volunteers devote to civil society organisations is significant, and the value thereof is not accounted for in this study
Second generation	Second generation costs	Second generation costs made up 2% of the total cost of GBV in Australia in 2004, and given the difficulties in quantifying second generation costs, this is also likely to be an underestimation

Given the extent of the problem, one could be forgiven for thinking that we do not have much in the way of legislative and policy structures to manage and respond to GBV in South Africa, however this is where one would be wrong – South Africa has one of the most robust anti-GBV legislative and policy frameworks in the world. The following section will provide some detail of this infrastructure and discuss some of the gaps that result in the extraordinary disconnect between the law/policy and the reality of GBV in South Africa.

South African legislative framework and gaps

South Africa's legislative framework is underpinned by the Constitution of South Africa and the Bill of Rights.[17] One of the most foundational pieces of legislation giving expression to the Bill of Rights is the Promotion of Equality and Prevention of Unfair Discrimination Act, 4 of 2000 (PEPUDA), which prohibits unfair discrimination and forbids hate speech and harassment on the basis of race, gender, pregnancy, family responsibility or status, marital status, ethnic or social origin, HIV/AIDS status, sexual orientation, age, disability, religion, conscience, belief, culture, language and birth. Giving expression to these two foundational pieces of legislation, South Africa has a number of policies and legislation in place to respond specifically to gender-based violence. Most significant are the:

- *Criminal Law Amendment Act 105 of 1997*, which established mandatory minimum sentences for certain rapes;

- *Criminal Procedure Second Amendment Act 85 of 1997*, which allowed for bail conditions to be tightened in cases of those charged with rape;

- *Domestic Violence Act 116 of 1998*, which set out to offer options to survivors of abuse through identifying certain obligations on law enforcement bodies and making provision for interim protection orders and restraining orders;

---

17 Section 9: Everyone is equal before the law and has the right to equal protection and benefits of the law. Section 10: Everyone has the right to inherent dignity and the right to have their dignity respected and protected. Section 11: Everyone has the right to life (Republic of South Africa, 1996). Perhaps we can divide these footnotes up, so a/b/c etc. will be explanations like this, and 1/2/3 etc. will be references?

- *Criminal Law (Sexual Offences and Related Matters) Amendment Act 32 of 2007*, which broadened the definition of rape and other sexual offences and introduced new offences that relate to gender-based violence, including digital distribution of pornography, etc.[18, 19]

In addition to the fairly comprehensive library of legislation, there have been numerous attempts by the state to co-ordinate a response to GBV. These include, amongst other things, the underfunded and largely dysfunctional Department of Women, which like most interventions achieved little success.[20] However, there have been some significant movements in the last few years.

In 2016, the Department of Monitoring and Evaluation commissioned a review of the state's response to violence against women and children, which provided important insights into the gaps in the state's GBV response.[21] At the same time, a coalition of civil society organisations called the Stop Gender Violence Campaign produced a *National Strategic Plan on Gender-Based Violence Shadow Framework*, which also identified gaps, mostly relating to implementation. Through the report, the campaign was able to both apply pressure to, and assist, the state in addressing the identified gaps. It is important to note that civil society has always been instrumental in the state's response to GBV, providing important expertise and capacity.

However, it was in August 2018, when an intersectional movement of women known as #TheTotalShutdown mobilised thousands of people to march to Parliament to deliver a memorandum articulating the failure of the state to keep women safe, as well as a list of 24 demands to the President of the Republic of South Africa, that momentum increased. These demands included, amongst others, a strong message from the office of the President against GBV, the development of a national action plan on GBV, and the establishment of accountability and oversight mechanisms to ensure the implementation of any National Plan.[22]

In direct response to this Memorandum, President Cyril Ramaphosa hosted a Presidential Summit on GBV, and published a document making a number of declarations on commitments to addressing GBV.[23] One of those commitments was the development of a National Strategic Plan to address GBV.

---

18 Stop Gender Violence Campaign, 2017.
19 Interim Steering Committee on Gender-based Violence and Femicide, 2019.
20 Stop Gender Violence Campaign, 2017; Interim Steering Committee on Gender-based Violence and Femicide, 2019.
21 Department of Planning, Monitoring and Evaluations, 2016.
22 #TheTotalShutdown, 2018.
23 Presidential Summit on Gender-based Violence and Femicide, 2018.

However, in August 2019, protests rocked the country once again. These protests were led by students to mourn and express anger at the deaths of Uyinene Mrwetyana[24] and Jesse Hess[25], two young women students from the University of Cape Town and the University of the Western Cape, respectively. In September 2019, President Ramaphosa re-committed that the decisions of the Summit would be prioritised for implementation at all levels of government, that legislative amendments would be made, and that substantial funding would be made available for interventions to address GBV.

The first draft of the *National Gender-Based Violence and Femicide Strategic Plan 2020-2030* became available in August 2019.[26] The Plan builds specifically on the review conducted by the Department of Planning and Evaluations and civil society on the *National Strategic Plan on Gender-Based Violence Shadow Framework*. Importantly, this plan is supported by resourcing.

One of the key reasons for the development of the National Strategic Plan is to plug the numerous gaps in the state's response to GBV, including the co-ordination and implementation of the legislative and policy frameworks. For us to understand why GBV remains so prolific in spite of what looks like a robust state response, it is useful to understand these gaps.

Gaps in the response to GBV

The *National Strategic Plan on Gender-Based Violence Shadow Framework* provides the most useful description of the gaps in the state's response to GBV, under five main themes. These themes are related to: the definition of GBV; gaps in implementing laws and policy; psycho-social services for survivors; investment in prevention, intervention, research and documentation; and accountability measures. Importantly, the new *National Gender-Based Violence and Femicide Strategic Plan 2020-2030* addresses all of these issues to a greater or lesser extent. Whether it does so adequately will be determined in the ongoing consultation phase and, of course, implementation.

a.   Limiting definition

Any discussion about GBV must start with a very important distinction between gender-based violence (GBV) and violence against women (VAW).

Gender-based violence (GBV) is:

> *"an umbrella term for forms of interpersonal violence characterized by gendered power imbalances. Fitting within this, intimate-partner violence refers to emotional, spiritual,*

---

24 Uyinene Mrwetyana was a student at the University of Cape Town. She was raped and murdered on 24 August 2019 by a Post Office employee at a Post Office in Cape Town.

25 Jesse Hess was a student at the University of the Western Cape. She was found murdered with her grandfather in their apartment in Cape Town on 30 August 2019.

26 Interim Steering Committee on Gender-based Violence and Femicide, 2019.

physical, sexual and financial abuse between people who are intimate. It also fits within broader subcategories of gender-based violence, namely family and domestic violence. It has been recognised under both international and local law as a fundamental barrier to the enjoyment of full human rights".[27]

Violence against women (VAW) refers to:

"any act of gender-based violence that results in, or is likely to result in, physical, sexual or psychological harm or suffering to women, including threats of such acts, coercion or arbitrary deprivation of liberty, whether occurring in public or in private life".[28]

These two terms are often conflated in both discourse and practice, and most state interventions primarily address VAW. For example, the '16 Days of Activism' campaigns use the terms 'violence against women and girls' and 'gender-based violence' interchangeably. There is no differentiation between groups that are at high risk for experiencing GBV, such as sex workers, prison inmates or refugees, and there is no mention of LGBTQIA++ communities.[29]

However, it is important to recognise that GBV is not only directed at cis-gender women[30]; GBV is violence targeted at someone on the basis of their gender and characterised by gendered power imbalances. Power imbalances can result from queer and gender non-conformity and identities that challenge hegemonic gender norms, for example, the violence transgender individuals experience is a form of GBV. Thus, GBV includes violence against LGBTQIA++ individuals and gender non-conforming men. This is an important development in understanding and responding to the kinds of violence individuals experience in relation to their gender. Although cis-gender women remain the largest social group globally (and nationally) who experience violence related to their gender, and it is important that interventions to stop VAW are as crucial as ever, not considering queer and gender non-conforming individuals leaves an enormous omission in both our understanding and our ability to respond to GBV.[31]

GBV is also different in another way to VAW. The GBV lens brings an expanded view of violence beyond physical, sexual and psychological. It includes systemic definitions of violence such as economic and state violence in which women, girls and LGBTQIA++

---

27 Ibid, p. 7.

28 United Nations General Assembly, 1993.

29 South African Government, 2019.

30 Cis-gender refers to gender that conforms to the sex assigned at birth. A cis-gender woman is someone who identifies as a woman and who was assigned female at birth. Cis-gender is used to differentiate from trans-gender. This is when someone identifies as differently from their sex assigned at birth.

31 Interim Steering Committee on Gender-based Violence and Femicide, 2019; Stop Gender Violence Campaign, 2017.

individuals are denied access to critical basic human rights, such as sexual and reproductive health care and participation in the economy. It also includes the hidden and normalised violence of institutionalised exclusions. These kinds and acts of violence rarely feature in state GBV responses, resulting in a serious gap.[32]

b.   Gaps in implementing existing laws and policies

The list of gaps relating to the implementation of laws and policies reads like a very long and very bad report card. It is not possible to relate them all in this chapter, but a detailed account can be found in the *National Strategic Plan on Gender-Based Violence Shadow Framework.*

The *Shadow Framework* identifies seven areas where the state has direct legal responsibilities with regards to GBV.[33] Of course all departments must respond to GBV in their respective contexts, for example the Department of Higher Education and Training and the Department of Labour, but the seven listed entities are collectively responsible for the anti-GBV infrastructure.

The main themes that emerged out of the analysis shared by the *Shadow Framework* are listed below:

- A **lack of co-ordination** between all the responsible parties, at both national and local levels. It is crucial in a system that is interconnected in the way the GBV-response infrastructure is, that all the relevant parts work together, however there is a serious lack of co-ordination across our South African systems. In rape cases, for example, information often goes missing between SAPS and the forensic and medical examiners and prosecutors, jeopardising the possibility of conviction.

- **Under resourcing** is a major problem and features across all seven of the responsibility areas. From South African Police Service (SAPS) stations that do not have Victim Friendly Rooms or trained staff to deal with GBV survivors, to a serious shortage of social workers, completely under-resourced forensic facilities that often do not provide adequate analyses to lead to convictions, overburdened prosecutors, and under resourced schools that can barely conduct their core business, never mind provide the necessary care, attention and education required to address GBV. It is clear that for any law or policy to find traction in practice, it must be adequately and sustainably resourced.

---

32 Interim Steering Committee on Gender-based Violence and Femicide, 2019; Stop Gender Violence Campaign, 2017.

33 These include the South African Police Service, National Prosecuting Authority/Department of Justice and Constitutional Development, Department of Social Development, Department of Health, Department of Basic Education, Department of Correctional Services and Department of Co-operative Governance and Traditional Affairs.

- **A lack of training** is linked to the problem of under resourcing; there is a desperate shortage of social workers, forensic scientists and nurses. SAPS is also often guilty of not correctly or fully processing GBV cases, while prosecutors are known to be insensitive, and in some cases unknowledgeable, about the sociocultural aspects of GBV. Teachers are not sufficiently trained to handle GBV cases at their schools, nor are they able to navigate the complicated legal processes.

- It is not only due to poor training that SAPS and the prosecuting authorities are insensitive or do not process cases correctly. **Patriarchal attitudes** are a big contributor, with survivors often being victim-blamed, slut-shamed, or indeed ignored and dismissed. Secondary victimisation by the legal system is one of the reasons survivors do not report their assaults.

c.   *Improving and expanding psycho-social services for survivors*

GBV is highly traumatising, leaving survivors (and others affected like children who witness GBV) with life-long psychological scars. There is currently insufficient capacity to provide sufficient psycho-social support for survivors of GBV, due to a serious shortage of state-employed social workers and trained psychologists. This, in part, has to do with debilitating budget cuts for the Department of Social Development (DSD) from 2010, which further reduced their already stretched capacity. Currently, there is a heavy reliance on NGOs to do the work of psycho-social support, which, given the funding challenges NGOs face, is not sustainable.

d   *Prevention, intervention, and research and documentation*

Although progress has been made with regards to policy and law-making, there has not been enough focus on preventative interventions as well as secondary interventions, which mediate the long-term impact of GBV on individuals and communities.

Where preventative interventions have been conducted there are often challenges. For example, there is often no collective analysis before intervention, i.e. programmes rarely spend the necessary time building relationships and shared understandings of GBV that facilitate meaningful change before blundering into the said intervention. Efforts are often individually, rather than collectively, focused, which limits the intervention's capacity to make broader meaningful change. Interventions are often siloed, leading to duplication or even conflict.

For a comprehensive and meaningful preventative effort that can really shift the behaviour of communities of people, there needs to be a deliberate effort to research and understand the causes, prevalence and impact of GBV, and this needs to be rigorously funded.

e.   Accountability mechanisms and insufficient resources

Although an Inter-Sectoral Committee for the Management of the Sexual Offences Matters was mandated by the Sexual Offenses Act (of 2007), this body was slow and unresponsive. There is still no integrated information system across all departments at the national or local level. Overburdened and understaffed Parliamentary Portfolio Committees means that poor reporting is often not adequately scrutinised. Departments are often late and inconsistent with their reporting, and the SAPS' poor quality reporting means that the obligations are often not met. Without proper reporting, accountability becomes nigh impossible.

A THEORETICAL FRAMEWORK FOR UNDERSTANDING GBV

Feminist scholars have been writing about the apparent disconnect between legislative and policy frameworks and reality for many years. One can identify gaps in implementation and a lack of resourcing, but there is something much more fundamental than a simple implementation gap at play. At the heart of our inability to significantly address GBV, in spite of all these structural measures, is the continued investment of our society in patriarchy. The following section of this chapter provides a brief overview of this feminist analysis. This analytical framework will lay the foundation for our consideration of lessons we can learn from higher education and its recent response to GBV.

A feminist analysis would broadly agree that "GBV results from a confluence of individual-, relationship-, community-, and structural factors which are underpinned by pervasive patriarchal norms".[34] Social norms that promote notions of masculinity which are constructed around the control of women, male sexual entitlement, compulsory heterosexuality and acceptable male violence, as well as notions of femininity which encourage women's subordination to men, are amongst these.

However, it is important to note that 'feminism' is very diverse in both its analyses and praxes. Race, class and other intersections constitute the experiences, concerns and politics of different women differently.[35] Kiguwa provided a useful breakdown of at least eight different versions of feminist analyses, ranging from 'Marxist feminism' to 'womanism', making the point that although all versions of feminism agree that women are oppressed, they differ in what they consider to be the causes of this oppression, and subsequently the most appropriate means by which it must be eradicated.[36]

---

34 Interim Steering Committee on Gender-based Violence and Femicide, 2019, p. 18.

35 Crenshaw, 1995.

36 Kiguwa, 2004.

Rape culture

Rape culture is a key conceptual lens for anti-GBV scholars, activists and practitioners. Although the concept of rape culture has been around in feminist circles since the 1970s, it has more recently been invoked by students in places such as the USA and Europe to describe and explain the pervasiveness of gender-based violence, especially sexual violence, on university campuses. The concept found particular traction in South Africa during the #EndRapeCulture student protests of 2016.

Gqola argued that South African society is deeply saturated in rape culture. She shared the story of Fezekile Ntsukela Kuzwayo, or 'Khwezi' as she became known, and how she was harassed and threatened by a vicious public when she brought a charge of rape against the then Deputy President, Jacob Zuma, in 2006. Her harassment was so severe that she needed to leave the country to ensure her and her family's safety. Similarly, the author of a book detailing the trial from a feminist perspective called *The Kanga and the Kangaroo Court,* Mmatshilo Motsei, was harassed to such an extent that she had to retreat from public life.[37]

"Rape culture renders rape acceptable."[38] Rape culture is embedded in our broader societal and more specific institutional cultures. Located deep in patriarchy, it is the way in which through the acceptable, everyday behaviours, norms and attitudes of these cultures, rape is rendered 'normal', 'inevitable', even 'acceptable'. Gqola recalled, for example, watching television as a child, where men were speaking openly about what was clearly rape, without shame or concern, and referring to it as 'sex'. What struck her was how 'ordinary' they were and how 'normal' the idea of rape was as part of ordinary, everyday life.[39] It is the 'ordinariness' of rape culture that lies at the heart of understanding why rape and other forms of GBV continue to happen at the scale that they do in our society.

---

37 Gqola, 2015.

38 Ibid.

39 Ibid.

Figure 7.1: Rape Culture Pyramid (Version 5)[40]

The Rape Culture Pyramid visually articulates how ordinary everyday attitudes, behaviours and norms contribute to an environment that lays the foundation for, and enables the more violent form of, GBV and rape. Normalisation lays the foundation for and enables degradation, and degradation lays the foundation for and enables assault. Understood this way, rape is not the isolated act of one deranged individual – it is deeply contextual act, enacted by perfectly 'normal' men who are enabled and even encouraged by a whole substructure of cultural cues that render the act acceptable (under certain circumstances). At the bottom of the pyramid are those behaviours and attitudes that, underpinned and firmly embedded in patriarchal cultures, are fairly common in any context – many, even most, individuals subscribe to them. These include sexist attitudes, rape jokes and 'locker room banter'. These kinds of behaviours and attitudes may not be so bad in and of themselves, but they serve to normalise certain ideas about gender and power relations that lay the foundation for less common, but more degrading, behaviour and attitudes. These might include non-consensual photos, groping and survivor shaming. These behaviours and attitudes, in turn, lay the foundation for more violent acts of assault such as molestation and rape. There are less acts at the top of the pyramid, but their behaviour has been made possible, even acceptable, by those at the bottom. This is rape culture, and it is something that we all participate in, to a greater or lesser extent.[41]

---

40 Chandre & Cervix, 2018.
41 Chandre & Cervix, 2018.

One of the significant features of rape culture are 'rape myths'. These myths circulate at the bottom of the pyramid as everyday attitudes and beliefs, quietly 'making excuses' for rape and other forms of GBV, and socially punishing the survivor for their 'behaviour'. Gqola listed the following common 'rape myths':

- **Perpetrators are monsters who are abusive all the time.** Rapists are ordinary, everyday men who can be wonderful people most of the time.

- **Rape is inappropriate sex.** Rape is not sex, it an act of violent dominance.

- **There is a proper way to respond to being raped.** This myth is that if a survivor did not fight, they were consenting. Survivors respond in many ways, for many different reasons.

- **Rape is when a man rapes a woman using his penis to forcibly penetrate her vagina.** Anyone can be raped and can involve instruments, as well as other body parts.

- **Rape myths are just harmless ignorance.** Rape myths have very real consequences in terms of who is considered accountable for a sexual assault, or even whether a sexual assault occurred.

- **Real rape victims/survivors lay charges with the police because they have nothing to lose.** Studies show that only very few survivors report their rapes due to, amongst other things, fear of stigmatisation or victimisation.

- **Rape is about male arousal and the need to have sex.** Rape is about power and domination. Arousal does not need to occur for rape to occur.

- **Dressing a certain way or being visibly drunk invites rape.** Old fashioned victim-blaming – there is absolutely no correlation between what survivors' wear and whether they are attacked.

- **Rapists are strangers who abduct women in public and rape them in unknown places.** Most sexual assaults occur in our homes. Rapists are loving fathers, brothers, uncles and friends.

- **Sex workers cannot be raped.** Sex workers can say 'no' and, as such, can be raped.

- **Women are accidentally raped because they play hard-to-get.** The idea of 'playing hard to get' is a function of rape culture which enables, usually, men to pursue someone even when women have said 'no'.

- **Rape looks a certain way. It leaves a specific imprint on the body.** Rape has no specific imprint, as it is different for everybody.[42]

---

42 Gqola, 2015.

These myths will be familiar to us. They are the everyday 'common sense' we hear around us all of the time: in the media, around the braai, in boardrooms and in classrooms. Every one of these myths represents an 'excuse' for the behaviour of rapists, rendering it acceptable and even innocent. These excuses say: 'It is fine to punish a survivor for the short skirt she wears; fine to excuse the male Professor who sexually harasses his students and colleagues, overly sexualising them, making inappropriate comments that the woman student is obliged to think of as compliments to stay alive.'[43]

It is rape culture that leads to the trivialising, widespread denial of, or refusal to acknowledge, the harm caused by rape, which leads to sexual violence further becoming so normalised that rape and gender violence are not viewed as serious problems.

GBV IN HIGHER EDUCATION IN SOUTH AFRICA

Higher education is one of the few sectors in South Africa that is developing a comprehensive response to GBV. It is also globally, and locally, the most researched sector, in terms of the prevalence and nature of GBV and organisational responses. The rest of this chapter will focus on the higher education sector in South Africa (with a specific focus on the last five years) and reflect on the question of why it is that higher education as a sector, and universities as institutions, seem to be further ahead than other sectors and institutions in addressing GBV.

Contextualisation

Just like with the national statistics, data detailing the prevalence of GBV within the higher education sector are not reliable. However, there is a body of research which provides us with some insight into this sector.

Research on sexual harassment and violence in the 1990s showed higher education to be a complex and significant site for the prevalence of various kinds of sexual violence.[44] From these studies emerged a number a key themes, namely: the vulnerability of junior staff in the context of hierarchical cultures; the presence of coercive transactional sex (especially between teaching staff and students); the 'threat' of women's sexuality'; the link between sexual violence and traditional patriarchal institutional cultures; and the difficulty and associated fear of reporting sexual violence. Overall, they found little evidence of sexual harassment policies being integrated into campus-based discourses and practices.[45]

---

43 Ibid.
44 At this point the discourse, and therefore the analytical lens, was related to sexual harassment and violence, rather than GBV.
45 Bennett, Gouws, Kritzinger, Hames & Tidimane, 2007.

The picture is much the same today. A 2018 survey conducted at Wits University to ascertain the extent and nature of GBV (from sexual harassment to rape) experienced on campus revealed that 70% of academic staff, 65% of admin staff and 68% of students (surveyed) had experienced sexual harassment, while 25% of academics, 28% of admin staff and 27% of students (surveyed) had experienced sexual assault and rape. In the vast majority (82%) of these cases the survivors were cis-gender women, and the perpetrators cis-gender men (84%). Worryingly, only a handful of the incidents reported in the study had been reported to the university or the police.[46]

A study conducted at Ayoba[47] University showed similarly alarming results. Twenty seven percent (27%)[48] of respondents had been asked for sexual favours, experienced sexual advances and been sexually harassed by male lecturers, while 14% had been pressured and 12% had actually failed a male lecturer's subject because they had refused sexual advances. An alarming 68% of respondents knew of lecturers who had exploited female students and believed that sex for the exchange of grades was practiced in the institution. As with the Wits study, only a handful of respondents reported these incidents.[49]

Other studies show the highly normalised experiences of coercive transactional sex, with young women again being most severely affected.[50] Overall, the primary experience of, especially cis-gender, women students on campus is that of fear, which severely curtails their freedom of movement.[51]

In-depth cases studies of three high profile universities on the impact of institutional policies on sexual harassment[52] found little evidence of sexual harassment policies being integrated into campus-based discourses and practices. They found that the implementation of sexual harassment policies was not a core interest in the advancement of democratic cultures on campuses.[53] These policies were always very marginal in official university and individual staff discourse. In the study conducted at Stellenbosch University, Gouws and Kritzinger found, for example, that only nine out of 16 Heads of Department were familiar with the sexual harassment policies and procedures of the university; two stated that they had never heard of the policy. Of the students who were surveyed, only 12 out of 50 were familiar with the details of university sexual harassment

46 Finchilescu & Dugard, 2018.
47 Pseudonym, to protect the anonymity of the university in question.
48 It is important to note that there were only 63 respondents, making this a small sample. The percentages must be read in that context. All respondents were women in their third/final year of undergraduate studies.
49 Adams, Mabusela, & Dlamini, 2013.
50 Shefer, Clowes, & Vergnani, 2012; Clowes, et al., 2009.
51 Collins & Gordon, 2013; Sexual Violence Task Team, 2018; Gouws & Kritzinger, 2007.
52 Again, the focus was not on GBV, but sexual harassment and violence.
53 Bennett, et al., 2007.

policies and procedures. Of the two students who had experienced sexual harassment in the survey, neither had reported it. It was clear from their elaboration on why this was, i.e. that there were serious barriers in place that disabled reporting. Most significant of these was that, because of the relative silence from the institution on matters of GBV and what felt like insufficient sanction of known perpetrators of GBV by the institutional structures, survivors did not trust these structures to protect them.[54]

However, although our universities are microcosms of South African life and therefore, as the above attests to, plagued by the same kinds of violence as the rest of our society, there is something particular about the way in which the sector has responded to this challenge that it faces.

In 2015, student protests to 'decolonise' higher education (#RhodesMustFall) and to fight for free higher education (#FeesMustFall) flared up all over the country. From the beginning of #RMF, young black feminists inserted a feminist sensibility and agenda into the movements under the hashtag #PatriarchyMustFall and the banner: 'This revolution will be intersectional or it will be bullshit.' "They were not afraid to speak in a feminist register, from the vantage point of intersectional, radical African feminism."[55] In 2016, frustrated at what they saw as the inaction of the university to do anything about a series of alleged rapes on campus, students at Rhodes University/UCKAR[56] released a list names of alleged rapists on social media. This action started a new wave of protests under the rubric of #EndRapeCulture at universities across the country, to express anger at the ways in which universities were dealing with sexual violence.

Students at Stellenbosch University (SU) also expressed their frustration at the way rape and sexual harassment were handled on campus. In 2016, students who were aligned with #OpenStellenbosch protested a number of concerns around rape culture, including the trivialising of GBV and the stigmatisation of survivors.[57]

In response to these concerns about GBV in higher education (now being made visible by student protests), the Department of Higher Education and Training established a Sexual and Gender-Based Violence Technical Task Team in February 2017 to "gather and use research and evidence-based best practice to inform a sector-wide strategy to tackle GBV". The Higher Education and Training Health, Wellness and Development Centre (HEAIDS) was mandated to lead key stakeholder engagements, research and planning processes.[58] There was also progress at the institutional level, for example, as a result of student

---

54 Gouws & Kritzinger, 2007.
55 Gouws, 2018, p. 3.
56 University Currently Known as Rhodes.
57 EndRapeCulture Task Team at SU, 2017.
58 Department of Higher Eduation and Training, 2017.

efforts, both Rhodes University/UCKAR and SU established task teams to examine the universities' responses to GBV and make recommendations. Both task teams released comprehensive reports with recommendations ranging from revising sexual harassment policies and processes for managing sexual violence cases, to curriculum change.[59]

However, although much work was being done, many in higher education did not feel that formal processes were translating into tangible changes on university campuses. In early May 2019, 12 South African academics sent a letter to the then Minister of Higher Education and Training, Dr Naledi Pandor, urging the Department to take a more active stance in addressing GBV on university campuses. In June 2019, in response to this letter, another Task Team (this team a ministerial one) on Sexual Harassment and Gender-based Violence in the University Sector was established. Its role was to advise the Minister specifically on the implementation of the *Policy Framework to address Gender-based Violence in the Post-School Education and Training Sector* and consider the possibility of a nationwide enquiry into GBV on university campuses.[60]

However, in August 2019 Uyinene Mrwetyana and Jesse Hess were murdered and students across the country again took to the streets. As with #RMF and #FMF (albeit on a smaller scale), a number of university-based movements were formed around the country. These movements were able to put enormous pressure on university administrations to make good on their promises of two years earlier and make substantive changes to institutional infrastructure and cultures. Students across the country re-engaged their respective institutions with protest actions and memoranda.

The final version of the *Policy Framework to address Gender-based Violence in the Post-School Education and Training Sector* was published in March 2020. It set out to do a number of things to support institutions in their anti-GBV work, by expanding the definition of GBV and providing guidance on the necessary structures and implementation strategies. It also, importantly, compels higher education institutions to prevent incidents of GBV, in ways that have not been compelled before.[61]

Lessons from higher education

Although most activists would argue that we are nowhere near to realising the desired outcomes of their various campaigns and memoranda, and that patriarchal institutional cultures continue to flourish within universities across South Africa, they would also acknowledge that there has been some significant progress since 2015. The higher education sector in South African has seen unprecedented amounts of activity in relation

---

59 EndRapeCulture Task Team at SU, 2017; Sexual Violence Task Team, 2018.

60 Department of Higher Education and Training, 2019.

61 Department of Higher Education and Training, 2020.

to GBV in the last five years. There is no other sector in the country which has seen this level of active intervention with regards to addressing GBV in terms of stakeholder engagement, policy making, monitoring and resourcing.

So, what is it that has catapulted higher education so far along a path of attendance to GBV compared to other sectors? There are lessons in this unprecedented progress. The following section will consider the conditions and character of this progress over the last few years and reflect on what has enabled the development of a relatively robust response to GBV within higher education.

Lesson 1: Feminist activism

The most important lesson emerging from the recent responses to GBV we see in South African universities is the way that it has been driven by feminist activism. Bennet et al. pointed out that "research on sexual harassment policy implementation shows evidence of an on-going contest between core principles of feminist activism and ideas which erase gender from a general approach to questions of social justice, an erasure quintessentially rooted in intellectual and philosophical fear".[62] What they mean by this is that it has required constant activism by feminists to ensure that gender has remained central to our engagements on questions of social justice and equality.

This is certainly the case in higher education. In fact, Gouws and Kritzinger made the point that even when institutions have failed to take gender seriously, feminist activism by women on and off campus have contributed to 'forcing' many to formulate policies to deal with GBV.[63] For example, it was the years of research and activism by a small and committed group of feminist activists at SU that enabled the ratification of the first sexual harassment policy.[64] Interestingly, Bennet et al. also found a link between international, national and local levels of feminist activism, i.e. that the implementation of policy at the local (institutional) level related to broader international and national developments.[65]

However, this activism has been important beyond a clear location of the work as a political project in the service of social justice and equality. It has also provided important theoretical framing or analytic proficiency to grasp and articulate the phenomenon of GBV and how it relates to, for example, institutional culture. Melissa Steyn suggested that "an informed analytical orientation that enables a person to 'read' prevailing social relations as one would a text" is one of the most important characteristics of truly transformative diversity interventions (which would include anti-GBV work) in complex

---

62 Bennett et al., 2007, p. 99.
63 Gouws & Kritzinger, 2007.
64 Bennett et al., 2007.
65 Bennett et al., 2007.

21st century organisations. Feminism, although contested and complex, provides this analytic ability in matters pertaining to gender.

For example, if we consider the Rape Culture Pyramid as a (feminist) theoretical framework, it allows us to see something like 'locker room banter' (characteristic of a culture) as underpinning and enabling an act such as sexual harassment (another characteristic of the culture). Without the lens provided by the 'Rape Culture Pyramid' we would see these two characteristics as unrelated, and not consider responding to the characteristic of 'locker room banter' in an effort to address GBV. Feminist understandings of gender, as constructed, as fluid, as characterised by relationships of power, have been crucial to the inclusion of LGBTQIA++ communities into the frame of GBV, and of GBV as more than VAW. If we look at most demands made by student anti-GBV movements of university administrations to address GBV on campuses over the last five years (e.g. the *SU Anti-GBV Movement Memorandum to the Rectorate of Stellenbosch University*)[66], they include LGBTQIA++ communities as key stakeholders and identify institutional culture as a primary concern. As a result, the institutions are compelled to address these issues.

Lesson 2: Protest

With #PatriarchyMustFall and #EndRapeCulture, feminist activism has become much more publicly emboldened and demanding, forcing universities into further action aligned with the feminist agendas of the movements.

From this point emerges the second lesson from university responses to GBV – that they are driven by a powerful and vocal stakeholder group, in this case, students. These stakeholders have the capacity and the social currency to disrupt operations of the university in ways that, arguably, other stakeholders do not.

Unlike union-led strikes and demonstrations, the student-led demonstrations of #RhodesMustFall, #FeesMustFall and #EndRapeCulture garnered mass public support. Of course there was also criticism of the more violent protest action of many of the 2015 student protests, but this did not deter from the fact that there was much public support for the cause, if not the method. The deaths of Uyinene Mrwetyana and Jesse Hess, and the subsequent anti-GBV protests, drew even more public support. South Africa has, for a number of years, witnessed increasingly violent and gruesome GBV and femicide. These rapes and murders were clearly morally reprehensible. Around the time that Mrwetyana and Hess were murdered there were a series of similar cases, and there was a growing sense of public helplessness and frustration in the face of these horrors. The student anti-GBV protests gave people, in general, an avenue to express their own pain and frustration, and a renewed sense of hopefulness that, as a society, we could do something about this scourge; students had a very public morality and anger on their side.

---

66 SU Anti-GBV Movement, 2019.

What they did through their protests was insert a very clear feminist analysis and language into the public moral concern. They used language such as 'rape culture', 'misogyny' and 'patriarchy' in their public gatherings, media postings and documents. They very publicly joined the dots between the horror and immortality of GBV and feminism to explain and address it. All of a sudden, this language, which had been marginal[67] and even chastised by university administrations, was making its way into mainstream leadership, managerial and administrative discourse.

An example can be seen in the story of a little booklet called *Talking Transformation*, which was published by the SU Transformation Office as a guide to 'transformation vocabulary'. Included in the booklet were concepts such as rape culture, sexual harassment and victim blaming.[68] However, the booklet became very publicly controversial, even catching Helen Zille's attention (the former Premier of the Western Cape province). At the heart of the 'controversy' was the idea that the Transformation Office/University was forcing Marxist (sic) doctrine down the throats of students.[69] The Transformation Office was instructed to remove the booklet from circulation, which members of the Transformation Office and more progressive students and members of staff understood as being a move to placate powerful conservative elements within the university. However, a year later, the university was itself using this language in its official communications and documents. In fact, a quick search of the Stellenbosch University website reveals that the university's official public communication around 'rape culture' peaked in 2016 (during the #EndRapeCulture protests), emerged slightly again when the #EndRapeCulture report was released in mid-2017, and then all but disappeared when anti-GBV protests sparked up in August 2019.[70] A similar trend was observed across the Wits' and Cape Town Universities' websites.[71]

Although some might argue that it is common sense that institutions would respond more during these times of public protest, this is exactly the point. It is these very public, moral and, importantly, feminist protests that forced the universities into a position where they had to engage with GBV. However, it is not just *that* they engaged – universities are always doing the work of dealing with GBV in some capacity – but *how* they engaged; specifically in the feminist register of the student protests, and subsequently in the form of commensurate actions. Although small groups of feminist academics and support staff had been advancing this analysis and these actions for years, it took the public 'shaming' of institutions to pull this into the mainstream discourse of universities.

---

67 Tucked away in transformation and anti-discrimination policy, gender units and courses.

68 University of Stellenbosch Transformation Office, 2018.

69 Zille, 2018; Slade & Botha, 2018.

70 University of Stellenbosch, 2020.

71 University of Cape Town, 2020; University of the Witwatersrand, 2020.

Students used public platforms to share their positions, gathered in public protests, formed partnerships with NGOs working in the anti-GBV sector, wrote articles in the press, and garnered vast public support. They also garnered government support, with government officials interacting directly with student leaders without university administrations present. The public and growing governance and public relations pressures became such that universities had to respond constructively to the students' demands; not doing so would start to get them into hot water with the authorities and could damage the reputation of the universities, both of which could seriously contribute to undermining their core business.

The risk that reputational damage posed to the core business has, in part, to do with the nature of the universities as being (ostensibly) more enlightened, progressive and responsible organisations with a concern for social justice – which can often be seen in extensive articulation of visions and strategic frameworks (see, for example, the *SU Vision 2040* and *Strategic Framework 2019–2024*).[72] Responding meaningfully and helpfully to the ills of our society is a core business of a university, be it through teaching or research. In the context of this mandate, not responding enthusiastically to a very public and 'obviously' moral request by students to respond to GBV would seriously undermine their credibility.

Lesson 3: Co-constructed process and leadership

The third lesson from university responses is in the shape of internal processes put in place to respond to the demands of anti-GBV efforts. In this case I cannot speak for other institutions, but can speak to how SU responded, which presents lessons in how to engage stakeholders to generate meaningful and long-term infrastructure and cultural shifts. Importantly, this is not to suggest that the SU response has been without fault or unproblematic. It is also not to suggest that the co-construction of processes to engage these questions were/are the modus operandi of universities, or indeed SU.

In fact, it was the protestors' political framework which dictated the terms of the engagement; there was never space for a top-down, hierarchical approach. From the beginning, students insisted that they must be represented in the highest levels of decision-making during the response to their demands. Members of the Anti-GBV Movement sat in meetings with senior leadership to design processes for implementing their demands. Importantly, the Anti-GBV Movement continued with extensive stakeholder engagement throughout their work with senior leadership. This co-constructed approach to problem-solving is a feature of political frameworks, such as feminism, that value egalitarianism and the co-creation of knowledge.[73] The Movement was not only forcing the university to

---

72   University of Stellenbosch, 2018.
73   Harvey et al., 2016.

act, but it was forcing it to do so in a way that fundamentally undermined the hierarchies and deeply-embedded power structures within the institution, and inserted an (unusual) egalitarian ethos into the culture of the institution.

In addition to this pressure, there was also one senior member of leadership who was very skilled and experienced at leading large-scale collaborative processes. Her leadership style was very much what we might refer to as a form of 'servant leadership', which was seemingly unconcerned with asserting power and more concerned with drawing students into dialogue and solution-making processes. As such, a process was developed involving the establishment of 'Working Groups', which over the course of 2020 considered the full extent and nature of the problem, as well as the best way to address it, under six thematic areas.[74] Students from the Anti-GBV Movement were key participants in defining these themes. Included in the work of the Working Groups was a full review of the Stellenbosch University residence system, which has long been identified as a serious concern for GBV on campus, and a review of reporting and disciplinary procedures for GBV. The Working Groups were co-ordinated by a senior member of staff and consisted of relevant (to function) and self-nominated staff and students, including those from the SU Anti-GBV Movement. This was intended to ensure that all experiences and relevant expertise were brought to the table to ensure more robust solutions. They also engaged directly with the Rectorate to ensure that there was accountability at the highest levels.

An important aspect of the collaborative, co-creation process is trust, which is essential to ensure the functionality of the process and to generate meaningful outcomes. This is not simply a matter of 'getting buy-in' which so many top-down attempts at collaboration are often reduced to, but a genuine attempt at a collective solution. Unfortunately, due to a long history of mistrust, students were still wary of the university administration paying lip service to their processes. It remained necessary for the institution to demonstrate its commitment to the actual process, as well as the principles embedded in the work, so it was important for the same senior leader who initiated this process to act unequivocally when a men's residence bullied their Residence Head and sexually harassed his wife. When another men's residence was implicated in the homophobic bullying of a Welcoming Monitor, swift action was taken. These actions sent a clear signal that the university was indeed committed to addressing GBV on campus, and that it could be trusted. This process of trust-making and reaffirming relationships is one that is necessary throughout the entire process of co-creation.

Although the criticism that this form of 'co-operative' process may also lead to the bureaucratisation, dilution and placation of the activist impulse, and this must be guarded against, it can also be one that can create lasting structural and cultural changes. This kind of less hierarchical, co-operative engagement is rare in most institutions and

---

74 University of Stellenbosch Department of Student Affairs, 2020.

organisations, which remain largely skewed in their hierarchy of power. However, it is the only way to drive meaningful and lasting change.

CONCLUSION

This chapter has presented a picture of where South Africa is in relation to GBV. It has done so through a review of the prevalence and nature of GBV, as well as the legislative framework governing the state response to the problem. It has considered the gaps in this framework, which go some way to explaining the vast disconnect between policy and reality. It has also considered theoretical explanations for the extremely high incidence of GBV in South Africa. However, in the face of this reality, it has identified a sector that seems to be making progress in response to GBV, specifically at a structural level. Driven quietly and consistently by feminists within institutions and thrust into public scrutiny and action by student protests, the higher education sector has been forced to find ways to address GBV at universities across the country.

There are lessons to be learnt from this tumultuous journey about what is necessary to drive meaningful structural and cultural change. First, an appropriate analytical frame and praxis that can accurately define the nature of the problem we face and develop an appropriate response, in this case feminism, is needed. Secondly, unwavering activism from within is key. Meaningful change will always require constant work in the face of both active and passive resistance from champions within an institution, organisation or sector. Thirdly, pressure from key stakeholders that starts to impact on organisational 'core business' is necessary, and finally, co-created processes to find, identify, implement and sustain the necessary changes are critical.

To reiterate, higher education is nowhere near where it should be with regards to addressing GBV, however the progress that has been made thanks to its key stakeholders, students, has been remarkable. It is an important site for those of us in the fight against GBV to continue engaging, not just for the scholarship and knowledge it produces, but for the praxis it is developing with regards to transforming itself.

KEY TAKEAWAYS

1. South Africa has one of the highest incidences of gender-based violence in the world, costing the country between R28.4 billion and R42.4 billion per year. This does not include the costs of pain and suffering, healthcare or other secondary costs.

2. Although significant policy and implementation gaps exist, one of the main challenges in addressing GBV in South Africa is our society's (and institutions') continued investment in patriarchy and the pervasiveness of rape culture.

3. Feminist activism has been instrumental in advancing anti-GBV work in South Africa, specifically in the higher education sector, and provides a useful model for other sectors.

4. Feminist activism provides the necessary analytical proficiency to see and understand the complexity and range of GBV, like the inclusion of LGBTQI++ communities and institutional culture in the analysis.

5. Feminist activism can generate the necessary pressure on institutions, compelling leadership to act. In the case of higher education in South Africa this was done through public protest. It can also provide democratic and collaborative methodologies for stakeholder engagement that can facilitate long-term, sustainable and socially just solutions to GBV.

Chapter 8

DIVERSITY IN THE WORKPLACE THROUGH A GENERATIONAL LENS

Prof. Linda Ronnie

Baby boomers

Generation X

Millenials

Gen Z

INTRODUCTION

In 2020, the office chatter about the clash between entry-level millennial employees and their baby boomer managers felt exhausting. For ten years, our watercooler conversations, news articles and viral memes had been overrun with debates about how the "new generation" of employees and their avocado toast were changing our organisations. In this time, we were consumed by questions about how to reconcile the differences in the values, goals and ways of working between people of different generations in our workplaces, yet this all happened for good reason. Our millennial co-workers have taken a great deal of flack in all this discourse for their role in disrupting things – something their generation seems to specialise in. But their entry into the workforce has awakened us to the reality of what it means to work in an organisation that is generationally diverse, and the challenges that come with it.

As we have started prioritising diversity of all kinds in our workplaces in more meaningful ways, we are increasingly recognising age as a key dimension of diversity. It has become unavoidable as organisations now house a greater number of generations than in previous decades, and a trend of older employees reporting to younger managers has emerged.[1] As with other dimensions of diversity, managing generational differences with the right policies and practices is a crucial part of maximising the effectiveness of our organisations.[2] Failure to address generational differences in work values and beliefs can result in workplace conflict, misunderstanding and miscommunication, lower productivity levels, and ultimately, problems with employee retention and turnover.

---

1 Cogin, 2012.
2 Kupperschmidt, 2000.

In South Africa, the challenge of generational mix is influenced by other key social factors, namely education. Part of South Africa's Apartheid legacy is a dysfunctional education system with varying levels of quality and unequal access to education across race and class. This results in the paradox of the South African labour market: an over-abundance of low-skilled employees and a shortage of intermediate- and high-skilled individuals.[3] Although the country has one of the highest rates of education expenditures in Africa at 20.32% as a share of total government expenditure[4], and despite gains made in the last 20 years, many pending educational challenges are impacting the supply of skilled workers for the labour market. This skills mismatch serves to exacerbate the divide between entry-level employees and their colleagues, and challenges organisations to devise creative policies to fill the gap.

This chapter discusses the challenges of managing the South African age-diverse workforce in an environment struggling with deep change, and proposes solutions toward integrating the workforce, fostering understanding between individuals, and creating an organisational culture of inclusion, encouragement and flexibility.

Generations in the South African context

A generation can be defined as a distinguishable group that "shares birth interval, location, and significant life events at critical development stages".[5] Because of the experiences that people within a generation share at the same life stage, they can also be thought of as "a cohort of individuals born and raised within the same historical and social context, who consequently share a common worldview".[6] Given that major socio-political and cultural events often shape the boundaries of generational cohorts[7], these events influence the attitudes and values of individuals within that group, and affect individuals' personal and professional lives in specific ways.

While generational descriptions are often assumed to be universal, characteristics that are typical in developed countries may not apply to developing countries. In South Africa, we must account for the unique differences following from the Apartheid regime that controlled the country between 1948 and the early 1990s, where various races were affected differently, i.e. Black and White South Africans have different generational outlooks due to different upbringing and experiences. More generally, the defining events of Apartheid resulted in generational cohorts in South Africa that differ from those of the USA and the UK (see Table 8.1).[8]

---

3   Horwitz, 2013.
4   South African National Treasury, 2020.
5   Kupperschmidt, 2000, p. 364.
6   Lyons, Duxbury & Higgins, 2005, p. 769.
7   Colakoglu & Caligiuri, 2010.; Rasch & Kowske, 2010.
8   Deal et al., 2010, p. 283.

Table 8.1: Generational cohort comparison (USA, UK and South Africa)

USA	Baby Boomers [1946-1963]	Generation X [1964-1979]	Generation Y / Millennials [1980-2000]	
UK	Baby Boomers [1946-1960]	Generation X [1960-1979]	Generation Y / Millennials [1980-2000]	
SOUTH AFRICA	Apartheid Generation [1938-1960]	Struggle Generation [1961-1980]	Transition Generation [1981-1993]	'Born Free' Generation [1994-2000]

Source: Adapted from Deal et al.[9]

The Apartheid Generation (1938-1960) has no national memory prior to the institutionalisation of Apartheid and its legal machinery which enforced racial segregation. While all races in this generation were exposed to protest action and its ramifications, Black South Africans were more aware.[10] The material conditions under which the various racial groups existed shaped their outlook on life and consequently racialised relationships in the workplace.

The term 'Struggle Generation' (1961-1980) was coined because of the countrywide protests that gripped the country in the mid-1970s, although there were different experiences across racial lines. The majority of the oppressed participated in some form of resistance, while many of the White population, and especially White men who were conscripted into the army and Defence Force to fight against the struggle for freedom, were silent and often complicit in actions against the Black majority.

The Transition Generation (1981-1993) entered adolescence in the post-democratic period but retained memories of the Apartheid regime. Due to educational challenges, this generation experienced high levels of unemployment and similar levels of economic and physical insecurity as prior generations.[11]

The 'born free' generation[12] (1994-2000) have no memory of living within the restrictive Apartheid structures forced upon previous generations, and can live and work without any official limitations.[13] While this generation is defined largely as Black due to current demographics, it is believed that young South Africans of different races enjoy more

---

9   Deal et al., 2010, p. 283.

10 Deal et al., 2010.

11 Ibid.

12 It needs to be acknowledged that the 'born free' label is problematic because many believe that the name is more aspirational than real and less homogenous than indicated. For the purposes of this discussion, tensions are acknowledged by showing contested terms in quotation marks.

13 Mattes, 2011.

in common with each another than previous age groups in the country.[14] Additionally, because they did not grow up amidst legally-mandated racial segregation, the 'born frees' are more culturally integrated with others in their generation.[15]

Recently, a new study on age segmentation in South Africa that incorporated the latest statistical data[16] proposed a change to the previously accepted parameters (see Table 8.2). The landmark events used to segment these proposed age cohorts are the Soweto uprising in 1961, the first democratic election in 1994, and the birth of the Fallist movements in 2015. This segmentation introduces the most recent generational cohort, Generation Second Wave, more commonly known as Generation Z.[17]

Table 8.2: Proposed new age cohorts and estimated size

Pre-Apartheid Generation [<1933]	Apartheid Generation [1933-1960]	Struggle Generation [1961-1979]	Transition Generation [1980-1999]	Generation Second Wave [2000-2020]
177,324 (0.3%)	5,345,025 (9.3%)	10,732,683 (18.8%)	20,504,754 (35.8%)	20,491,467 (35.8%)

Adapted from Lappeman, Egan and Coppin[18]

The Generation Second Wave (2000-2020) is similar to the 'born free' generation in having a shared identity that is more universal, following again from technological influences. As this generation will soon be the primary constituency of the entry level workforce, they will be the target of most organisations' attraction and retention agendas. Understanding their shared characteristics will be essential for effective management strategies. Although it may be too early to say for sure, they appear to have characteristics that contrast starkly with those of their Generation X and baby boomer counterparts. Members of Generation Z are described as multi-taskers, flexible, intrinsically motivated, value-driven, independent and entrepreneurial, yet they also have higher levels of vulnerability.[19] They are, at least in part, the product of their classroom experiences, where generally speaking, current educational practices encourage a culture of debate and participation.[20] They are also the first generation born into a fully technological environment – a world where being connected, being digital, and having mobile phones or tablets is a matter of course. This makes them more advanced in searching for information and figuring things out

---

14 Martins & Martins, 2010.

15 Malila, 2015.

16 StatsSA, 2019.

17 Lappeman, Egan & Coppin, 2020.

18 Ibid.

19 Bencsik, Horváth-Csikós & Jubász, 2016.; Bornman, 2019.; Chillakuri & Mahanandia, 2018.; Vetter, 2017.

20 Cameron & Pagnattaro, 2017.

on their own, while expecting fast and immediate responses.[21] These descriptions are anticipated to hold true for graduates who have just entered the South African labour market. However, race- and class-related disparities within the cohort are likely to paint a less favourable picture.

In spite of their unique experiences related to Apartheid, South Africans generally hold similar beliefs to generational cohorts in other emerging economies that face similar challenges of inequality, political instability, financial volatility, disparate living conditions, larger birth rates and similar demographics. However, in recent years, the influence of technology has played a significant role in shaping a common modern identity for younger generations that spans across national borders.[22] Younger generations in South Africa are therefore more similar to their counterparts in developed counties; they are more proficient with technology than previous generations and use social media to collaboratively solve problems that enable innovation.

These unique experiences of the different cohorts are important in the employment context because they can result in different values, expectations and work relationships between younger generations and older generations.[23] This affects all organisations in the private, public and non-profit sectors, however critics of multi-generational theory assert that there is sparse evidence for these claims, citing a lack of theoretical foundation and outcomes of studies in this area being, at best, mixed. This is because much of the published work in the popular press is based on observation rather than large-scale empirical findings.[24] Studies in South Africa show that differences do indeed exist between generational cohorts across a wide range of factors such as turnover and commitment;[25] autonomy; engagement and meaningful work;[26] the desire for interesting, motivating, flexible and efficient work environments; and opportunities for learning.[27]

The South African work environment

South African organisations exist in an environment that is still recovering from the traumatic effects of a system of institutionalised discrimination. The inequalities created by Apartheid are a daily reality that continue to hinder growth in employment and impact the educational sector.[28] The education system itself is at the root of many problems as

---

21 Opris & Cenusa, 2017.
22 Edmunds & Turner, 2005.
23 Benson & Brown, 2011.; Ng, Schweitzer & Lyons, 2010.; Papavasileioua & Lyons, 2015.
24 Cogin, 2012.
25 Ronnie, 2016.
26 Hoole & Bonnema, 2015.
27 Nnambooze & Parumasur, 2016.
28 Horwitz, Heng, Quazi, Nonkwelo, Roditi & van Eck, 2006.

it struggles to overcome years of Apartheid-era neglect in the form of under-funding and poorly trained teachers, particularly in the racially marginalised sections of the community.[29] Meanwhile, the ineffectiveness of national training facilities and the Sector Education and Training Authorities (SETAs) adds to the national skills shortage.[30] As a result, South African organisations, which are already challenged to find talented and skilled employees in their developing economy, are faced with a limited pool of candidates.

However, there are forward-thinking organisations that are outsmarting competitors in nabbing sought-after employees by using "people management differentiation".[31] This involves attracting talented individuals, engaging and motivating them to attain high productivity, and retaining them in organisations as a fundamental business priority. To be sure, South African companies are already compelled to increase their productivity to compete in the global economy. This means that they must rely on skilled employees' contributions to foster innovation and attain continuous productivity improvement.[32] Highly skilled workers in the workplace – regardless of generational cohort – play an essential role in increasing national economic development, building an inclusive society, and enhancing the national capacity to compete globally. However, there are a number of multi-generational differences that may pose a challenge to the different aspects of people management.

Recruitment and retention across generations

Employee attraction

Based on the different motivations, needs and values of the different generations, employees are attracted to organisations by different things. An organisation's reputation or brand is as valuable as a competitive edge in South Africa as it is worldwide. It is also a critical factor for attracting employees who are the best fit for the organisation.[33] Organisations that outwardly demonstrate their commitments are able to attract and retain new recruits seeking to match values of their own. As organisations develop recruitment strategies for entry-level employees, however, they find a growing gap between the demands and motivations of the future workforce and the existing pool of seasoned employees. South African organisations have the dual challenge of offering skilled, young prospective employees an attractive employment contract, while competing intensely with other organisations for the scarce talent.[34] In order to attract and retain

---

29 Breier, 2009.; Mattes, 2011.
30 McKechnie & Bridgens, 2008.
31 Markova & Ford, 2011.
32 Horwitz, 2013.
33 Moroko & Uncles, 2008.
34 Bussin & Moore, 2012.

talented employees across generations, organisations need to understand their unique motivations and needs.

Generation X – the equivalent of South Africa's Struggle Generation – is often considered more sceptical, less loyal and fiercely independent than other generations.[35] They approach their workplace with positive, pragmatic approaches to problem-solving, creativity, independence, innovation and technical ability, and are comfortable with change, diversity and multi-tasking.[36] They are the mid-career employees and rising managers within our organisations – those who have acquired an appreciable degree of maturity, but still have the energy of people on an upward trajectory. Generation X is also resourceful and independent.[37] Importantly, they are motivated by the ability to influence and hold authority over others.[38] In them, we have the potential for great leadership in the near future.

By contrast, younger generations show a greater interest in forming meaningful relationships and doing meaningful work within an organisation based on shared values. Beyond remuneration, young employees are attracted by prospects of career growth, work/life balance, a strong sense of purpose, investment in and use of technology, opportunity to travel, and professional development.[39] They are the doers within the organisation who want to be immersed in the practical but challenging operational work that drives the core mission. One of the key attractions for these new employees is the certainty that the organisation will continue to show interest in their learning capacity. Ongoing training and development is an area 'born frees' demand as part of their employment package and career development, including partial or full study reimbursement[40], and this is likely to be true for Generation Second Wave as well. Their desire to learn and grow reflects a deeper desire to continuously add more value to their work. In them, we see both the drivers of innovation and the engines of our organisations over the long-term.

In response to these different demands, some organisations have opted for a recruitment strategy that accommodates variation in the workforce. The use of idiosyncratic deals (or i-deals) is one way organisations can offer a customised arrangement for employees. An i-deal allows all workers to achieve their preferred employment conditions by negotiating them with employers from the onset.[41] For example, seasoned Generation X

---

35 Glass, 2007.

36 Smola & Sutton, 2002.; Southard & Lewis, 2004.

37 Kupperschmidt, 1998.; Lancaster, L., & Stillman, 2002.

38 Macky, Gardner & Forsyth, 2008.

39 Deloitte, 2016.

40 Bussin & Van Rooy, 2014.

41 Rousseau et al., 2009, p. 980.

employees, having experienced the most organisational change through retrenchments and reorganisation during their careers, tend to be a little wary and cynical.[42] They know the rules and the realities of how organisations work, and are therefore more interested in concrete benefits that are secure. Thus, an example of an i-deal for this cohort would be ample paid leave.[43] Meanwhile, younger employees who are newer to the workforce and more mission-focused want to feel that their contributions to the organisation are meaningful and valued. An i-deal for these employees would include a suitable, market-related base remuneration, and assurance that there is room for progression in the organisation.[44] For older employees who are at more mature career stages – the baby boomers – who have fewer years left in the workforce but an abundance of valuable knowledge, their concern is more about ensuring personal security as they transfer that information to organisations, either as leaders or mentors. For this group, pensions and share schemes would be the most attractive i-deal.[45]

Employers need innovative ways to attract and retain skilled staff. I-deals are crucial because they offer win-win employment situations and encourage organisations to identify opportunities for people management customisation. Personalised deals should be considered by employers because these deals have shown a positive impact on organisational commitment as an element that plays a significant role in employees' motivation and retention.[46]

Employee retention

Two areas that employers need to focus on for retaining employees are: a) providing clear performance feedback for career development; and b) meaningful performance recognition. Frequent and effective communication is at the heart of these concerns for employees. Most employees want ongoing reassurance that they are valued and they want frequent feedback from managers who are supportive and nurturing.[47] Within the South African work environment, there is an excellent example of this in practice. Open Box Software is a South African software company that specialises in the development of innovative solutions for real estate firms, the so-called 'proptech' industry. The company features a flat organisational structure and open communication policies with a focus on a collegial environment.[48]

---

42 Erikson, 2010.

43 Nnambooze & Parumasur, 2016.

44 Bussin & van Rooy, 2014.

45 Benson & Brown, 2011.

46 Ng & Feldman, 2010.

47 Weick, 2003.; Weick, Prydun & Walsh, 2002.

48 Metcalf, 2011.

A unique aspect of the people management system is the appraisal process, where employees receive feedback on a weekly basis. Junior employees' feedback focuses on the development of individual skills, technical issues that arose during the assessment period, and how things can improve in future. This is in contrast with senior employees, where feedback is less technical and more focused on broader concerns that include entire project plans, project specifications, communication and inter-personal skills, and performance appreciation. Growing numbers of prominent global organisations are also abandoning traditional performance assessment systems, such as annual reviews, that contain obsolete information, and substituting them with frequent performance feedback to improve performance and employee engagement. With executive commitment, the type of approach used by Open Box Software leads to highly committed staff and can be applied in all industries and sectors.[49]

Mobility concerns pressure employees "to differentiate themselves in terms of developing distinctive competencies and generating options to pursue personal and career goals"[50], therefore the retention of employees is challenging. Given the high costs associated with job rotation and recruitment, it makes financial sense for employers to deploy effective retention programmes. The shortage of talent and 'brain drain' in South Africa, along with the retirement of baby boomers, is increasingly challenging for organisations in a precarious position regarding the pipeline of suitably skilled employees.

Employee commitment and engagement

Millennials reportedly show lower levels of allegiance to their employer and higher levels of loyalty to their work and peers. When problems arise in the workplace, the highly skilled among them are more inclined to leave their employer than to stay. Deloitte noted that 53% of South African millennials expect to leave their current organisation during the next two years given the choice, while only 26% would stay on with their current employer beyond five years.[51] Of those surveyed, 96% would consider joining the gig economy. Securing career and developmental opportunities are important for young employees because they are in the early stage of their career.[52] Skilled millennials are highly sought after in South Africa and abroad, where opportunities for the exchange and acquisition of new knowledge exist.[53] This is a serious challenge to South African organisations employing large numbers of 'born frees' and the growing numbers of Generation Second Wave.

---

49 Lee, Idris & Tuckey, 2019.
50 Rousseau, 2001.
51 Deloitte, 2019.
52 Hess & Jepsen, 2009.
53 Breier, 2009.

This newest generational cohort, Generation Z, is reported to have little issue with staying loyal to their employer, however their commitment levels are low, particularly if their organisational desires are not met.[54] Compared to other generational groups, Generation Y has shown lower levels of commitment, both in terms of affective commitment (the emotional attachment, identification, and involvement in and to the organisation) and continuance (the costs or implications of leaving the organisation).[55] Older South African employees have higher levels of affective commitment and normative commitment (a perceived obligation to stay with the organisation).[56] Turnover, or the intention to leave, is therefore influenced by several factors across generational groupings. These differences have the potential to redefine retention strategies for employers, and may give rise to new forms of organisational development.[57]

A way to ensure ongoing engagement and heightened motivation levels across all generational cohorts is to create alternative career paths in addition to traditional linear expectations. Organisations can meet employees' interests when they are aware of their needs and desires in terms of career progression – including lateral/lattice career moves.[58] One organisation that has integrated such an approach to balance the needs of its junior employees with existing opportunities is the food processing company Namib Mills in neighbouring Namibia. Faced with a large workforce that stretched across three complex business units, the company opted for a flat organisational structure to distribute leadership to lower levels of the organisation. This also meant eliminating middle management positions to which young employees could aspire. The company therefore encouraged horizontal career progression, where employees could seek to upskill in different technical areas across the company. Their aim was to keep talented employees engaged with different challenges or areas of innovation, encouraging them to stay within the ecosystem by satisfying their desire to learn and try new things.

Lateral moves provide opportunities for a wider range of careers that may expand personal satisfaction, offer new career trajectories, and open prospects to undertake further professional challenge within their organisations.[59] Most employees – regardless of age – show eagerness to move on when there is clear opportunity elsewhere to learn something, be involved in substantial change, and contribute meaningfully.[60] The use of the lattice strategy of horizontal career paths within organisations may enhance the

54 Chillakuri & Mahanandia, 2018.

55 Lub, Nije Bijvank, Matthijs Bal, Blomme & Schalk, 2012.

56 Ferreira & Coetzee, 2010.

57 Cronley & Kim, 2017.

58 Wilson, Squires, Widger, Cranley & Tourangeau, 2008.

59 Helvey, 2016.

60 Hobart & Sendek, 2014.

engagement and loyalty of both younger and older existing employees, and allow an organisation to differentiate itself from its competitors.

Managing the multi-generational mix

The diverse preferences and skills of different generations of employees means that these cohorts have the potential to make unique contributions to organisations, and yet, generational differences also challenge organisations to find unique ways of integrating the cohorts to create a harmonious, cohesive and efficient working climate.[61] South African organisations must therefore develop effective strategies that manage the expectations of skilled employees and optimise the contribution from each generation.

Teamwork

One of the challenges for organisations with baby boomer executives and Generation X managers is the need to balance work demands with the desires of both 'born free' and Generation Second Wave employees, who are willing to make more meaningful contributions given their current level of competency. A psychological contract is the concept that defines the mutual expectations in the employer-employee relationship based on perceptions of the two parties' commitments to each other.[62] Managers play a critical role in establishing, developing, or breaking psychological contracts with employees. Breach of the psychological contract can cause irreparable damage to work relationships and result in employees withholding effort and commitment, or resigning from the job.[63] South Africa's current skills shortage and depressed labour market place additional pressure on this contract, and can further negatively impact productivity levels.

Organisational success hinges on the effective coordination of people from across cohorts at the team level. Here again, the generations have different approaches to teamwork. For example, one study showed that baby boomers prefer teamwork where they are in charge, while Generation X favours teams where individual contributions are valued, and millennials enjoy teamwork but require some supervision.[64] While Generation Z values independence, they also do not shy away from collaboration.[65] Therefore, managers must be aware of these dynamics when planning teams to optimise team design, task allocation and process design.

---

61 Dols, Landrum & Weick, 2010.
62 Chartered Institute of Personnel Development, 2016.
63 Conway & Briner, 2005.
64 Van der Walt & Du Plessis, 2010.
65 Ozkan & Solmaz, 2015.

A cautionary note: the perceptions of baby boomers who worked during the Apartheid years can be quite different from those who joined the workforce in the era of democracy.[66] Policies implemented to redress past imbalances – such as employment equity – have created burdens in the South African workplace.[67] A key objective of this Act is to achieve a diverse workforce. Compliance with the legislation thus requires organisations to meet targets related to the recruitment, retention, training and development of different groups identified as Black people, women and people with disabilities.[68] A recent study showed that young people agreed that the affirmative action law is necessary and enhances their autonomy in the workplace.[69] Although this is encouraging, the implementation of this legislation means organisations must use positive employment practices as envisaged in the Code of Good Practice: Human Resource Policies[70], including a regular analysis of the workforce, a review of people management policies and procedures, an analysis of the working environment, and surveys to gauge employee experience of diversity management within the organisation. These audits should include an analysis of the barriers faced by Black people, women and people with disabilities regarding their recruitment, promotion, advancement and retention, as they can introduce real changes in organisational culture.[71] Age should be added as a further factor in this analysis to dispel ageist beliefs that can reduce the harmful effects of ageism, particularly for older employees.[72]

Inclusionary practices

Regardless of generational differences along values, motivations and attitudinal beliefs, organisations must be prepared to deal with tensions and conflict that arise when implementing inclusionary practices for improved performance. Ultimately, South African organisations must secure the right resources to achieve the innovation and continuous performance improvement that will lead to increased productivity and competitiveness at the local, national and global level. Strategies for effectively diversifying the workforce must therefore incorporate approaches that inherently promote employee satisfaction and organisational performance. Four key recommendations are suggested for organisations dealing with inter-generational challenges: building a culture of respect, cross-generational activities, using Generation X as a bridge, and rethinking people management strategies.

---

66 Shrivastavaa, Selvarajaha, Meyerb & Dorasamy, 2014.
67 Lloyd, Roodt & Odendaal, 2011.
68 Republic of South Africa, 1998.
69 Mula, 2014.
70 Department of Labour, 2005.
71 Booysen, 2007.
72 Nelson, 2016.

1.   Building a culture of respect

One way to enhance inclusion in organisations is to focus on shared values. In South Africa, forward-looking organisations are drawing on the concept of *ubuntu,* an old African philosophy that has gained increasing attention. It is particularly relevant for today's organisations as many consider the revival of *ubuntu* as "an attempt to (re) discover African cultural values eroded by colonialism and Apartheid".[73] It therefore speaks directly to the unique challenges of our generations.

Ubuntu is the practice of embracing values of generosity, hospitality, friendliness, care, and compassion among human beings.[74] Desmond Tutu explained that individuals who share these values are willing to affirm others and be accessible themselves. It therefore centres all activities in the organisation around the priority of community and togetherness, which inherently speaks to bridging generational divides, among others. In organisational settings, specifically, there are five key values underpinning *ubuntu*:

•   Survival (sustainability).

•   Compassion (helping others).

•   Solidarity (being part of a collective).

•   Dignity.

•   Respect (courtesy, organisational citizenship and consideration).[75]

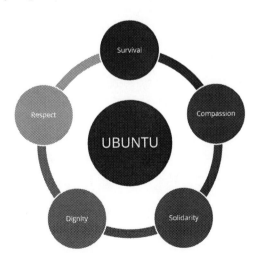

Figure 8.1: Key values underpinning ubuntu
Source: Mbigi[76]

73 Beet & Le Grange, 2005, p. 1200.

74 Tutu, 2000.

75 Mbigi, 2000.

76 Ibid.

Practicing *ubuntu* involves deploying strategies to build and consolidate relationships between groups in the workplace. The adoption of the *ubuntu* philosophy leads to the strengthening of a specific organisational culture. This culture promotes the formation of a unified identity where everyone acts in the interests of the self, as well as in the interests of the team to achieve the organisation's objectives. Therefore, anyone who values themselves is able to value and support the interests of others. A unified identity is crucial to fill gaps in South Africa's fractured past and an understanding of the other is critical for acceptance and inclusion.

In practice, organisations achieve this culture of inclusion and *ubuntu* in a few key ways. In terms of leadership from managers or other positional decision-makers, a democratic leadership style that invites participation from throughout the organisation is essential. By holding strategic meetings or planning sessions that intentionally include employees from different generational cohorts and who occupy different roles in the organisation, leaders can enhance tolerance and the understanding of differences across generations, gender, race and culture.

Relatedly, inclusive communication among leaders and employees, which involves showing genuine sensitivity to individual concerns, upholding others' self-esteem, and win-win conflict resolution, is vital to consolidating the success of *ubuntu* cultures.[77] For instance, executives can create open-door policies where employees of all ages and levels of experience can approach them to discuss important professional and personal matters. Particularly between executives and entry level employees, where the generational gap is likely the widest in the entire organisation, the use of direct and purposeful communication in the form of individual or group meetings can go a long way to bridging the generational divides overall, which are also widened by the power differential. And these do not have to be formal meetings. In fact, casual but deliberate conversations – watercooler chats – are some of the most effective tools for shaping a culture, building relationships and enhancing learning. Then, to seed these actions throughout the organisation, effective employee training programmes with continuous assessment of results is the best way to lead organisations into meaningful interactions.

Promoting tolerance using *ubuntu* through a variety of methods empowers employees, offers independence and strengthens inter-dependence. This leads to increased employee participation, a higher level of work satisfaction, and engagement where all employees – across generational groupings – assume responsibility for their actions and outputs.

---

77 Shrivastava et al., 2014.

2. Cross-generational activities

Organisations in all industries and sectors should create opportunities for cross-generational mentoring to promote knowledge transfer among employees and increase work satisfaction that benefits all the participant cohorts. For example, younger employees may seek to gain new, practical knowledge while baby boomers wish to share the experience they have developed over time. But there are also suitable strategies that reverse the case, where baby boomer and Generation X employees are mentored by young employees familiar with the latest tools, techniques and information. 'Reverse mentoring' can be an effective approach to shifting attitudes to benefit organisations.

A related activity consists of integrating cross-generational teams to participate in volunteer or corporate social responsibility (CSR) activities. Joint activities that are ancillary to core operations help to engage younger generations with their inherent desire to be productive citizens, serve society, and work for organisations with good ethical records. Meanwhile, Generation X, who enjoy goal-directed activities, and baby boomers, who are committed to a track record of giving back through social initiatives, help organisations improve productivity and social inclusiveness. Organisations that show interest in giving back to society and supporting these initiatives reinforce their reputations and offer strong attraction for both new recruits and existing employees.

3. Using Generation X as a bridge

At this particular point in time, a unique opportunity presents itself to South African organisations. Baby boomers are moving towards retirement and Generation X managers are poised to take on more senior management roles. This has the potential to change the way organisations traditionally deal with their employee relationships. Generation X managers have seen and experienced, first-hand, rapid and ongoing organisational change, and have faced downsizing, delayering, economic uncertainty, outsourcing, and the advent of new technology.[78] Because they understand the consequences of these changes – job insecurity, lowered morale, loss of the right mix of people in terms of skill and experience, erosion of motivation and loyalty, and poor organisational communication – Generation X managers are better prepared to create conducive conditions for both new and existing employees to function optimally.

In South Africa, this is also the Struggle Generation, who have faced many hardships and overcome them. Because of their own experiences, Generation X is ideally suited to address organisational inefficiencies by prioritising employee collaboration, respecting and appreciating diversity, and embracing complexity. Because of their experiences,

---

78 Erikson, 2010.

they can bring a sense of realism and insight to organisations[79], while also seeming relatable to younger employees. Older executives eyeing members of Generation X as their successors should therefore be aware of this aspect of their leadership potential and start taking advantage. They might, quite literally, use Generation X managers and employees as conduits to younger employees to gather information about their needs and contributions. They might also delegate the task of designing strategies for multi-generational diversity directly to Generation X, knowing that they are best positioned to see the fuller picture of age diversity and will one day champion these strategies at the highest levels of leadership.

4.   Rethinking people management strategies

There are several recommendations to address productivity in multi-generational workplaces[80], including radical changes to the ways of working. Instead of presenting employees with a generic value proposition, this approach focuses on re-thinking processes entirely to make the experience of producing more enjoyable for all involved. As the prospects for promotion and increased remuneration narrow for employees in increasingly flat organisations that are treading water in a developing economy, process and culture become the primary levers for organisations to incentivise productivity. New processes that change how employees do their work, such as introducing flexible working practices, reconfiguring office design with deskless offices and communal workspaces, or creating child- and pet-friendly spaces, allows for customised work experiences that accommodate employees' different needs and allow them to contribute more.

One way organisations can use the cultural lever to both develop people management strategies and incentivise commitment in tandem is to include employees in the design of the strategies. Leaders can engage employees in structured or informal conversations about how processes can be changed, analyse their views and motivations, and design policies accordingly. Their input may range from some of the flexible working processes cited above, to more behavioural, normative practices that contribute to the culture, such as regular socials, rituals, and other activities that are not directly related to work, but which boost morale and foster connection between employees – and generational cohorts.

It is, of course, useful for managers to develop policies that are informed by the desires of employees, but this approach also has the effect of demonstrating a culture that prioritises diverse employee input, signalling a commitment to multi-generational coordination and feeding employees' desire to be part of an inclusive organisation. Another important aspect of this approach is that often, each generational cohort believes they bring unique strengths to the workplace. Organisations should therefore use this engagement with their teams as an opportunity to identify the areas of commonality and strengths of each

---

79 Erikson, 2010; Glass, 2007; Southard & Lewis, 2004.
80 CIPD, 2008.

group, and build on these to ensure that diversity can be embraced through inclusionary practices and an inclusive culture.[81]

On an individual level, diversity management interventions of this nature have many advantages, including improved communications and friendships, an increase in trust, and a decline in stereotyping.[82] In an inclusive workplace, individuals have the opportunity to realise their potential within the group and contribute to an organisation's sustainable competitive advantage.[83]

What's next for the South African workplace?

Young employees, more so than older generations, want to have a voice regarding their employment conditions and interactions in the workplace. In South Africa, where this 'voice' was denied to so many for so long, this interaction is even more significant, both for those generations who remember the indignity and those 'born free' of it. But organisations must be cautious to avoid the risk of stereotyping along generational lines. South African organisations are very familiar with the effects that negative racial stereotyping can have on individuals, teams and productivity. They must therefore guard against the same thing happening with generational stereotyping, which can happen when people fixate on minor differences and take them out of context. By failing to appreciate and acknowledge the similarities between cohorts, organisations could be missing out on important opportunities. More than that, the differences between generations might be less significant when you look past the superficial differences to the deeper core of employees' motivations, goals and values. Research shows that all employees want the same things: challenging, meaningful work; opportunities for learning, development and advancement; support to successfully integrate work and personal life; and fair treatment and competitive compensation.

Central to matching these shared values are the behaviours of an ideal leader – a person who leads by example is accessible, acts as a coach and mentor, helps employees see how their roles contribute to the organisation, and challenges others and holds them accountable. Implicit in these behaviours is a sense of respect – of self and others – consistent with the ethos of *ubuntu*. In business, as in life, the fundamentals of mutual respect go a long way in building positive workplace cultures. Respect will also be key in managing multi-generational teams. For leaders, enacting respect for this purpose means taking a common sense approach that maintains a focus on individual needs, honours each person's contribution, and strives to keep older workers engaged alongside newer hires so as to avoid losing institutional knowledge. It may also help to remember

---

81 Nnambooze & Parumasur, 2016.
82 Joubert, 2017.
83 Hugo, Sauerman, Schutte, Schutte & Van Eeden, 2019.

that each generational shift evolves organically – and so, too, will the workplace, if we are open to allowing it to do so.

KEY TAKEAWAYS

1. The shared experiences and values that define generational cohorts translate to different motivations, goals and ways of working between generations in the workplace, which affect the people management practices of organisations.

2. In order to remain competitive and secure highly sought-after talent, South African organisations must adopt strategies that create awareness of the unique characteristics of the different generations in organisations, and actively promote collaboration across generational divides.

3. Organisations must address the issues of employee attraction, retention and commitment along generational lines through policies and practices that accommodate the needs of employees with different values and at different life stages. These include customised policies such as i-deals, regular feedback systems and lateral career pathways.

4. There are four strategies that organisations can use to address the challenges of a multi-generational mix: building a culture of respect, cross-generational activities, using Generation X as a bridge, and rethinking people management strategies.

5. In particular, embracing the philosophy of Ubuntu can foster an inclusive culture that intrinsically bridges divides and drives organisational performance on the basis of a unified identity, where everyone acts in the interests of the self as well as in the interests of the team to achieve the organisation's objectives.

Chapter 9

INCLUSIVE SOLUTIONS TO MENTAL HEALTH CHALLENGES: CREATIVE RESISTANCE FROM THE MARGINS

Cal Volks, Gabriel Hoosain Khan and Dr. Sianne Alves

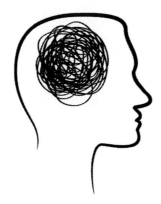

INTRODUCTION

Managing diversity and inclusion within the mental health sector is a fundamental part of delivering services and enabling integration in society. Understanding whether mental health services are inclusive towards all its users requires increased and regular discussion and debate. Mental health conditions are apparent among South African youth and are exacerbated by exposure to one or more variables such as violence, economic inequality and co-morbid diseases.[1] In the South African context, decolonial contemporary scholars have raised important questions about how Western mental health classifications contrast with African therapeutic practices. Mkhize[2] argued that in African practice, a person's connection to their present, their past and their ancestors as spiritual guides are integral to their healing. The contrast between Western and African mental health approaches is contextually relevant for this chapter, as it is based on our engagements with adolescent participants who were concerned by mental health questions and the societal variables that exacerbate them.

In this chapter, we focus on inclusive mental health services for marginalised youth. We present two separate case studies of youth from various marginalised backgrounds (including youth of colour, LGBTIAQ youth, young women, etc.) living in Cape Town.

---

1   Kaminer & Shabalala, 2019.

2   Mkhize, 2004.

The thrust of our research focuses on the effect of intergenerational trauma, structural oppression and exclusion on the mental health of marginalised youth. In assessing the experiences of these groups of youth, we explore how marginalised youth employ awareness, expression, disruption and collaboration to build inclusion in the face of inequity, oppression and intergenerational trauma. Utilising Freirean theory,[3] which is both useful and challenging, the case studies include the participants' analysis and construction of solutions to overcome the challenges that they identify.

CASE STUDIES

Case Study One: The Creative Change Laboratory (CCoLAB)

In Case Study One, the Creative Change Laboratory (CCoLAB) is introduced as an immersive learning space in which young, excluded people can experiment with unconventional solutions to problems in their communities, including mental health. Unlike most art-based projects, CCoLAB was designed as a long-term intervention; one that introduces participants to diverse creative modes and allows them to develop and test original prototypes. Its overall objective is to enable marginalised youth to respond to the problems they face, using art. Unlike previous projects, CCoLAB aims to expose participants to multiple ways of analysing and responding to their positions in the world. In addition, CCoLAB supports participants over a six month period to develop a prototype solution that responds to a social challenge emerging from their analysis.

The CCoLAB intervention and the Creative Resistance methodology that underpins it harnesses the transformative potential of art to process lived exclusion experiences[4] among youth in Cape Town. CCoLAB and Creative Resistance are based on the extensive work of Judy Seidman and Charlotte Schaer of the Curriculum Development Project (CDP).[5] Both the CDP and Creative Resistance methods draw on theories of popular education, including those developed by Paulo Freire and Augusto Boal. These methods prioritise collective and experiential modes of learning that are grounded in lived experiences. For the purpose of this chapter, the works of three participants are shared below, as these works (See mini documentary, "The Creative Change Laboratory Journey" for more information (CCoLAB, 2019)[6] centre narratives responding to mental health.

---

3   Freire, 2007.
4   Marnell & Khan, 2016.
5   Seidman & Schaer, 2010; Seidman & Schaer, 2011.
6   Khan, 2019.

"Ema o Eme" – Masechaba Khoza

Masechaba is a young woman from Vosloorus in South Africa who identified challenges of poor mental health and trauma faced by people living in an impoverished area. In her community, few young people have access to green spaces such as parks or gardens, and there are few safe spaces for young people. She suggested that this inhibits young people's ability to heal trauma. She responded to these challenges by developing a mobile green box that includes a chair, a plant box and an audio recording. The audio recording comprises a calming meditation, suggesting how the user can interact with the natural elements in the green box. The chair and enclosed space offer momentary safety and a solitary retreat from the busy outside space. She asserted that when installed in a school or library, this prototype would change the structure of the space to make it safer and more affirming to young people struggling with their mental health.

"Walk on Bye" – Diego de Abreu

Diego is a young gay man from Durbanville who has struggled with poor mental health for much of his life. As a gender non-conforming person, his gender expression has often led to a negative backlash from his school and community. Diego was interested in exploring the relationship between being a queer and gender non-conforming person and the implications this had on his confidence, self-esteem and mental health. Diego's prototype was an art installation – a white fabric throne adorned with several pencil sketches – Diego who sat on the throne whilst wearing a red dress. A video of Diego walking the streets of Cape Town was projected over Diego and the fabric throne. Diego's performance on the throne involved only facial expressions, which invoked and expressed the emotions he felt when he received negative pushback from people. The emotions and sounds expressed were a powerful reminder of the often-hidden visceral responses we have to discrimination. Diego's prototype used art in a powerful and evocative manner to raise awareness of the lived experience of those struggling with their mental health.

"On the margin" – Zintle Olayi

Zintle is a young gender-non-conforming person from Stellenbosch who expressed that poor mental health is a huge challenge for youth activists. However, on platforms used by young people – like Facebook, Instagram and WhatsApp – there wasn't a simple way to access information on mental health services. Zintle was interested in addressing this lack of easily accessible information, so created a prototype of a series of video clips and a documentary film that highlighted the mental health services available at organisations based in Cape Town. These video clips centre around the story of one staff member at each organisation, giving the organisation a human face. The clips were developed so that they could be easily disseminated on social media platforms.

In the three examples provided by CCoLAB, young people on the margins of Cape Town grapple with mental health and exclusion in a range of ways. From safety in township settings and being gender non-conforming in the city, to the lack of availability of resources, young people were able to creatively make sense of, and respond to, their lived experience.

Case Study Two: Intergenerational trauma

In the second case study, we reflect on personal resilience in the absence of support. The students in this case study explored the multi-dimensional experience of being in a relatively privileged position at a university whilst their parents were denied the opportunity of higher education. The students also reflected on the distress of being a second-generation Apartheid trauma survivor, a carrier of intergenerational trauma, and continually negotiating spaces where White privilege is at work. These complex layers weaved together to form a narrative for the students, which helped them make sense of their experiences of alienation. It is these complex narratives that students bring to the university space that require that the university's response to mental health is inclusive and sensitive to these layered experiences of marginalised youth. (Pseudonyms have been used.)

Kellerman asserted that intergenerational trauma may be transferred from parents to children biologically, through relational parenting, socio-cultural means, or family system operations.[7] This may result in "difficulties in forming relationships... a pervasive sense of guilt; a need to achieve and overachieve (to compensate for parental loss); insistence on perfectionism... and intense fear of punishment".[8]

---

7   Kellerman, 2001.
8   Hoffman, 2005, p. 56.

Sivu Sishoba

One of the research participants, Sivu, was an HIV positive, 19-year-old, heterosexual Health Sciences Faculty student in her second year at UCT, repeating her first year of study. Learning that she was HIV positive led to the family realising that Sivu's mother was HIV positive, and that she had transmitted it to her daughter in utero. The stigma of HIV was strong and the family banished Sivu's mother. No one in Sivu's family was allowed to speak about her HIV status.

At university, Sivu's experience of HIV stigma was just as apparent. Sivu's friend told her, "If you got HIV, I'd laugh at you", which resulted in silencing her. Only when Sivu was excluded from university did she disclose her HIV status to her academic course supervisor, explaining how much she had struggled with her health in her first year. Sivu battled multiple traumas, and the anti-depressants she was put on were not effective. She stated that, "Whenever I came back from campus I would go to my room and at night I would cry myself to sleep".

Aaron Ncingwana

Aaron identified himself as a gay, Black, HIV positive, 24 year old, post-graduate Commerce student. His mother worked casually as a domestic worker. It is clear that Aaron's mother's economic position was directly influenced by the impact of Apartheid. Aaron feared disclosing his status to his mother who he described as "fragile". Acquiring HIV through a homophobic gang rape when he was in grade 10, Aaron's belief was that the police would not take this 'form' of rape seriously. His expectations of being treated in an inclusive way in the face of assault regarding his sexual orientation were so low that he chose to minimise further hurt to himself by not reporting the rape.

Thabo Radebe

The third student, Thabo, identified as a Black, HIV positive, heterosexual, 19 year old Science student. He spoke of daily financial struggles resulting from existing structural oppression, as a result of Apartheid. These financial struggles influenced and affected Thabo's ability to thrive academically.

All three students interviewed in 2012 spoke about how difficult it was to adjust, coming from their school environments in so-called previously Black areas under Apartheid group areas laws where they were at the top of their classes, to the university environment where they struggled academically and were pitted against students from privileged education backgrounds. They were also economically juxtaposed with students from economically privileged backgrounds. It is of further importance that out of the three students in Case Study Two, only Aaron felt that he could find some form of support from mental health care services in the university.

In addition, Sivu, Aaron and Thabo clearly demonstrated some of the traits that Hoffman[9] identified in second and third generation survivors whose parents and grandparents had experienced political violence. These include the need to achieve against all odds, the guilt of the students in telling their parents that they are less than perfect, and the shame and judgement of not being able to seamlessly rise above the oppression inherited from older generations.

Understanding the interplay of intergenerational trauma, along with experiences of exclusion economically and academically for students (despite their relative privilege being at a university), sheds light on structural changes that need to be made at universities to enable inclusion. Students require economic support as well as mental health interventions that acknowledge the complicated legacy of being second generation Apartheid trauma survivors. The research relied on participants being able to reflect in a Freirean way around aspects of their life where they had more agency, power or privilege than others (e.g. being allowed into a University, as opposed to their parents who did not have that chance), as well as aspects of their life where they still felt oppression (e.g. the University spaces were still dominated by White privilege). Freire's philosophy that learners must be made aware of political domination in educational settings relies on participants being willing to engage in the research and acknowledge the power imbalances. If the participants were unwilling to have these realisations, the research would not have been possible.

Discussion

Through our analysis of the case studies, the following concepts emerged in relation to youth, mental health and marginalisation in higher education.

Resistance to oppression can be therapeutic

Rudley, Cole and Goodley's research drew on the concept of resilience to define what may constitute inclusive mental health services for marginalised groups.[10] Through

---

9   Hoffman, 2004.

10 Rudley, Cole & Goodley, 2013.

a complex dance between the relationships young people find themselves in, their sometimes marginalised identities, disparities of power, and the communal strength that emerges through participatory processes, young people can resist oppression.[11] As seen in Case Study One, the ability to connect, even for a moment, outside the alienating and oppressive world is a form of resistance to oppression. Resilience can also be a powerful mechanism for building solidarity and a sense of community, which, in some cases, can last beyond the end of the intervention. For example, the art interventions created by participants continues to live on as moments and places (physical and online) where people can continue to connect. Case Study One further emphasises how awareness of structural barriers and resisting violence and oppression could become a therapeutic response to feeling marginalised.[12] In both case studies, the participants highlighted the tension between their individual efforts in response to marginalisation, and the need for broader structural changes in their communities. For example, a mobile green box, a virtual social media platform and peer networks can provide reprieve to marginalised groups, but these solutions should not take away from the need to confront townships or universities themselves as unsafe and marginalised spaces.

Value of a community

Mkhize pointed out that in indigenous thought, one attains personhood by being in community with others, and that good mental health is necessary for the maintenance of the advancement of the community.[13] In Case Study One, participants came together to unify their thinking and build solidarity by witnessing each other's lived experiences, collaborating and supporting each other's work, and physical proximity. These practices of witnessing, collaborating and connecting can have beneficial effects for mental health.[14] In this group, inclusion was achieved through a democratic process which brought participants together through making art or joining in a fun activity. The students in Case Study Two were not able to experience the social cohesion of a group due to prevalent and suppressive stigma. These case studies highlight the importance of connecting marginalised groups to community support, which in turn assists with better mental health provision and care.

Recommendations for inclusive practices

Selection of participants

Kumashiro suggested that despite best efforts to create equal, inclusive and meaningful engagement, it is simply impossible to address the needs of every marginalised person

---

11 Ibid.
12 Watts, 1997.
13 Mkhize, 2004.
14 Runswick, Cole & Goodle, 2013.

in one engagement.[15] Thus, while the case studies listed here prioritised marginalised youth, the authors acknowledge that the methods for enrolment in Case Study One and Case Study Two, such as an online enrolment, university posters or peer networks, may have influenced who could participate. While the participants in the case study groups were diverse, the methods of enrolment inadvertently favoured university-educated applicants who are well versed in current Euro-American articulations of identity politics. Future interventions on diversity and inclusion in mental health may need to rethink selection processes and more carefully identify a target cohort to counteract trends of privilege and power. While diversity is a strength in all the interventions, it is also important to safeguard that facilitators and researchers can sensitively negotiate differences to ensure all participants feel fully included and their particular experiences are valued and respected.

Long-term facilitation for social change

In Case Study One, sustaining funding for long-term interventions on mental health, diversity and inclusion was found to be a challenge, yet mental health, systemic inequalities, HIV and intergenerational trauma are complex problems that require long-term sustained work. Long-term interventions aim to work with the same group of participants over an extended period of time (often six months or longer) and come with a unique set of challenges. For example, Case Study One consisted of 42 full-day sessions held over three learning blocks. For each component, the facilitators developed a learning process rooted in popular education methodologies. The methods used for this intervention – practice-based learning, arts-based analysis, prototype development, etc. – are primarily used in shorter workshops (lasting a maximum two to three weeks). The length and intensity of the interventions left the participants and facilitators feeling emotionally and physically exhausted, frustrated, and at times overwhelmed by the number of structural barriers needing to be confronted for social change. A learning process that is facilitated around social change with regards to diversity, inclusion and mental health involves a higher level of emotional engagement and conceptual thinking than those found in traditional classroom settings. For participants, the longer the process went on, the more difficult it was to remain committed due to study responsibilities or social pressures. For facilitators, it became increasingly difficult to hold the space, and in some instances, the emotional dependency on them by participants increased. For long-term facilitation or interventions to be practical and effective, new types of practice may need to be developed and employed in order to sustain the intervention and accommodate shifting needs/expectations. As we deepen our thinking about improving facilitation with marginalised youth, we also need to consider multi-modal structures of mental health support that are separate to, but also work in tandem with, the facilitated workshops.

15 Kumashiro, 2000.

The limits of a Freirean approach when doing diversity work

Both case studies used Freirean approaches in the form of participant agency and/or collective decision-making as essential characteristics of the learning space. However, these useful principles can sometimes conflict with some of the broader objectives of a project. It can be difficult for facilitators to adhere to the values of democratic learning if participants make choices that facilitators think might limit potential valuable learning opportunities for participants. For example, in Case Study One, facilitators grappled with how to respond if a participant opted out of learning an art method that they were uninterested in or they perceived would be too confronting. What if a participant rejects the processes of sharing and reflection, perhaps because they regard other people's feedback as stifling or too confronting when they are making themselves vulnerable? On the one hand, the agency of participants cannot be compromised as there is a need to protect participants from feeling the exclusion they have come to the workshop to work through. However, it is also worth remembering that a pedagogy of discomfort[16] may sometimes enable people to gain insights about themselves, if facilitated in a thoughtful, respectful manner. While this tension was not new or exclusive to the listed case studies, it can be more pronounced here than in some other projects. This highlights the need for facilitators to develop training in mental health and critical diversity that assists in facilitating the complexity of needs of participants.

Reflections on results

How do we determine if the case studies were a success or a failure? Do we couch our assessment solely within the vocabulary of corporate monitoring and evaluation, measuring positive quantifiable outcomes for participants (which did materialise)? In many ways, the case studies were a success as they worked with a group of participants to creatively respond to mental health challenges and exclusion. However, even in projects like this, there are limitations to outcomes. There were moments when facilitators and participants misaligned, and even in the best-case scenario, the interventions did not entirely end or sustainably disrupt systemic exclusion. However, activism is always evolving through learning. The ways in which participants pushed back against the process allowed us, as facilitators, to recognise the limits of the employed methodologies and broader praxis, as well as the shortcomings of current theoretical frames. This offers a useful opportunity to rethink the potential of long-term art-activism interventions; the role of facilitators in such processes; and what we might understand as 'failure' and 'success' within a multi-faceted learning process.

---

16 Zembylas, 2015.

CONCLUSION

This chapter outlined two case studies on working with marginalised youth facing mental health challenges and exclusion. The case studies emphasise how youth-centered and youth-led approaches can build more inclusive, equal and diverse spaces for young people experiencing mental health challenges. Even in the face of intergenerational trauma, oppression and exclusion, the youth participants became aware of complexities in lived experiences and/or worked collaboratively to respond to the mental health challenges they were facing. The chapter also noted the need for practitioners to think carefully about selection processes for such initiatives, expanding Freirean approaches to facilitation, and assessing or evaluating success. These points highlight useful tension points for strengthening praxis.

The approaches employed in each case study highlighted a key tension between structural oppression and methods which foreground individual change. While collective and individual resistance to exclusion can be empowering and therapeutic, it is also important for mental health care services to adapt and transform to support marginalised students experiencing mental health challenges. Building inclusivity is a dialogue between individuals who experience discrimination, and structures which unwittingly produce exclusion. Through this dialogue, communities of support can emerge as indigenous mechanisms for support and cohesion.

KEY TAKEAWAYS

1. The case studies show that young people reflecting individually and as peers about whether they have agency or not can help them to conceptualise and lobby for structural change in mental health services for marginalised young people.

2. Young people reflecting on whether they have agency (individually and as groups) allowed the authors to recognise both the value and the challenges of the employed methodologies and broader praxis of current theoretical frames.

3. Establishing and sustaining peer support groups (acknowledging this depends on the willingness of peers to do this) physically and/or virtually can improve mental health care services to ensure further accessibility, relevance and inclusivity.

4. Facilitators of creative resistance to exclusion require skills to sensitively facilitate vulnerable groups.

5. Long-term interventions are required for programmes that seek to respond to mental health among youth. These interventions require skilled facilitators, resources and structural support in order to succeed.

Chapter 10

UBUNTU ETHICS AND HUMAN RIGHTS: IMPLICATIONS FOR REHABILITATION PRACTICES IN INDIGENOUS AFRICAN FAMILIES OF PERSONS WITH DISABILITIES (PWDS)

Prof. Gubela Mji and Dr. Chioma Ohajunwa

INTRODUCTION

The focus of this chapter is on children with disabilities (CWD) living in a rural setting in the Eastern Cape province of South Africa. Persons with disabilities (PWDs) in low- and middle-income countries are often deprived of basic human rights and are over-represented among the poor. Compared to those without disabilities, they generally have lower educational attainment and employment rates.[1] Stats South Africa,[2] using the Washington Group tool, has reported a prevalence of 10.7% of CWD in South Africa.

In South Africa, despite its relative wealth compared to other countries in the region, poverty is still rampant for a large majority of the population living in rural areas. The rural areas are the poorest, most under-served and historically most neglected areas of South Africa, despite the fact that 52% of South Africa's total population live in rural areas. They are also where 75% of the poor are situated, with the Eastern Cape having the most people living in poverty.[3]

---

1   Grut, Mji, Braathen & Ingstad, 2012.

2   Stats South Africa, 2010.

3   Statistics South Africa, 2016.

In the face of this widespread poverty, social grants have become the main source of income and livelihood for many families in rural areas. Yet while this money may prevent complete destitution for individuals and families, it is not enough to escape poverty completely.[4, 5]

CWD also are recipients of disability grants and, unlike other children who receive child support grants, CWD receive care dependency grants of R1,860 per month, until the age of 18. This grant is three times that of child support grants because CWD are seen as having greater needs. The fact that CWD are now the recipients of disability grants have resulted in the mushrooming of community homes for CWD within a rural context. The argument for building these homes is that they will provide better care and rehabilitation, which the managers of these institutions believe CWD are not getting at home. There is also a perception that CWD will be protected from the abuse that many experience in their private homes, either from relatives or strangers within the community. What is not clear is how these new community homes for CWD are adequately regulated, and how they link with the original private homes and families of CWD.

Joan, in her paper on creating caring institutions, asked: How do we know which institutions provide good care?[6] She expanded on this by claiming that the best way to think about care institutions is to model them on how they link to families. Joan's paper argued that good care in an institutional context has three central foci: the purpose of the care; a recognition of power relations; and the need for pluralistic, particular tailoring of care to meet individuals' needs. The 1994 Constitution of South Africa gives an opportunity to all South Africans to reflect on issues of human rights and human dignity. Central to this reflection is how do South Africans, including those residing in rural areas, support PWDs and their families. Challenging fixed identities and perceptions about PWDs, and imagining a future of equality for all, are what the Constitution espouses.[7] CWD are still busy developing their own identities, and central to this formulation are their families and communities.[8] Many CWD in rural areas come from indigenous households, with many of them not having gone through formal education. These households still adhere strongly to indigenous practices such as Ubuntu, which might include holding back one's needs for the greater need of the family and greater good of the community.[9,10] What is not clear, then, is how the newly developed institutions/community homes bridge the divide between the scope of practice of the institution to that of the home, thereby

---

4   Surender, Ntshongwana, Noble & Wright, 2007.
5   Maistry & Vasi, 2010.
6   Joan, 2010.
7   The Constitutional Assembly, 1996.
8   Murugami, 2009.
9   Boon, 1996.
10 Keane, 2008.

ensuring that the child with a disability spends part of her/his time in the institution, and still remains rooted within his/her family and community. For this chapter, we present a case study that will highlight some of the challenges that emerge from uprooting children with disabilities and placing them in an institution in the rural South African context. These challenges are exacerbated when there is little or no consideration of ensuring a connection, or nurturing of a relationship, between the home and the institution.

Conceptual framework and literature review

The conceptual framework for this chapter includes disability, Ubuntu ethics, human rights and rehabilitation. These concepts are examined further in this section, highlighting the various interpretations that influence their application within the South African context.

Disability is, and often has been, a very problematic concept to define due to the fact that disability is a heterogeneous, intersectional concept, and persons with disabilities experience disablement in different and subjective ways.[11] Garland-Thomson argued that the understanding of disability is influenced by how disabled bodies interact with their environment, i.e. disability is socially constructed.[12] Some of these lenses include varied models such as the individual medical model, the functional model, the environmental model, the socio-political model and the transactional model.[13] However, facets of all these models are condensed within two main interpretations of disability that influence how society locates it, i.e. the medical/individual model and the social model.

Disability can be defined in terms of the impairment a person has, which prevents participation in daily life activities (the medical model or individual model). This model asserts that disability is caused by the impairment a person has[14], hence the focus is on the impairment and the healthcare professionals who try to 'fix' the impairment/disability. Another framework for understanding disability is the social model of disability. The key assertion of this model is the separation of the impairment a person has from the experience of disability. While this thinking has been powerful in creating certain, advantageous advances in the field of disability, it has been critiqued for its perceived lack of consideration of the impact of impairment on a disabled person, and the relevant roles played by medical professionals.[15] Some disability scholars believe that there is no clear demarcation between disability and impairment, as both concepts co-create the experience of disability.[16] Stienstra and Ashcroft argued that an individual,

---

11 Nwanze & Sciences, 2016.
12 Garland-Thomson, 2005.
13 Nwanze & Sciences, 2016.
14 Nwanze & Sciences, 2016.
15 Mckenzie & Ohajunwa, 2017.
16 Shakespeare & Watson, 2002.

whether disabled or not, exists in more than one dimension, therefore disabled persons are more than the sum of their various experiences.[17] They reasoned that disability is a human state. Disabled people carry more than just their impairment and disability; they rather exist within complex, rich, unique and diverse lived experiences, from which their impairment and disability are not excluded, including their culture.

Within Africa, there is a multiplicity of understandings given to disability based on both the diverse contexts and belief systems, as well as the varied experiences that various African indigenous communities have been subjected to. In terms of oral history, medical and missionary (mainly Western) influences of segregation and categorisation, and definitions ascribed by various world international instruments and funding organisations[18], still impact on these communities. These categorisations neglect the more collectivist approaches favoured within these indigenous communities.[19] The functional abilities of community members, although relevant to the survival of their families and communities, are no determinants of their humanity. So, within this chapter, we go beyond the traditional ways of understanding disability to a more community-based understanding. We therefore perceive disability as a human state.[20]

Yeo and Moore, cited in Munsaka and Charnley, stated that disability has also been perceived as a causative factor, and an outcome, of poverty.[21] Disability narratives within indigenous African communities have either reflected the collective approach, where disabled family members are supported by their families and community to continue to perform their roles as family and community members, or described the further marginalisation that disabled people face within their families and communities. It is safe to assume that the understanding, and therefore lived experiences, of disability are expressed differently within various African indigenous communities. The definition, for instance, of a human rights model that enshrines individual autonomy presents challenges when being implemented within African indigenous contexts by healthcare professionals.

Approximately 15% of the world's population have a disability, and 80% of those live in the Global South.[22,23] This statistic is, of course, not surprising, as disability is closely associated with poverty, which the African continent is plagued with, amongst other

---

17 Stienstra & Ashcroft, 2010.
18 Berghs, 2017.
19 Stienstra & Ashcroft, 2010.
20 Ibid.
21 Munsaka & Charnley, 2013.
22 WHO (World Health Organization). 2011.
23 Ndlovu, 2016.

factors. The World Bank estimate[24] that 20% of the world's poorest are disabled clearly reflects the positioning and relationship between disability and poverty in the Global South. Various lenses, including the human rights framework (described below), have been used to address the various challenges, and support the full participation of PWD on an equal basis within rehabilitation work.

THE HUMAN RIGHTS APPROACH

The ideology of human rights, and equality of all humans, existed and was debated even before the term "human rights" was coined, but its origins remain in the West.[25] Human rights are "those rights that belong to all just because we are human".[26] The human rights framework is made up of 30 articles that attempt to cover all aspects of human life, arguing for an understanding of rights that are ascribed to every individual regardless of their nation, location, language, religion, ethnic origin or any other status.[27] These rights are applicable everywhere and at every time, in the sense of being universal, and they are egalitarian, in the sense of being the same for everyone.[28]

Further emphasised by the UN's Alma Ata Declaration of 'Health for All', the human rights approach enshrines equality, respect and dignity for all human beings as its foundational principles. This approach has been an influencing lens that has driven the creation of various disability policies. Its principles are reflected within policies and practice guidelines that impact on vulnerable and disadvantaged populations, of which indigenous communities and PWD are a part, including services offered to these populaces.[29,30,31,32] The human rights approach has also informed the development of one of the most pivotal policies for PWD, the *United Nations Convention on the Rights of Persons with Disabilities* (UNCRPD)[33], which has been instrumental in many gains within disability activism.

Within the South African context, some policies that have disability foci, and which are crafted from the human rights ideology, include the *Integrated National Disability Strategy* (INDS) – promotion and protection, integration;[34] the *National Rehabilitation*

---

24 Meekosha, 2008.
25 Cobbah, 1987.
26 Healy, Hampshire & Ayres, 2003.
27 United Nations, 2006.
28 Hanna & Vanclay, 2013.
29 Toebes, 1999.
30 Amin et al., 2011.
31 MacLachlan et al., 2012.
32 Gilbert & Lennox, 2019.
33 United Nations, 2006.
34 ODP, 1997.

Policy (guidelines on planning, developing, implementing and monitoring rehabilitation services for PWD)[35]; the *Strategic Policy Framework on Disability for the Post-School Education and Training System*[36]; and the *White Paper on the Rights of Persons with Disabilities.*[37] The human rights approach has predominantly guided the current understanding of disability, as well as current explorations of the lived experiences of disability within the South African context. However, this is often done without taking cognisance of the prevailing contextual philosophies that already exist at the context of implementation and consciously planning with these pre-existing influences in mind.[38,39,40,41] This imposition equally has the potential to defeat the aims of healthcare and rehabilitation interventions for PWD within African indigenous communities if these epistemological challenges are not addressed.

Despite these lofty ideals and egalitarian goals, however, the implementation of the human rights approach has not been without challenges, and the concept has its fair share of critics. Moral maturity within the human rights concept is conceived through independence and autonomy, which has been critiqued for being too individualistic and posing a challenge to more collectivist societies.[42] Stammers argued that the concept of human rights is embedded within certain social power relations that influence the context, and processes, of implementation. Therefore, any exploration of the concept of human rights must equally take cognisance of these integral power dynamics that are inherent to the concept.[43]

Disability studies, as a discipline, is informed by these power dynamics within the human rights discourse and emanated from a troubled past within the Southern context. This domination of Northern narratives have constantly negated the lived experiences of disabled people in the South, who not only live with current challenges to inclusion, but also exist with the historical marginalisation and trivialisation of their lived experiences.[44] This is particularly rife within African indigenous communities, where the majority of the African knowledge systems are marginalised, including varied understandings of disability that emanate from these contexts. There is a need to understand how African indigenous communities theorise disability and unpack the implications of these perspectives on the

---

35 Mji et al., 2017.
36 Department of Higher Education, 2018.
37 National Department of Health, 2016/17.
38 Chilisa, 2012.
39 Owusu-Ansah & Mji, G. 2013.
40 Easby, 2016.
41 Ohajunwa, 2019.
42 Gouws & Van Zyl, 2014.
43 Stammers, 1995.
44 Meekosha, 2008.

lived experiences of these communities. The understanding given to disability influence these outcomes. One of the philosophical worldviews of the South African indigenous communities, which influences this chapter, is Ubuntu.

The African indigenous worldview and disability

In the Latin language, the term 'indigenous' means 'born of the land', which could equally be understood as 'born of its context'.[45] This would suggest that the term 'indigenous' is very much connected to its context physically, emotionally and spiritually, hence every aspect of indigenous peoples' lived experiences are shaped and imbued with contextually-laden influences and meaning-making. This would then imply that indigenous research, and indeed any indigenous engagement, should be influenced by an understanding that is not only related to, but actually emanates from, the relevant indigenous context.[46] The understanding and definition given to disability is no different.

Within South Africa, Ubuntu is an indigenous moral, social and psycho-spiritual ethic that influences the understanding of life and all of existence as relational.[47,48,49,50] Ubuntu is about a shared humanity. This philosophy guides relationship-building and lived experiences within African indigenous communities, of which PWD are members.

Ubuntu is an African moral and ethical discourse that posits a person in relation to another[51,52,53,54]; as an ethical orientation, it is multi-faceted and all encompassing. Dreyer posited Ubuntu as the good, which is about *virtue ethics*; as an issue of the right, which speaks to *duty ethics*; and about the wise or wisdom, which is about *situation ethics*[55]. Ubuntu existed and originated from oral tradition, long before it existed in printed format. Ubuntu was practiced as a lived philosophy, on the continent of Africa, that is evidenced by a person's behaviour and conduct towards the other. Ubuntu is a fluid concept, embodying a spirituality that has the ability to transcend difference and create a shared experience for all.

---

45 Cardinal, 2001.
46 Ibid.
47 Metz, 2007.
48 Edwards, 2011.
49 Wanless, 2007.
50 Dreyer, 2015.
51 Wanless, 2007.
52 Battle, 2010.
53 Gade, 2012.
54 Dreyer, 2015.
55 Ibid.

We need to understand disability in the context of humanity, realising that care, therefore, is a human transaction. Being informed by Ubuntu when engaging with PWD gives us a larger framework and understanding of humanity. As an indigenous ethic, Ubuntu has the capacity to support a contextually and culturally relevant re-conceptualisation of rights, as applied to disability. This will potentially enable PWD and their families, within African indigenous contexts, to access rights and opportunities that are currently inaccessible to them.

The study setting

The study setting was the Mbhashe municipality in the Eastern Cape province. The people in the study setting are amongst the Xhosa of the old Transkei, who are known as a Xhosa clan that hold staunchly to their rituals, traditions and belief systems. The majority has not received a formal education, and the clan believes that the greatest indicator of good health is to live, and exist, according to the characteristics of the clan.

The process of the acculturation of rural South Africa, which affected thousands of Africans to mainly work as labourers in the country's mines, was largely orchestrated by the industrial powers. This resulted in the breakdown of the tribal economy, which forced rural South Africans towards rapid cultural change.[56] Now the community in the study is left to struggle in poverty, and is blighted by diseases such as TB and HIV and AIDS.

There is a secondary hospital and nine clinics linked to that secondary hospital. Rehabilitation professionals are based in the secondary hospital. Stellenbosch University has had several research projects and postgraduate students (PhD and Masters) conduct research in this area. The majority of research outcomes from these studies link problems, identified in this setting, to social determinants of health. There is generally a high prevalence of disability in the area, with high numbers of children with disabilities as consequences of social determinants of health. As part of research dissemination and the translation of research evidence, researchers have worked with the community on strategies to respond to some of the problems that appear to be blighting this area. Our approach has been a participatory action research one, with the community guiding us on projects that should be prioritised. The issue of vulnerable children, including those children with disabilities, was presented by the community as a priority area in one of the workshops. We intend to present a case study of Noluthando Home for Children with Disabilities (pseudonym).

---

56 Jansen, 1973.

Case study of Noluthando Home for Children with Disabilities

The home was started by a couple from overseas, who felt that there was a need to open a home for CWD. They approached the Chief of the area, who was able to offer them a sizeable piece of land to build the home and a farming area. CWD were drawn from neighbouring villages who were able to pay boarding fees using 100% of their disability grants. Children in the home were only able to go home during the school holidays. Employment for young people was a major problem in the area, so it was easy for the couple to draw on young people to be employed in the home as caregivers for the children. The home thrived in the area as a result of its gardening activities, however it was not clear whether there were clear goals and outcomes for the CWD. Some key informants who visited the home in 2010 raised concerns with regards to the health and well-being of the CWD. At that time, the couple running the place were away on a visit to Cape Town and could not meet with the key informants.

As a research team, we started visiting the home in 2018. At that time, the couple who were driving this project had left, leaving the caregivers (CGs) to manage the project. The CGs assisted us to understand the running of the home; below is a report on some of the challenges they experienced as the new managers of the home after the previous managers left:

The CGs reported that they had been running the home since their supervisors left two years prior. They had 16 CWD with different type of disabilities under their care but they were not sure of the types of disabilities that the children had, nor how to manage them. They felt that they needed training on how to look after CWD. It appeared that they did not receive formal training to look after CWD. Although there were rehabilitation professionals at the secondary hospital, when they visited the hospital with their managers they were not included in the management and the rehabilitation of the children. As a result, they were finding it difficult to link with the rehabilitation professionals at the hospital, who would have been well suited to assist them with the training they needed. It also appeared that the home had not developed the necessary relationship with the community, as CGs were not attending community meetings. These meetings would have provided ideal opportunities to exchange more detailed information regarding the CWD and their impairments, and would have provided a platform for gaining community support regarding some of the challenges that the CGs were facing. The Chief was the only member of the community that they had links with, thus the CGs felt isolated, from both the rehabilitation professionals and the community.

They further spoke about the relationships that they had with the parental homes of children with disabilities; it appeared that the only time the CGs had links with the parental homes was during school holidays when the children left the institution to go home and their parents had to come and pick them up, or when they were delivered to their parental homes. Of concern was the fact that, while back at their parental homes, the CWDs were susceptible to abuse during their school holidays. An additional concern was that during the time that the CWDs were in the institution, they used part of their disability grants to buy clothes, and these items were often given to other siblings who were not disabled and attending normal schools. This appeared to be a bone of contention to the caregivers, who felt that the parents of the CWD were not sensitive and caring to their CWD. The CWD were integrated into the home because they were neglected at their maternal home, in the first place, and secondly, when attempts were made to improve their situations, these were undermined during school holidays.

The case study of Noluthando Home for Children with Disabilities left us, as researchers, with lots of unanswered questions, which we will analyse in the discussion. The discussion is guided by a contextual and an interpretive approach (Denzin & Lincoln, 2005), which is well suited when the aim is to explore the multi-dimensional relationship between disability, ethics and human rights. This relationship played out within an indigenous context that still strongly clings to its cultural roots, with notions of Ubuntu quietly existing as a community guiding- and governing instrument.

Discussion

In our discussion we use, as a starting point, key discussion areas that emerged from the introduction and case study:

- The perceived marginalisation of children with disabilities that are encased in households of indigenous families.

- The exposure of children with disabilities to rehabilitation practices that can potentially alienate them from their families and the cultural practices of their communities.

- Disability as a social construct, and the need for rehabilitation services to be informed by the social context and cultural practices of these indigenous spaces.

Perceived marginalisation: Encased in households of indigenous families

Dura-Vila expanded on the challenges for both parents and families who are raising a CWD in a rural context.[57] The extended family, who are usually expected to offer support during times of crisis, often distance themselves from both the parents and the CWD. There is usually speculation and stereotyping of the child's disability among community members, often due to inadequate information about the condition.[58] Ingstad, in a study conducted in Botswana, stated that in poorly resourced rural settings, mothers of children with disabilities were more often unemployed, and depended on the extended family for support.[59]

Most importantly, the issues of access to health care and rehabilitation services are major challenges to be prioritised for parents/CGs of CWD living in rural areas.[60] For poor parents of CWD, who typically are already facing multiple challenges, access to health and rehabilitation services become an additional burden.[61] A lack of knowledge and understanding of how to respond to the needs of the CWD might create a picture of uncaring parents. Several studies, amongst them Gona, Mung'ala-Odera, Newton and Hartley[62] and Gona, Newton, Hartley and Burning[63], on caregiver challenges in rural contexts confirm that, in dealing with disability diagnosis and coping with challenges, some parents resort to neglecting their children. The parents are quickly labelled as uncaring, which fuels the institutionalisation of CWD. There is a need to question whether the institutionalisation of children with disabilities supports access to rehabilitation and prevents abuse. Institutionalisation also separates CWD from their culture and communities, therefore it is not clear whether the institutionalisation of children with disabilities does not undermine their fundamental rights.[64]

Disability and the concept of rehabilitation have historically been understood and practiced in various ways around the world. In many cases, PWDs have been marginalised and denied their rights to participate in societies on an equal basis.[65,66,67]

57 Dura-Vila, 2010.
58 Gona, Newton, Hartley & Bunning, 2018.
59 Ingstad, 1997.
60 Vergunst et al., 2017.
61 Ibid.
62 Gona et al., 2010.
63 Gona, 2018.
64 Constitutional Assembly, 1996.
65 Connell, 2011, pp. 1369-1381.
66 Van Rooy, Amadhila, Mufune, Swartz, Mannan & MacLachlan, 2012, pp. 761-775.
67 Hollinsworth, 2013, pp. 601-615.

This conceptualisation of disability and rehabilitation within societies is influenced by identity politics and historical foundations[68], which exist in each context.[69, 70]

This is especially notable between the Global North and the Global South. For the North, although the understanding and practice of disability services are influenced by an egalitarian intent, they remain mainly individualistic in their approach. Other influencers of the disability framework from the Global North are the recognition and regard given to formal learning and scientific explanations, industrialisation and so forth.[71] It appears that this is the lens that was driving the international external agents who were responsible for the building of Noluthando Home for Children with Disabilities. The argument for building these institutions/homes is that they will provide better care and rehabilitation than the managers of these institutions believe the children are getting at their parental homes.

Alienation: Rehabilitation devoid of connection to family and community

As explained earlier, the lack of health and rehabilitation services for CWD has opened a gap for the mushrooming of homes/institutions for CWD in this rural community. On the one hand, it is not clear how these homes/institutions further link with the original homes of the CWD and the community to ensure that the children are not separated from their culture. CGs, who could assist the home managers by introducing community and parental home cultures into the institution, are typically overlooked by the managers, and are only deemed useful to do labour-related caring. In addition, the managers have not been educating the CGs about the disability-related problems and impairments that the children are struggling with, including how the children can be, and are being, rehabilitated. On the other hand, the managers themselves miss opportunities to potentially learn about the culture of the community that the CWDs come from. While it appears that the managers of the home made an initial attempt to link with the indigenous leader of the community, it is not clear whether that knowledge transfer was fully utilised. When the managers attended some village meetings, there could have been reciprocal learning, for example the managers learning about cultural practices that could influence the growth and development of the CWD under their supervision, and the community being regularly informed about various impairments and disabilities from a rehabilitation perspective.

This side-lining of the caregivers, who could assist in bridging the cultural divide, was also overlooked by these managers even during visits to the rehabilitation unit at the

---

68 Mpofu & Harley, 2002.
69 Meekosha & Soldatic, 2011.
70 Soldatic, 2015.
71 Mpofu & Harley, 2002.

hospital. The caregivers continue to play the role of general carers, without having benefited from the transference of skills or receiving a holistic understanding the entire rehabilitation cycle within the hospital and community, including what is available for them as consumers of rehabilitation services. As a result, once the managers left the institution, the caregivers were left to their own devices to manage the institution and did not know who to turn to. On one hand, they felt alienated from the community and the parental homes where the children came from, and on the other, they had not been trained for the individual approach of rehabilitation services that draws its knowledge base from the West. Joan explained that the best way to think about care institutions is to model them on how they link to the families.[72] This particular institution for CWD does not appear to have fully adopted Joan's principle of linking with the families or their communities.

Mpofu and Harley[73] and Setume[74] highlighted how the Global South conceptualises disability from a metaphysical-spiritual location of disability, utilises more collectivist approaches, and is less industrialised than the North. The lens utilised for the exploration of disability, as a concept, and the lived experiences of disability, have predominantly emanated from the Global North until now.[75;76,77] These understandings of disability are constructed through social processes and philosophical influences that inform and position groups within society, instituting a hierarchy of people and groups.[78] Eurocentric philosophies permeate healthcare delivery within indigenous communities (Nielsen, Stuart & Gorman, 2014), creating hurdles to sustainable healthcare provision.[79]

The mainstream idea of science that influences formal healthcare and rehabilitation practices is crafted in the Global North and presented as a universal truth, akin to the biomedical understanding of disability. However, science "is not something that exists outside the culture and society that produce it".[80] Therefore, the concept of human rights, although egalitarian in its intention, bears within it the inherent thinking and philosophies of its context of origin. This is similar for disabilities. It seems safe to assume that it is presumptuous to attribute universality to any concept that emerges from only one aspect of the global context. While the idea of a concept may sometimes not be problematic, it does, however, present challenges in terms of its intrinsic values adopted

---

72 Joan, 2002.
73 Mpofu & Harley, 2002.
74 Setume, 2016.
75 Martin & Mirraboopa, 2003.
76 Meekosha, 2011.
77 Meekosha & Soldatic, 2011.
78 Connell, 2011.
79 Nielsen, Stuart & Gorman, 2014.
80 Connell, 2011.

from its contextual historical origin. This history, and its impact, cannot be isolated from disability, as this has informed service delivery for CWD and their families within indigenous contexts.[81,82] When this Eurocentric understanding of disability is uncritically transferred and utilised, without some adjustment within different contexts, challenges can often emerge.

Disability as a social construct: The role of context and indigenous cultural practices

The human rights lens influences rehabilitation services delivery for CWDs, their families and their communities. In his discussion about bioethics and belief systems, Durante asserted that although there is a similarity between human rights egalitarian intentions within various other traditions, the manner in which these tenets are interpreted and applied is influenced differently by context.[83]

The manner in which disability is conceptualised and interpreted influences policies and the practice of rehabilitation within each global context.[84] Even the language used to describe disability creates a frame of reference that has a powerful impact on how support is structured for persons with disabilities.[85] Therefore, the imposition of Northern values on the South means that the discourse and implementation of disability in the Global South does not accurately reflect Southern realities about disability.[86] Hollinsworth further argued that these historical foundations are often downplayed, while 'othering' marginalised knowledges when related to formal disability practice.[87]

Southern perspectives are important for the discourse of disability. The social constructionist approach of understanding disability has challenged the hegemonic dominance of the biomedical lens, through the recognition of social embodiment.[88] Social embodiment is the collective, reflexive process that embroils bodies in social dynamics, and social dynamics in bodies.[89] The concept of social embodiment emphasises an interaction between social dynamics and bodies in certain ways to recreate disability. The focus here is on the "interaction" that occurs within social processes to create the lived experience of disability. Taking an example from Noluthando Home for CWD, one can begin to see how social embodiment theory plays out. The external influences who

---

81 King, Brough & Knox, 2014.
82 Sherwood, 2017.
83 Durante, 2009.
84 Mpofu & Hartley, 2002.
85 Devlieger, 1999.
86 Grech & Soldatic, 2015.
87 Hollinsworth, 2013.
88 Connell, 2011.
89 Ibid, p. 1370

opened the home/institution perceived disability in a particular way that influenced their interactions with the community, as well as the caregivers. The children were isolated within this home, not engaging regularly with their families and community. This did not augur well for the social determinants of the health of the caregivers and the children when the initial owners went back to Europe. The capacity of social dynamics and processes to influence determinants of bodily outcome is not new, and was recognised by the WHO in the *Social Determinants of Health Report of 2008*. The UNCRPD supports comprehensive inclusivity[90,91,92,] however for CWD in indigenous settings, sadly this theme of inclusion often stops at the policy level. Inclusion should be continuous and inform actual practice within the context of implementation.

The goal of rehabilitation is to reintegrate a person within their community and to contribute to a better quality of life for CWD and their families. Hence, isolating CWD without duly considering more holistic perspectives for engagement between them and their families within their contexts, defeats this goal.[93] This action would equally reflect the hierarchical approach reflected by Noluthando Home, which is evident in the lack of transference of skills for caregivers, and the lack of transparency when the facilitators take the children to the secondary hospital for rehabilitation. As things stand, the caregivers are not trained or included within this process.

Cultural beliefs are important factors in the conceptualisation of disability[94] and parental understanding of their CWD as informed by their culture, and impact the development of their CWD and the treatment choices they make.[95] An understanding of the complex belief systems that exist in a community is critical to successful rehabilitation.[96]

African indigenous contexts often operate with both an indigenous and modern perspective.[97, 98,99,100,101] In sub-Saharan Africa, for instance, proverbs, ceremonies and moral teachings are used within indigenous communities to philosophise on existentiality and the insecurity of life as related to disability.[102] Whatever the belief systems that exist

90 Harpur, 2012.
91 McKenzie, Mji & Gcaza, 2014.
92 Series, 2015.
93 Stone-MacDonald, 2012.
94 Ibid.
95 Danseco, 1997.
96 Stone-MacDonald, 2012.
97 Mpofu and Harley, 2002.
98 Setume, 2016.
99 Ndlovu, 2016.
100 Stone-Macdonald, 2012.
101 Devlieger, 1999.
102 Ndlovu, 2016.

within Africa, it is clear from the discussion above that ignoring or imposing Northern values on rehabilitation services within African indigenous communities, without taking note of the existing contextual values, will continue to cause many challenges.

Bearing the above in mind, we propose an approach to understanding disability that recognises a space of our shared humanity, and provides a conducive space to support a co-creation of knowledge on disability and rehabilitation through Ubuntu – which seemed to be absent from the original managers of the home for children with disabilities. Dupré discussed a pluralistic model for understanding disability, which took cognisance of the prevailing philosophies in the context and culture of implementation.[103] The outcomes from the case study on Noluthando Home reveal the relevance of aligning disability understandings with the local context, or else the ultimate goal of re-integration may be lost when CWD end up becoming isolated from their families, cultures and communities.

Rethinking a contextually relevant rehabilitation service model

The newly developed homes for CWD emphasise that they will provide the children with rehabilitation services, which they are not currently receiving in their parental homes. Although there are recent definitions to rehabilitation[104], in this chapter we draw key points from the comprehensive operational definition of rehabilitation by Hellander, who maintained that rehabilitation includes measures aimed at reducing the impact of disability on an individual, and enabling the achievement of independence, social integration, a better quality of life and self-actualisation.[105] He continued that rehabilitation not only includes the training of disabled people, but should also include interventions at a society level (the elimination of physical and attitudinal barriers), equalisation of opportunities, adaptations of the environment, and the promotion and protection of human rights.

There are four rehabilitation service models: (1) inpatient/institution-based rehabilitation, designed for patients requiring intensive interdisciplinary rehabilitation services; (2) outpatient-based rehabilitation on an appointment basis; (3) outreach programmes, which take the rehabilitation service from a health facility closer to the communities; and (4) community-based rehabilitation (CBR). For this chapter, with regard to some of the challenges experienced by parents of CWD, we focus on the CBR service delivery model. CBR is a strategy within community development for rehabilitation, which is focused on the equalisation of opportunities and social integration of PWDs. CBR is implemented through the combined effort of PWDs, their families and communities, and the appropriate health, education, vocational and social services.[106] Its principles are applicable at all

---

103 Dupré, 2012.
104 WHO, 2011.
105 Hellander, 1992.
106 WHO, 2010.

levels of service. CBR provides and delivers effective rehabilitation services, as it takes an inclusive development approach to working with persons with disabilities.[107] CBR has five domains or sectors, viz., education, health, livelihoods, social life and empowerment. It is envisaged as a complex, local set of specific processes carried out by a range of agencies and actors, with the full participation of PWDs and their families.[108] When one looks at these five domains of the CBR strategy, one can see that it is a strategy that would benefit both the children and parents of children with disabilities in the study setting.

Like all strategies developed by the WHO and the UN, there is always a need to domesticate them to fit the context. For a CBR strategy that has to be contextually relevant and culturally responsive, one needs to understand the context, including the indigenous clan that underpins this context. We hear from the description of the study setting that this clan believes in rituals and traditions from birth to death. The question is thus, when children with disabilities are in an institution that separates them from their communities, when and how regularly do they link back with their families to go through these rituals and traditions?

In the past, many regulations and laws prevented CWD from being integrated into 'typical' schools, and adolescents and adults were barred from vocational training and employment. There was a reluctance on the part of society to integrate PWDs into public life, and authorities sought special solutions in terms of separate facilities for schooling, living and employment. Recent policies, constitutional reforms and democratisation have made governments more responsive and receptive to proposals that promote human rights for PWDs, however, including integration of PWDs with their families. Some of the challenges experienced by families of CWD is gaining information about their child's impairment or disability.

In counteracting the cultural and socio-economic challenges faced by parents/caregivers of children with disabilities, as suggested by Gona et al.[109], empowering communities with information on disabilities and participating in discussions that challenge stereotypes is usually the best approach. Thus, if we are to respond appropriately to the health and support needs of children with disabilities, it is crucial to understand the social context and interpretation thereof by their families and caregivers alike. Community-based rehabilitation would be a malleable health and rehabilitation strategy that could respond to the needs of rural children with disabilities, as it will have the ability of developing a contextually relevant rehabilitation strategy that is undergirded by ethics and human rights, with Ubuntu running underneath as the guiding tool.

---

107 Ned, Cloete & Mji, 2017.
108 Sherry, 2016.
109 Gona et al., 2018.

CONCLUSION

This chapter has attempted to highlight some of the challenges of separating children with disabilities from their families and communities by moving them to an institution that is based within the community. The challenges of linking the children with their cultural backgrounds and activities, including the interpretation of ethics and human rights within an indigenous context and how Ubuntu is interpreted within ethics and human rights, were also highlighted. The chapter further highlighted the need to link children with disabilities to their cultural practices. CBR was seen as a rehabilitation strategy that could bridge the gap between the institution and the home.

KEY TAKEAWAYS

1. Persons with disabilities and their families who live in rural communities in South Africa are twice marginalised in terms of their disability and indigenous belief systems.

2. Rehabilitation services offered to these communities are based on a human rights approach, which although egalitarian, often alienate children with disabilities from their families and communal practices through institutionalisation.

3. There is a critical need for rehabilitation services within these rural communities to be imbued with the philosophical concepts that inform the lived experience of the communities for more sustainable outcomes.

4. The inclusion of indigenous ethics would support connectivity between communities and institutions, contributing to a reduced alienation of children with disabilities while supporting an increased sense of belonging for children with disabilities in their communities.

5. We propose that Ubuntu is a moral and ethical framework that should inform service delivery, which could be supported by the principles of human rights, so as to ensure that a contextually relevant rehabilitation practice is offered to rural communities in South Africa.

Chapter 11

RELIGIOUS DIVERSITY AND SOCIAL COHESION – THE IMPORTANCE OF MEDIATED INTER-GROUP CONTACT IN THE WORKPLACE IN SOUTH AFRICA

Prof. Dion Forster

INTRODUCTION

We would not blame you if you asked why a chapter on religion should be included in a book on diversity and inclusion in South Africa. In much of the Western world, religion seems to have been relegated to the private sphere. It is something that one practices in one's free time and in privatised spaces (such as the home or a designated religious building), and it is frowned upon to 'bring' religion into the world of work. Contemporary research shows, however, that such views are outdated – religion and spirituality are more present in contemporary life than they have been for decades. Africa, and particularly Southern Africa, has pushed back against the scholarly and popular notions of religious decline made popular in the late 19th and early 20th centuries by persons such as Auguste Comte, Herbert Spencer, Emile Durkheim, Max Weber and Karl Marx, who contended that religion would weaken and eventually vanish in both public and private life.[1] It has not done so in Africa. An important policy document from the African Union, *Agenda 2063: The Africa We Want,* notes that, "Africa is a continent of people with religious and spiritual beliefs, which play a profound role in the construction of the African identity and social interaction".[2]

This chapter does not wish to make a case for religion and the religious in public life. Rather, it will show how and why religion and spirituality matter for identity and social

1   Kotze, 2019, p. 3.
2   African Union, 2015, p. 2.

cohesion in Southern African society. We will consider various quantitative and qualitative metrics that will help us to understand the extent of the importance of religion in South African public life.

The reason why this should be included in a book on diversity and inclusion is that religion plays an ambivalent role in public and private life. We will see that religion and spirituality can be sources of meaning, resilience, discipline and virtue, however religion can also be a source of bigotry, judgement, division and conflict.

As with all forms of diversity and inclusion, certain strategies can be considered, and carefully employed, to facilitate constructive and positive engagement among people with differing beliefs, social practices, and expectations for the freedoms to exercise their beliefs. This chapter will propose two important theoretical frameworks that can serve to enhance the appreciation of religious diversity, the deepening of respect for difference, and responsible engagement across the lines of religious difference.

First, we shall consider the importance of authenticity in religious diversity, and second, we will consider the importance of positive inter-group contact among people with diverse religious convictions and practices. The intention is to provide you with insights and resources that can aid in diversity management and social inclusion strategies for the sake of safeguarding the dignity and rights of people within your sphere of influence, while also contributing towards a more just and inclusive public life for all South Africans.

Case study – The complexities of religious diversity in South Africa

It was just before noon and Rashied was trying to respond to a last urgent email before leaving the office to get to the Claremont Mosque in Cape Town for Friday prayers. He was a devout Muslim and the congregational prayers were important to him. They helped him to gain strength for his work and life, and he believed that they made him a better person. However, his boss, Candice, was quite critical of religion, and described herself as an atheist. Candice had often asked Rashied to attend work functions or remain at work on a Friday afternoon – forgetting that he had permission to attend Friday prayers. Whenever Rashied had raised this issue with her it had created some minor conflict. Now Rashied felt that Candice was not treating him in the same way that she treated Thando, his colleague. Thando was also religious, however as a Christian, his worship services took place on Sundays and thus seldom impacted his work. Thando had offered to stand in for Rashied at times; he realised that the dominance of Christianity in South African history and social life meant that his faith perspective was more easily accepted and protected in the work environment. The fact that Sunday was not a work day was related to South Africa's historical relationship to western Christendom, and the values and rhythms of Christianity had even shaped secular activities such as the structuring of the work week. Rashied had considered taking up Candice's disregard for his religious convictions with the Human Resources department as he knew that he had certain rights and freedoms under the South African Bill of Rights, but he was worried that if he did pursue the matter, he may harm his career prospects and create conflict in their team. He wished that Candice had the same kind of understanding that Thando did. It would make his work life so much more meaningful and pleasant if he were able to integrate this important part of his identity, freely and responsibly, into every aspect of his life.

This case study highlights the complexities of managing religious diversity in contemporary South African life. As we see with Rashied and Thando, and will also read in this chapter, religion plays an important role in the majority of South African's lives. However, South Africa has a rich diversity of religions, each with its own set of values, beliefs and practices. The history and social dominance of some religious traditions – as well as perceptions about the public/private nature of work and faith – can mean that people like Rashied live and work with a great deal of tension due to their inability to fully integrate this important aspect of their life and identity. In this chapter we will consider some ways in which we can cultivate an awareness of religious diversity, sensitivity towards difference, and some strategies for managing inclusion and minimising exclusion.

The role of religion in (South) African public life

John Mbiti stated in *Concepts of God in Africa* that, "African peoples are not religiously illiterate".[3] He is quite correct. Religion did not arrive on the African continent with the missionaries. African traditional religions, African cultures and African philosophies have long played a very significant role in the shaping of African identities, African theologies, and African religious beliefs and practices.[4] Of course some religions, like Christianity and Islam, arrived on African soil via missionaries and colonisers. Africans embraced these religious traditions, and now African expressions of Christianity and Islam are among the fastest growing in the world. For example, there are more Christians attending Church services in the city of Cape Town on any given Sunday than there are in the whole of the United Kingdom – from which Christianity first came to the Cape in the 17th and 18th centuries.[5]

---

3   Mbiti, 1970, xiii.
4   Mbiti, 1990, pp. 3-4.
5   Gledhill, 2009.

Religion and existential security in (South) Africa

Why does religion feature so prominently in the lives of South Africans? In part, South Africa conforms to the general trends for religiosity and public life that apply to sub-Saharan Africa.[6] Some of the prominent reasons for pervasive religiosity in Africa relate to social, political and economic vulnerability, and the influence of culture on worldviews. Norris and Inglehart, two leading researchers in this field, suggested that religious sentiments and adherence to formalised religion "persists most strongly among vulnerable populations, especially those living in poorer nations, facing personal survival-threatening risks".[7]

Norris and Inglehart's research focuses on the qualitative measure of "existential security" that religion provides, rather than just quantitative studies of church membership and attendance at religious services and rituals.[8] In order to qualitatively evaluate the importance of religion in people's lives, one needs to adopt an axiomatic approach that engages two primary realities – the 'security' axiom and the 'cultural traditions' axiom.[9]

Since many Africans remain vulnerable as a result of poverty, war, natural disasters, inadequate state structures, and globalised exploitation of both natural and human resources, they score much lower on the 'security axiom' than their counterparts in the West. This reality is borne out in many global indices, such as Gross Domestic Product per capita, the GINI Coefficient and the Human Development Index, to name a few such metrics. One of the clearest illustrations of vulnerability is to be found in measuring where different African nations sit on the pre-materialist/materialist/post-materialist continuum. In Inglehart's important book, *The Silent Revolution*[10], he charted the move from materialist to post-materialist values in various Western societies. Materialist societies are those in which survival and the maintenance of physical well-being are a primary concern, whereas post-materialist societies tend to emphasise 'softer' issues, such as those related to self-expression and quality of life. A materialist society is concerned about economic and social security, whereas a post-materialist society is dominated by issues such as work satisfaction and personal fulfilment. Kotze argued that because of the extreme vulnerabilities that many Africans experience, they could be classified as existing on the 'pre-materialist' end of such a continuum.[11] Pre-materialist measurements include working towards providing shelter for all people, providing clean water for everyone, making sure that everyone is adequately clothed, ensuring that everyone can go to school, providing land for all people, and providing everyone with

---

6   Kotze, 2019.

7   Norris & Inglehart, 2011.

8   Ibid, p. 4.

9   Kotze, 2019.

10   Inglehart, 2015.

11   Kotze, 2019, p. 7.

enough food to eat.[12] It is not yet dealing with the quality of these items or their ongoing provision (as in a materialist society), nor the experience evoked in relation to choices between quality options (as in the post-materialist society). A pre-materialist society is simply working to achieve the basic minimum for survival. Many Africans, and African societies, subsist on this side of the continuum and are extremely vulnerable. This is also the case in South Africa.[13]

The next axiom deals with the role that 'cultural traditions' play in the shaping of identity, values and beliefs. Traditional secularisation theories rest upon understandings of a decline in 'religious participation'.[14] Such measurement is based upon the presupposition that there is a separation between religion and everyday life. Such views are, however, inadequate to describe lived religion, pre-cognate theologies, cultural and social beliefs, and everyday spiritualities of most Africans. The 'cultural traditions' axiom assumes that "the distinctive worldviews that were originally linked with religious traditions have shaped the cultures of each nation in an enduring fashion".[15] Indeed, John Mbiti rightly claimed that Africans are not religiously illiterate, and they never have been.[16]

One identifiable characteristic in many African philosophies and religions, which differentiate them from their Western counterparts, is the continuum of 'connectedness' between the 'sacred' and the 'secular'. Cornel du Toit wrote that for Africans in general,

> ...there are no ontological gaps between existing entities. The Western natural-supernatural dualism is foreign... God, humankind, extra-humans and sub-humans are all regarded as integral parts of a single totality of existence. God's actions are not experienced as extra-ordinary.[17]

Of course, we should not be idealistic about this notion, as some have been. In many African contexts, individualism, secularism and materialism are increasingly evident, as they are in other parts of the globalised world. However, in large measure, all of reality, and indeed all of life in Africa, is still subject to what Charles Taylor described as "enchantment".[18] The concept is best explained as the opposite of the sociologist Max Weber's term "disenchantment" with life and reality.[19] The "enchanted world... is the world of spirits, demons, and moral forces which our ancestors lived in".[20] This enchanted view

---

12 Ibid.
13 Ibid, pp. 7-8.
14 Kotze, p. 9; Taylor, 2009, pp. 1-3.
15 Norris & Inglehart, p. 17.
16 Mbiti, 1970, p. xiii.
17 Du Toit, 2004, p. 30.
18 Taylor, 2009, p. 25.
19 Gane, 2009, pp. 20-27, 40.
20 Taylor, 2009, pp. 25-26.

of the world significantly influences how Africans, including of course South Africans, view the world. Whereas in some Western societies, religion and the religious are viewed with suspicion, distrust and even scorn, that is not the case in most African contexts.[21] It certainly is not the case for the majority of South Africans who integrate religious and cultural practices (such as ancestor veneration, African traditional religious rites and ceremonies, and aspects of Western religions, such as Christianity, in their individual and social lives). Religion plays a central role in what may be called the 'cultural imagination' and the 'social imaginary' of most African societies and the persons that constitute them. The same is largely true for South Africans, as we shall see shortly.

Many contemporary ethicists and philosophers agree that every person shapes their life according to a sort of 'cultural imagination'. Graham Ward, a Professor at the University of Oxford, explained that the cultural imagination is a set of inherited, unquestioned beliefs, values, and social commitments that a society adopts over time.[22] The 'cultural imagination' shapes what we think is possible, and impossible; it informs how we believe we should live, act and engage socially. It informs what we find attractive and unattractive, what we believe is morally and ethically right or wrong, and even what we believe to be true and good. For example, what some in the West consider corruption is viewed quite differently from the perspectives of some Southern African cultural and religious convictions. This can be a source of misunderstanding, and even conflict, in a globalised economic and political setting.[23]

Charles Taylor used a slightly different term to describe this phenomenon – he called it the modern "social imaginary".[24] This "social imaginary" constitutes those sets of beliefs, ideas and values that shape the ways in which people 'imagine' how their 'social existence' functions or should function. As was mentioned in relation to the 'cultural imagination' above, "social imaginaries" are not set in concrete, and they are not universal. Neither do they remain static throughout history. What is acceptable in one context may be completely unacceptable in another, and what was considered necessary at one point in history may be considered barbaric in another. Social imaginaries are thus the imaginative boundaries of our social and moral lives. Religion figures prominently in the cultural imagination and social imaginary of many African societies; it shapes morals, values, social interactions and political and economic structures. Indeed, as Elisabeth Gerle noted, "[r]eligion has always played an important role in [African] society. Its pervasive presence has often shaped shared world views. As a result, it is often almost impossible to differentiate between culture and religion".[25]

---

21 Forster, 2020, pp. xiii, 1-2.
22 Ward, 2018, pp. 10-11.
23 Prozesky, 2013, pp. 7-19.
24 Taylor, 2004, p. 23; Taylor, 2009, pp. 159-211.
25 Forster, 2019, p. xvii.

Thus, Africa, and Africans, tend to feature in a qualitatively significant manner on both the 'security axiom' and 'cultural traditions axiom' as religious individuals and religiously predisposed societies. As a result, it is not strange to see religion playing an overt role in the shaping of political life, economic systems, cultural values and societal norms in (South) Africa.[26] In this sense one could reasonably assert that, in Africa, the distinction between private faith and public faith does not operate, or need to operate, in the same way as it does in many secularised Western societies.

Why religion is an important consideration in diversity and inclusion in South Africa

As has been argued above, South Africa remains a deeply religious nation. In this section, we draw upon two important sources to gain some understanding of the demographic makeup of the religious population in South Africa, and consider how South Africans engage with religion in their public lives. The most recent survey of the South African population conducted by Statistics South Africa was in 2015, which showed that 86% of South Africa's citizens self-identified as Christian.[27]

Table 11.1: General Household Survey 2015: Religious affiliation

Religion (Names as stipulated in the survey)	Percentage
Christian	86%
Muslim	1.9%
Ancestral, tribal, animist or other traditional African religions	5.4%
Hindu	0.9%
Jewish	0.2%
Other religion	0.4%
Nothing in particular	5.2%
Refused to say or do not know	0.0%
Total	*100.0%*

These statistics[28] offer some helpful insights into the importance of engaging religion in relation to diversity and inclusion in South Africa.

---

26 Lugo & Cooperman, 2010.

27 StatsSA, 2015, p. 28.

28 Forster & April, 2020.

The first observation relates to *religious dominance and inclusion*. While the South African Constitution[29] recognises that South Africa is a multi-faith society, the Christian religion dominates numerically. This could hold some challenges for religious diversity and inclusion in public life and the world of work. Dominant groupings tend to be less inclusive of, and sensitive to, the religious convictions and faith practices of minority groupings.[30]

Secondly, we should take note of *religious diversity within religious groupings.* The statistics show that the 'Christian' grouping is diverse, thus it would be a mistake to regard them as a single, unified religious tradition or perspective. Research shows that the largest part of the group marked as Christian belong to what are variously known as 'African Independent Churches', but then there are also Catholics, Reformed, Pentecostal, Evangelical, and a host of independent Christian groupings.[31] There are significant differences in doctrine, belief, ritual and ethical commitment among these groupings, which frequently lead to rivalry and conflict around issues such as gender roles, sexual preference and moral values.[32] For this reason, any attempt at managing diversity and fostering inclusion in public life, general social settings or the workplace, will have to be sensitive to the internal diversity that exists within religious groupings, and account for differences in beliefs, practices and moral convictions.

Third, the statistics also show that there is not a direct correlation between numerical dominance and *social influence.* It is worth keeping in mind that the power relations of South African society, which are related to race, economic class and education, also intersect significantly with public religious identity and influence.[33] While some religious groupings may be numerically small, such as adherents to Judaism or persons who indicate that they are agnostic or atheists, these groups exercise a disproportionally significant influence on religion in public life, the media, and the formation of policies and laws related to religion and society. For example, almost all of South Africa's Jewish, agnostic and atheistic population are upper middle-class White South Africans. Because of South Africa's social and political history, persons in this segment of society are generally wealthier, more educated, and have greater economic influence and social influence. Their voices, and their concerns, are thus more readily represented in the mainstream media. For this reason, religious diversity management and inclusion in South Africa cannot be undertaken apart from other important demographic factors such as race, education and economic status (an intersubjective understanding is what is required). For example, if a company owner and their senior management share a similar worldview or set of historical religious convictions (e.g. Judeo-Christian values), these are

---

29 Matthee, 2019.

30 Carrim, 2015.

31 Hendriks & Erasmus, 2005, p. 3.

32 Palm, 2019, pp. 174-98.

33 See, Forster, 2019a, pp. 3-9, 177-210, 214-219.

likely to set the tone for what is acceptable and desirable in the company's culture. This could easily exclude minority religious perspectives or practices, and prejudice minority religions on matters such as time off work to practice one's religion, religious holidays, dietary laws, attitudes toward differing sexual orientations and/or gender relationships.

A fourth point, among many others that could be made, is that in South Africa, certain religious traditions are very closely associated with certain *cultures and geographically-located communities*. For example, Islam is most prominent among the so-called coloured communities of the Western Cape and Gauteng, with a much smaller presence among other cultural groups and geographic locations. The same can be seen with Hinduism, which is largely concentrated in KwaZulu-Natal and parts of Gauteng among persons of Indian descent. Among the African Independent Churches, the Zion Christian Church (also known as 'Boyne'), which has around 4.97 million members, is largely present in Limpopo and Gauteng. Similarly, the Nazareth Baptist Church (also known as *iBandla lamaNazaretha*, founded by Isaiah Shembe), which is believed to have around 6.7 million members, is largely located among the Zulu-speaking populations of KwaZulu-Natal and the Zulu diaspora in Gauteng. One could trace the social and cultural histories (often related to the arrival of missionaries in Southern Africa) to specific denominations and groupings – for example, the Dutch Reformed Church remains almost entirely White and Afrikaans speaking, while the Methodist Church of Southern Africa (the largest mainline Christian denomination in South Africa) is multi-racial and multi-lingual.[34] Thus, diversity and inclusion engagements will need to show an awareness of the cultural and historical informants of religion in different parts of the country, or among different population groups. For example, if one were working in a multi-national corporation, it may be necessary to have a common set of negotiated values, with some regional differences and concessions to allow for diversity and inclusion.

Religion and social identity, and values

In addition to what we can ascertain from religious statistics (which are largely quantitative in nature), there are some other important qualitative factors to consider in relation to religious diversity and inclusion. A 2010 *Pew Report* found that 74% of South Africans "indicated that religion plays an important role in their lives".[35] *The World Values Survey* (WVS) helps us to understand a qualitative aspect of this "important role" for religious South Africans. The findings of the WVS show that religious organisations remain among the most trusted institutions in society, enjoying higher levels of public trust and confidence than either the State or the private sector.[36] The report noted that "while trust in political

---

34 Forster, 2019b.

35 Lugo & Cooperman, 2010, pp. 3-4.

36 Winter & Burchert, 2015.

institutions recedes, in contrast, civil society organisations enjoy growing trust".[37] In the WVS, faith-based groupings are classified within the 'civil society' designation. Hennie Kotzé, the lead researcher on the WVS for South Africa, noted that, "Religion in general, and churches in particular, play an important political socialization role [for South Africans]".[38]

The previous points have shown us that religion is an important phenomenon in South African public life. Moreover, it occupies an important place in the establishment of personal well-being and social harmony. Yet, at the same time, South Africa is a religiously diverse nation with some demographic factors that could lead to exclusion and even religious intolerance or conflict. There are numerous strategies that can be employed to manage religious diversity and inclusion[39], however any strategy that is proposed will only function if there is a measure of individual and social awareness that allows for honest, critical and appreciative engagement among people from different religious traditions, or those who hold differing religious beliefs and views.

Intergroup contact theory and religious diversity and inclusion

Intergroup contact theory holds great promise for helping to facilitate the necessary conditions for the appreciation of religious diversity and inclusion. The notion that positive intergroup contact could be employed to facilitate the conditions under which better intergroup relations are developed, and prejudice of the other is reduced, was first put forward by Williams in *The Reduction of Intergroup Tensions*.[40] However, it was the social psychologist, Gordon Allport, whose work fully developed the notions of contact theory and intergroup contact theory within the broader academy.[41]

At the heart of Allport's contact hypothesis is the postulation that bringing people together in carefully mediated interpersonal encounters could reduce intergroup prejudice and conflict. Hermann Swart, a South African social psychologist, argued that there are two possible uses for intergroup contact theory that are of value working for social harmony – inclusion and the appreciation of diversity.[42] First, there is the traditional emphasis on *mediating the negative aspects of intergroup contact* and intergroup conflict. Second, there is the possibility of facilitating or fostering *positive intergroup relations*. While the former seeks to help us to structure our engagements so as to minimise conflict and misunderstanding among diverse population groups, the latter tends aims to build a more inclusive, just and diverse community.[43]

---

37 Ibid., p. 1.

38 Kotzé, 2016, pp. 1-17.

39 April, Makgoba & Forster, 2018, p. 223-63; Forster & April, 2020, pp. 94-114.

40 Williams, 1947, p. 153.

41 Allport, 1954.

42 Swart et al., p. 181.

43 Ibid.

Allport's hypothesis *The Nature of Prejudice* identified and presented a number of situational criteria for diminishing intergroup prejudice through facilitated intergroup contact.[44] Swart and Hewstone described these as the "moderators" and "mediators" of intergroup contact.[45]

Moderating factors indicate the conditions under which contact is most likely to have a positive effect, whereas *mediating factors* indicate how positive intergroup contact can best be achieved. While Allport's work was influential in identifying the moderators and mediators of positive intergroup contact, it was the work of later theorists, such as Pettigrew and Tropp, who showed how positive intergroup contact could be facilitated.[46] Swart and Hewstone noted that a major development since Allport's pioneering work "is that researchers have moved from merely demonstrating that contact works to showing how it works".[47]

Thus, what we have come to understand is that it is not mere contact between in-groups and out-groups that reduces prejudice. Rather, particular types of contact are necessary to reduce prejudice and create the conditions of inclusion and the recognition and appreciation of diversity. This has become known as positive intergroup contact.

It stands to reason that certain types of contact can fuel distrust or enforce stereotypes about the 'other'. Moreover, there are certain kinds of contact that are deemed to be physically or psychologically damaging. For example, while non-sexual touch between men and women is acceptable in some religious communities (e.g. among Protestant Christians), it is considered taboo in others (e.g. some Muslim groupings). In such settings, a lack of understanding of the reasons for one's own beliefs, and the reasons for the beliefs of others, can easily lead to misunderstanding, judgement and even conflict. This would not be considered a positive intergroup contact event or process. These kinds of unenlightened, unconscious or unintentional contacts are often categorised as 'negative affective mediators' of contact since they increase distrust of the other and often heighten prejudice.[48] Research in this area has shown that, to a large measure, the mediation of affect (emotion) can make a significant contribution towards facilitating positive intergroup contact between in-groups and out-groups. Hewstone and Swart wrote of such positively mediated contact, i.e. that it:

---

44 Allport, 1954.

45 Hewstone & Swart, 2011, pp. 375-76.

46 Allport, 1954; Pettigrew, 1998, pp. 65-85; Pettigrew & Tropp, 2006, pp. 751-55.

47 Hewstone & Swart, 2011, p. 376.

48 Swart et al., 2010, p. 313.

...exerts its effect on prejudice reduction both by reducing negative affect (e.g., intergroup anxiety) and by inducing positive affective processes (e.g., empathy and perspective taking).[49]

In my own research among Black and White South Africans, I found that mediated positive intergroup contact facilitates opportunities for re-humanisation, mutual recognition, cognitive reframing and empathy among groups of racially and culturally diverse Christians.[50] The notion of understanding and engaging prejudice is the foundation upon which subsequent studies on intergroup relations have been based.[51] At the heart of Allport's hypothesis is the notion that prejudice is the source of intergroup conflict and exclusion. Allport's "least effort principle" holds that the human brain tends to opt for efficiency in making sense of the world.[52] As such we tend to relate to other persons, and social structures, based on learned or received stereotypes about them – these are our prejudices. In general, individuals and communities find it difficult to honestly engage such overgeneralised categories, since this takes mental effort, and as Allport stated, "effort... is disagreeable" to the brain's efficiency system.[53] Allport did, however, concede that people and social groups are willing to engage and amend their prejudices, deconstructing their stereotypes in favour of more nuanced perspectives, when they are motivated to do so by some form of psychological energy (e.g. interest in a person or culture, friendship, or fascination) In such cases, we frequently come to understand that the larger whole, of which we have a prejudice (all men, all Americans, etc.), has subcategories (e.g. not all men are the same, not all Americans are the same). Thus, at its very core, his theory engages prejudice between in-group identity and out-group identity.[54] It is the expression of prejudice, or the experience of prejudice, that increases anxiety and limits the capacity for empathy. It was Allport's intention to address this aspect of social identity that formed his hypothesis on contact theory:

> Prejudice (unless deeply rooted in the character structure of the individual) may be reduced by equal status contact between majority and minority groups in the pursuit of common goals. The effect is greatly enhanced if this contact is sanctioned by institutional support (i.e., by law, custom or local atmosphere), and provided it is of a sort that leads to the perception of common interests and a common humanity between members of the two groups.[55]

---

49 Hewstone & Swart, 2011, p. 376.
50 Forster, 2018, pp. 77-94; Forster, 2019a, 177-210; Forster, 2019b, 77-88.
51 Zuma, 2014, p. 40.
52 Allport, 1954, p. 21.
53 Ibid.
54 Dovidio, Glick & Rudman, 2008, p. 40.
55 Allport, 1954, p. 281.

Prejudice is frequently a result of a lack of contact between in-groups and out-groups. For example, it is easy to misjudge a group of people that one has never met. However, some forms of prejudice are fuelled by unmediated or poorly conceived instances of intergroup contact.[56] Dixon noted that, "Allport wanted to highlight the importance of contextual prerequisites in promoting meaningful change".[57] Allport found that frequent superficial contacts could "strengthen the adverse associations we have" of the out-group.[58] Thus, Allport developed the "situational specifications" that would allow social psychologists to distinguish between favourable (positive) intergroup contact, and unfavourable (negative) intergroup contact.[59] The intention of this research was to understand the subtleties of both the frequency and quality of intergroup contact in order to identify and understand the "optimal contact strategy", and to "elucidate the conditions under which contact works most effectively to reduce prejudice and, by implication, to increase the possibility of social harmony".[60]

Positive intergroup contact theory suggests that at least four "situational specifications" need to be present for positive intergroup contact to take place. These overarching moderators of positive intergroup contact have proven to be effective in reducing prejudice through mediating anxiety and heightening intergroup empathy[61]:

- *Equal status within the situation:* Allport stressed the importance of facilitating equal status among the participants within the situation of the intergroup contact. Pettigrew pointed out that there is widespread consensus on the importance of equal status among the participants in an intergroup contact session to reduce anxiety and increase empathy.[62] If participants in the process feel that there is an imbalance

---

56 Booysen, 2013, pp. 3-6.

57 Dixon, Durrheim & Tredoux, 2005, p. 698.

58 Allport, 1954, p. 264.

59 Allport's contact theory has sparked a variety of different fields of research within the academy. Conceptually, some scholars have an interest in how, when and why certain situational variable "maximize prejudice reduction". Methodologically, a sub field has developed that has a particular interest in the empirical testing of the association between intergroup prejudice and more ideal forms of intergroup contact. Then there are scholars working in the applied sciences who are "attempting the translation of theory into practice" Dixon, Durrheim, and Tredoux, "Beyond the Optimal Contact Strategy," 698. Also, please see the work of Scheepers for insights into the complexity of social identity and political identities in relation to free choice and social pressure Tom WG Van Der Meer, Manfred Te Grotenhuis, and Peer LH Scheepers, "Three Types of Voluntary Associations in Comparative Perspective: The Importance of Studying Associational Involvement through a Typology of Associations in 21 European Countries," Journal of Civil Society 5, no. 3 (2009): 227–41; M. J. W. Gesthuizen, P. L. H. Scheepers, and M. J. Savelkoul, "Explaining Relationships between Ethnic Diversity and Informal Social Capital across European Countries and Regions: Tests of Constrict, Conflict and Contact Theory" 40, no. 4 (January 1, 2011): 1091–1107..

60 Dixon, Durrheim, & Tredoux, 2005, p. 699.

61 Pettigrew & Tropp, 2006.

62 Pettigrew, 1998, p. 66.

of personal or institutional power between the in-group and out-group, they are less likely to trust either the process or the participants who hold power over them. Thus, it is critical to structure the groups, and the intergroup contact between the groups, in a manner where power is largely equal and shared. This will include such aspects as age, gender, class, language, education and a variety of other variables within the representative groups. Moreover, there are some researchers who emphasise the importance of equal status among the participants as they enter the intergroup contact session. In other words, the expectation of equality is as important as the experience of equality in the intergroup contact session.[63] For example, in South Africa it will be quite difficult to facilitate groups in which there are no numerical, economic and power differences between participants. However, it would be wise for those who seek to facilitate positive intergroup contact engagements to manage power relations, to ensure that no perspective or group dominates the 'space' of the engagement, and to ensure that all voices and perspectives are given enough space and protection to be shared and considered. Thus, the selection of the participants for intergroup engagements, as well as the communication of the identity of the group participants, and the shared tasks, place of meeting and manner of facilitating the groups, should be undertaken in such a manner as to minimise power hierarchies.

- *Common goals:* The reduction of prejudice in contact among religiously diverse groups requires a common focus.[64] Inter-racial sports teams serve as a good illustration of this point. In striving to win a sporting game, inter-racial sporting teams show a need for one another, showcase respect for talents and abilities, and create opportunities for flourishing in order to achieve the common goal of winning the match. This mechanism in intergroup contact has become known as 'instrumental contact'.[65] Instrumental intergroup contact occurs when members feel that in-group and out-group contact can work towards the achievement of a shared and valued goal. However, the converse is also true. If the group perceives that their contact with the 'other' is counterproductive to an important goal or conviction that they hold, they will seek to sever the contact or diminish its effects on the in-group. The famous 'Robbers Cave' illustrates how subordinate goals serve to reduce intergroup prejudice.[66]

- *Intergroup cooperation:* Allport pointed out that where people from in-groups and out-groups cooperate in the achievement of shared tasks, without unhealthy competition, prejudice is lessened. What Pettigrew suggested regarding this point is that intergroup cooperation, without unhealthy competition, is required to lessen anxiety and increase empathy in order to create an opportunity for positive

---

63 Brewer & Kramer, 1985, pp. 235-36.
64 Pettigrew, 1998, p. 66.
65 Wilcox, 2011, p. 33.
66 Sherif, Harvey, White, Hood & Sherif, 1961; Wilcox, 2011, p. 33.

engagement within the intergroup contact.[67] Aronson's 'jigsaw classroom' has frequently been cited as an example of a mechanism or process in which such conditions for positive-intergroup encounter are facilitated.[68] In such a setting, students are assigned to learning groups where each group learns a different part of the new material, and after this the students are re-assigned to heterogeneous learning groups. In each of these new groups, one person from each of the previous learning groups has the responsibility to teach the others what they know about the subject. This creates an openness to learning from others and a reliance upon their knowledge and expertise for success.

- *Support of authorities, law or custom:* Allport identified that positive intergroup contact functions best when the participants know that they have the support of authorities, laws or customs in engaging the out-group in a positive manner. It would stand to reason that with explicit social sanction from figures or institutions of respected authority (government, Imam, Pastor, Priest, Rabbi, Pujari, Bhikkhu or Bhikkhunī), intergroup contact has a better chance of achieving a positive effect. If people participate in intergroup contact knowing that they will face shame, ridicule or persecution from authorities in their in-group, they are less likely to have a qualitatively positive engagement in which the affective mediators are constructively engaged. In unsanctioned settings, anxiety is likely to remain high and there will be little opportunity for vulnerability in the encounter with the other, that could lead to increased empathy.[69] This is particularly challenging in contacts with significant social consequences for disobedience to figures of authority or community rules, such as religious settings.[70] A person may fear the consequences of shifting their primary in-group identity to a position that is in conflict with that of the primary group of belonging, identity and care. Thus, it may be wise for the facilitators to seek formal permission, or sanction, from authoritative religious figures, before inviting members of different faith groups to engage one another.

Dixon et al.'s[71] review of the literature over the last 50 years, since Allport's first work, has led to the construction of the following, more detailed, list of situational specifications for positive intergroup contact:

- Contact should be regular and frequent.
- Contact should involve a balanced ratio of in-group to out-group members.

---

67 Pettigrew, 1998, p. 67.
68 Aronson, 1978, pp. 33-34.
69 Pettigrew, 1998, pp. 65-85.
70 Parker, 1968, pp. 359-66; Zuma, 2014.
71 Dixon et al., 2005.

- Contact should have genuine 'acquaintance potential' (i.e. enough time to get to know others in the group) .

- Contact should occur across a variety of social settings and situations.

- Contact should be free from unhealthy competition.

- Contact should be evaluated as 'important' to the participants involved.

- Contact should occur between individuals who share relatively equal status.

- Contact should involve interaction with a counter-stereotypical member of another group.

- Contact should be organised around cooperation towards the achievement of a superordinate goal.

- Contact should be normatively and institutionally sanctioned.

- Contact should be free from anxiety or other negative emotions.

- Contact should be personalised and involve genuine friendship formation.

- Contact should be with a person who is deemed both a positive example, and yet typical or representative, of another group.[72]

A careful consideration of this list of specifications shows that planned, facilitated intergroup contact is possible, and that it can hold great promise for the recognition and celebration of diversity and the inclusion of varying religious traditions, perspectives and beliefs.

CONCLUSION

This chapter argued for the importance of focusing on religion as an important category in studies of diversity and inclusion in South Africa. We started by showing how religion functions in (South) African social consciousness. In general, South Africans cannot be understood as secular. Religion plays an important role in addressing existential needs, and in forming social values and expectations. However, a study of South Africa's religious demographics shows that there are some challenges to inclusion and diversity that could lead to misunderstanding, prejudice and even conflict in public life. Finally, we considered how positive intergroup contact, which is facilitated under certain conditions, could contribute towards a decrease in intergroup contact anxiety, and an increase in the possibility for empathetic engagement. The intention of such efforts is to appreciate and recognise the important role that religion and faith play in the private and public lives of South Africans, yet to ensure that their convictions contribute towards a society that celebrates diversity, values inclusion, and works for the common good.

---

72 Dixon, Durrheim & Tredoux, 2005, p. 699.

KEY TAKEAWAYS

1. Religion remains a very important source of identity formation, meaning making and social belonging among South Africans. In the last South African General Household Survey, 86% self-identified as Christian, with only 5.2% of persons indicating that they do not hold any faith affiliation.

2. South Africa has a 'multi-faith' Constitution with a Bill of Rights that protects the freedom of religion and rights to free association of all citizens. These protections relate to both private and public life. This means that employers should give careful consideration to how the diversity of beliefs and religious practices will be approached in spaces such as the world of work.

3. In contexts, like South Africa, where there are religious traditions that have both numerical and historical dominance in society, far greater attention must be paid to maintaining the rights of minority religious groups.

4. The recognition and appreciation of religious diversity in society requires a critical self-awareness. For example, what are my beliefs and convictions? What practices and rituals do I find important? How might my beliefs and practices be perceived and experienced by others? At the same time, it is important to cultivate an openness towards, and an appreciation of, the beliefs and practices of others.

5. Positive intergroup contact theory gives us some important insights and resources that can be used in social systems (such as the work environment) to lessen the anxiety of engaging persons, practices and beliefs that differ from our own. Through carefully facilitated positive intergroup contact, an environment of recognition, respect and understanding can be created that can allow individuals to flourish and teams to function without unnecessary misunderstanding and conflict.

Chapter 12

CONSOLIDATION: CONNECTING THE DOTS IN A DIVERSE SOUTH AFRICA

Prof. Kurt April & Dr. Preeya Daya

Diversity is premised on the notion that none of us are completely similar; even siblings who grew up in the same household, attended the same schools, were parented by the same individuals, ate the same foods, and hung out in the same neighbourhoods. Human interactions, by their very nature, involve judgement by others, in which our superficial appearance, group assignment, primary capacities, ascribed roles and qualities of character are instantaneously assessed – and corroborative and corrective manifestations are not immediately likely, desired nor sort out. In fact, without purposeful action and consistent discipline, both individuals and organisations seemingly cannot escape the idea that the differences in people are intrinsic, innate and even essential. No picture of such judgement is complete without the consideration of the role of beliefs, prevalent assumptions and the maintenance of fiction/stories, as frames of reference, in a particular society's context. Underpinning such considerations are a number of social, political, economic, cognitive, psychological and emotional contributors. As a collective of authors, in this book we have explored a number of critical diversity strands that have significance in modern day South Africa, and posed a number of challenges and opportunities.

Racism, which has no genetic foundations, has been prevalent in South Africa ever since differential power engagements, forged through judgements, first took place on our land. It unfortunately persists, even after a compromised political settlement was reached in 1994 to formally end Apartheid, and a non-racial Constitution was written into law. For South Africans, its design took on new meaning during Apartheid and race classification has stayed with us ever since, even in the democratic dispensation of the country. Its prevalence, even though evident and personally and systemically experienced on a daily basis by ordinary citizens, has been treated largely with indifference by many professions, disciplines and organisations. Political and social power continue to fail to unseat the patterns of economic power and historic practices, embedded over centuries of oppression in South Africa. For most of the country's citizens, the outplaying of democracy in their everyday lives has had a rough ride against the backdrop of virtually no change in how the world and others have engaged them and continues to treat them. Additionally, race-based oppression has crippled the ways in which people of colour perceive themselves and their place in their birth country, to the extent that they need psychological freedom before they can hope to fully achieve political and economic freedom. We have addressed the dynamism of a number of the current narratives in the country: the unacceptability of the continued dominance of Eurocentric knowledge production in addressing our very unique challenges, which requires a shift (and demand) for the decolonisation of such knowledge production; the shift from overt to covert racism and political correctness; the academic skewedness and differential bases for academic preparation, to the call for levelling the playing fields and addressing the skewed pathway to skills and therefore better futures for all citizens; the shift in trying to address some of the country's challenges through affirmative action policies and enactment, to the difficult change processes of full transformation; the shift from open aggression to microaggressions; the shift from the gargantuan efforts by many to resemble something closer to being White, and the associated identity disassociation accompanying such efforts, to a seeking and fondness for new-found authenticity; the shift from silent acceptance of the embeddedness of prototypical management and leadership, to the battles and legitimisation of atypical pathways/career journeys towards atypical management and leadership; as well as the shift from Apartheid intolerance to tolerance, then multiculturalism, and ultimately to the hope of credible inclusion.

Political rights in South Africa have not led to significant socio-economic gains for the majority in the country, due mainly to the indifference of those with power, which, as a result, threatens the continuance of our current democracy. The changing narratives in the country are making such indifference intolerable, however, and, thankfully, unsustainable.

Over the decades since the fall of Apartheid, South Africa has been caught between the tension of globalisation and wanting (also needing) to be a market economy (the reification of markets), and the political imperatives of wealth and land distribution in a country plagued by persistent economic inequality and access. The invented social construction termed 'racism' continues to be used as an economic tool, as it has done throughout the centuries, and serves to sustain a number of privileges for a minority of people in the country. We explored privilege as one of the overarching determinants of oppression, which means that privilege comes at the expense of a disadvantaged 'other'. An additional takeaway is that complicity and ignorance hold privilege together, because by claiming that they are unaware of other peoples' disadvantage, the privileged are basically endorsing the status quo. This brings in the third takeaway, which states that privilege and disadvantage are interlocking systems – they are phenomena which are not static, but dynamic and complex, and subject to shift across time and space. As this book has shown, women, for example, find themselves feeling privileged in some spaces and disadvantaged in others. Fourth, people living in the 'margins of the margins' are endlessly dismembered, resulting in the fact that they are more likely to always be disadvantaged. These may include people living with disabilities, the poor, Blacks, women and queer people, all of whom are groups of people whose positionalities always mark out differences that limit access. In cases where a person has a multiplicity of these excluding identity markers, their lived reality is endless dehumanisation.

The last takeaway from this chapter asks of us to acknowledge and be cognisant of our privileged positionalities. This allows us to consider how our privilege thrives on the oppression of others, and that our occupation of dominant positionalities leads to implicit buy-in (in much the same way as 'silence' in the face of injustice is a form of approval).

In 1998, South Africa introduced the Employment Equity Act, which sought to promote equity in the workplace by ensuring that all employees receive equal opportunities, as well as to ensure that employees are treated fairly by their employers. Subsequently, national laws and organisational policies have been established to help deliver this goal, but sadly discrimination and inequality remain the norm. Despite a growing trend, more work needs to be done to increase the representation of Black Africans in top and senior levels, for instance. Part of the work that is required to make a tangible difference for this section of the working population is ensuring a more rigorous, and deeper, understanding of the individual and organisational issues that prevents the inclusion of Black Africans. Notwithstanding the slowly declining numbers, White South Africans still constitute more than 50% of top and senior management in organisations, and, incredibly, constitute the majority of new recruits and promotions at these levels. Even though the representation of women has grown in all occupational categories in the country, more focus is required on the full inclusion of Black females generally, and Black African females in particular.

Legislation is important in setting the agenda for transformation, but execution in keeping with the spirit of such legislation remains poor and is not enabling the country to get to the intended results. As businesses, the government, civil society, and the nation as a whole, we need to have frank and honest discussions about the prevalence of unfair discrimination and access in our organisations, specifically discussions around bias, systemic prejudice, stereotyping, colourism and micro-discrimination, followed by appropriate actions and sanctions for those not committed to the necessary transformation.

Gender, as an individual's innermost concept of self in relation to others, is an important part of who they are, and provides an important basis for their interactions with others. Possible psychosocial (such as child and parental characteristics) and biological factors (such as the effects of prenatal exposure to gonadal hormones and the role of genetics) have been shown to contribute to a gender variant identity. We assert that gender is not equivalent to biological sex (i.e. male or female). Instead, gender refers to the socially constructed and culturally determined roles of men and women in society. Gender identity, in fact, intersects with other categories of social difference, such as race, class, ethnicity and sexuality. In particular, Black women in South Africa experience such hybrid intersections of multiple subordinated positions, where they are continuously subjected to gendered racism, that they suffer mental and physical stressors as a result. Contemporary gender inequalities in South Africa have deep roots, shaped by its colonial, political, economic and social past. Despite the good intentions and legislative reforms of the new democratic South African government, the country continues to struggle with eradicating gender inequalities.

Achieving true gender transformation in South Africa means engaging with the complexity of gender in formulating policies and organisational practices to address inequality and oppression. Gender diverse others are still treated as abhorrent. We have presented differences within women as a grouping, as these provide important distinctions about the needs, behaviours and assumptions about women at work – which informs research design and organisational policy. Gender is experienced as an organised means for culturally-patterned ways, which upholds social relationships and reproduces norms/rules and patterns of expectation. Industries remain gendered in nature, insisting on normative masculine and feminine attributes, and have embedded inequities in pay and career opportunities. There are sufficiently qualified numbers of women, in all major disciplines, such that a parity in numbers of women equal to that of men can be achieved. Equality in numbers only, however, is missing the point – greater attention should be paid to organisational decisions that are taken along the lines of sameness or difference. As women become more economically independent, new dynamics are emerging in marriages, disturbing social expectations that women should primarily be homemakers, subsistence farmers and caregivers, and that they should expend a lot of energy on maintaining household relationships, including marriage.

Reports from around the globe during the covid-19 pandemic – due to the disproportionate role of women responding to the virus in community outreach, household responsibilities, care for older parents and children, and as frontline health workers – highlight the fact that many of the (minor) gains in gender equality and women's rights have been rolled back as a result of the dynamics related to the pandemic (also in the rise in violence against women and girls). The expectations emanating from the requirement of women to be superwomen lead to tension in the household, as well as in the workplace. An organisation that makes an assertion about gender equality should follow it up with measurement of such, however gender equity, which is more difficult to measure and structurally embed, should be vigorously pursued with thoughtful intent.

Violence against women and girls (VAWG) is a human rights violation, according to the United Nations and South African law. South Africa has one of the highest incidences of gender-based violence in the world, occurring in various contexts and costing the country between R28.4 billion and R42.4 billion per year. This does not include the costs of pain and suffering, healthcare, or other secondary costs. Although significant policy and implementation gaps exist, one of the main challenges in addressing gender-based violence (GBV) in South Africa is our society's and institutions' continued investment in patriarchy and the pervasiveness of rape culture. As stated above, the covid-19 pandemic lockdown stages have served to increase perpetrated violence, as security, health and money concerns heighten the already prevalent tensions and strains from cramped and confined living conditions in South Africa. Feminist activism has been instrumental in advancing anti-GBV work in South Africa – we specifically explored the core issues related to GBV in the higher education sector, as it provides a useful model for other sectors to consider. Feminist activism provides the necessary analytical proficiency to see and understand the complexity and range of GBV, like the inclusion of LGBTQI++ communities and institutional culture in the analysis. Feminist activism can generate the necessary pressure on institutions and compel its leadership to act. In the case of higher education in South Africa, this was done through very visible public protest. It can also provide democratic and collaborative methodologies for stakeholder engagement that can facilitate long-term, sustainable and socially-just solutions to gender-based violence.

The shared experiences and values that define generational workplace cohorts translate to different motivations, goals and ways of working, as well as management and leadership styles between generations in the workplace, which ultimately affect the people management practices of organisations. If employees from one generational cohort constantly blame individuals from another cohort when they fail to achieve their expectations, aspirations and personal goals, there will be ramifications, resulting in unwanted suspicion, purposeful rigidity, dysfunctional work attitudes, unnecessary politicking and organisational disharmony. In our treatment of generational workplace diversity we claim that, in order to remain competitive and secure highly sought-after talent, South African organisations must adopt strategies that create awareness of the unique characteristics of the different generations in organisations, and actively promote collaboration across generational divides.

Although it may seem like a monumental task for management and leadership, organisations must address the issues of employee attraction, retention and commitment along generational lines through policies and practices that accommodate the idiosyncratic needs of employees with different values, and at different life stages. These include customised policies such as ideals, regular feedback systems and lateral career pathways. We explored four strategies that organisations can use to address the challenges of multi-generational mix: building a culture of respect, cross-generational activities, using Generation X as a bridge, and rethinking people management strategies. In particular, we have argued that embracing the regionally-relevant philosophy of ubuntu can foster an inclusive culture – a culture that intrinsically bridges divides, and drives organisational performance, on the basis of a unified identity where everyone acts in the interests of the self, as well as in the interests of the team, to achieve the organisation's objectives.

Since 1994, South Africa has seen improvements in healthcare, living conditions and life expectancy for many (albeit with enormous and daunting challenges remaining), however the many improvements have been accompanied by an increase in depression, conduct disorder, schizophrenia, dementia and other forms of chronic mental illness. The covid-19 pandemic has exacerbated such mental health concerns for many in the country. It was previously believed that the listed conditions are on the increase because more people are living to the age of risk, however young people are not immune to similar, debilitating conditions – in both episodic and persistent forms. Research indicates multiple barriers to taking care of the mental health needs of youth, including a lack of services, a lack of awareness, myths, misconceptions, stigma, cultural dogma, and low priority to, and low funding of, mental health from institutions and government. Early identification and intervention for the problems remain vital to the solution.

Our case studies show that young people, reflecting individually and as peers about whether they have agency or not, can help conceptualise and lobby for structural change in mental health services for marginalised young people. The World Health Organization has warned of the consequences of not addressing adolescent and young adult mental health conditions, as they extend into adulthood and impair both physical and mental health, and ultimately limit the opportunities of people to lead fulfilling lives as adults. Young people have allowed us to recognise both the value and the challenges of the employed methodologies, and broader praxis, of current theoretical frames. We have discussed how the establishment and assistance of peer support groups (acknowledging that this does depend on the willingness of peers to do so), physically and/or virtually, can improve mental healthcare services to ensure further accessibility, relevance and inclusivity. Long-term interventions are required for programmes that seek to respond to mental health issues among youth. These interventions, however, require skilled facilitators, resources and structural support in order to succeed. Additionally, we have described the need for requisite skills to sensitively facilitate vulnerable groups when making use of creative resistance to address exclusion and break down barriers to inclusion. We conclude that those with more persistent mental health challenges usually do very well with treatment, peer and professional support and services, and a family and social support network.

Disability is one of the seven focus areas identified by the South African Human Rights Commission (SAHRC) within its mandate to promote, protect and monitor the realisation of human rights in South Africa. According to the SAHRC, people with disabilities (who currently account for 5.1% of the population aged five years and older in South Africa) continue to lack access to adequate health and basic education, and are at risk of economic isolation with no prospect of securing employment. In fact, persons with disabilities are also particularly vulnerable to the compounded effects of discrimination and abuse. We have shown how persons with disabilities, and their families, who live in rural communities in South Africa are twice marginalised in terms of their disability and indigenous belief systems. We noted that rehabilitation services offered to these communities are based on human rights approaches which, although egalitarian, often alienate the children with disabilities from their families and communal practices through institutionalisation. There is a critical need for rehabilitation services within these rural communities to be imbued with the philosophical concepts that inform the lived experiences of the communities, as this will allow for more sustainable outcomes. The inclusion of indigenous ethics would support connections between communities and institutions, contributing to a reduction in the alienation of children with disabilities, and would support an increased sense of belonging for children with disabilities in their communities. We believe that ubuntu is a moral and ethical framework that should inform service delivery, which could be supported by the principles of human rights, to ensure that a contextually relevant rehabilitation practice is offered to rural communities in South Africa.

Religion, in its different forms (such as formal religious traditions and beliefs, spiritual beliefs, spiritual practices, cultural beliefs or social beliefs), connects individuals through rituals and practices with something/someone larger than themselves, and ultimately shapes who the individuals are, how they interact with others, and how they engage with the world around them. Religion remains a very important source of identity formation, meaning making, and avenue for social belonging among many South Africans. In the last South African General Household Survey, 84.2% of the South African population self-identified as Christian, with only 7.6% of persons indicating that they do not hold any faith affiliation (the rest fell into ancestral, tribal, animist or other traditional African religions, as well as the Muslim, Hindu and Jewish faiths). South Africa has a multi-faith Constitution, with a Bill of Rights that protects the freedom of religion and rights to free association of all citizens. These protections relate to both private and public life. This means that employers should give careful consideration to how the diversity of beliefs and religious practices should be approached in spaces such as the world of work. In contexts, like South Africa, where there are religious traditions that have both numerical and historical dominance in society, far greater attention must be paid to maintaining the rights of minority religious groups. The recognition and appreciation of religious diversity in society requires a critical self-awareness on behalf of individuals, e.g. what are my beliefs and convictions? What practices and rituals do I find important? How might my beliefs and practices be perceived and experienced by others? At the same time, it is important to cultivate an openness towards, and an appreciation of, the diverse beliefs and practices of others. Positive intergroup contact theory gives us some important insights and resources that can be used in social systems (such as the work environment) to lessen the anxiety of engaging persons, practices and beliefs that differ from our own. Through carefully facilitated positive intergroup contact, an environment of recognition, respect and understanding can be created that can allow individuals to flourish and teams to function without unnecessary misunderstanding and conflict.

Along with innovation; rich perspectives; deeper understanding; less rework; better relationships and teamwork; greater understanding of markets, communities and other stakeholders; and many of the other phenomenal and constructive possibilities that diversity offers us, It also has a downside. When we encounter 'others' who are different from us, without our consent or knowledge, we are plugged into an automated structure that, unfortunately, ranks us – the social scripts that dehumanise us, judge us, treat us as 'less than', view us suspiciously, alienate us, and ensure that we do not gain access to social and economic capital. Many are unaware that there is a social ranking system or how it influences their lives, and how those beneficiaries of the system make use of the levers of power to sustain social injustice and reasons for the lack of reparations from themselves (the offenders), while others are profoundly aware of the system and its consequences. An orientation of inclusion offers individuals and organisations the opportunity to initiate the process of disengaging and rectifying the devastating, negative sides of this social system. The process may be disorienting and painful, but ultimately empowering, as we begin to notice the overt and nuanced injustices, unfairness and downright nastiness operating at individual levels (intent and choices, action and behaviour), organisational levels (systems, procedures and policies, peers and allies), as well as governmental levels (laws, diversity auditing capabilities, context-regional relevance). Inclusion in South Africa that draws from the best from our African heritage, the best from our Western heritage and the best from our Eastern heritage offers possibilities, a sense of belonging, and hope for the many who have been, and those who continue to be, marginalised.

REFERENCES

Chapter 1

Afrobarometer. (2019). *AD324: Despite progressive laws, barriers to full gender equality persist in South Africa*. Retrieved from: http://afrobarometer.org/publications/ad324-despite-progressive-laws-barriers-full-gender-equality-persist-south-africa

April, K., Ephraim, N. & Peters, K. 2012. 'Diversity management in South Africa: Inclusion, identity, intention, power and expectations', *African Journal of Business Management*, 6(4): 1749-1759.

Daya, P. (2014). Diversity and inclusion in an emerging market context. *Equality, Diversity & Inclusion*, 33(3): 293-308.

De Vos, P. (2013). *In black and white: the truth about 'unconstitutional' race quotas in universities*. Retrieved from: https://www.dailymaverick.co.za/opinionista/2013-03-12-in-black-and-white-the-truth-about-unconstitutional-race-quotas-in-universities/

Hearn, J.& Louvrier, J. (2015). *Theories of difference, diversity and intersectionality: What do they bring to diversity management*. In R.Bendl, I. Bleijenbergh, E. Henttonen, & A.J. Mills (Eds.), The Oxford *Handbook of Diversity in Organisations*. Oxford: Oxford University Press.

Mangelsdorf, M. E. (2018). The Trouble with Homogeneous Teams. *MIT Sloan Management Review*, 59(2), 43-47.

Milliken, F. J.; Martins, L. L. (1996). Searching for common threads: understanding the multiple effects of diversity in organizational groups. *Academy of Management Review*, 21(2), 402-433.

Nair, N. & Vohra, N. (2015), *Diversity and inclusion at the workplace: A Review of Research and Perspectives*, No. WP2015-03-34, Research and Publication Department, Indian Institute of Management Ahmedabad.

Post, C., De Lia, E., DiTomaso,N., Tirpak, T.M., & Borwankar, R. (2009) Capitalizing on Thought Diversity for Innovation., *Research-Technology Management, 52*(6), 14-25.

Socio-Economic Rights Institute of South Africa. (2018). *Informal Settlements and Human Rights in South Africa*. Retrieved from: https://www.ohchr.org/Documents/Issues/Housing/InformalSettlements/SERI.pdf

Spaull, N. (2013). *South Africa's Education Crisis: The quality of education in South Africa 1994-2011*. Retrieved from: http://www.section27.org.za/wp-content/uploads/2013/10/Spaull-2013-CDE-report-South-Africas-Education-Crisis.pdf

Statistics South Africa. (2000). *Stats SA Library Cataloguing-in-Publication (CIP) Data*. Retrieved from: http://www.statssa.gov.za/publications/SAStatistics/SAStatistics2000.pdf

Statistics South Africa. (2020). *SA economy sheds 2,2 million jobs in Q2 but unemployment levels drop*. Retrieved from: http://www.statssa.gov.za/?p=13633

Sutherland, C., Roberts, B., Gabriel, N., Struwig, J., & Gordon, S. (2016). *Progressive prudes: a survey of attitudes towards homosexuality & gender non-conformity in South Africa*. Other Foundation and the Human Sciences Research Council. Retrieved from: http://repository.hsrc.ac.za/bitstream/handle/20.500.11910/10161/9400.pdf?sequence=1&isAllowed=y

The World Bank. (2020). *Overview*. Retrieved from: https://www.worldbank.org/en/country/southafrica/overview

Wray, D., Hellenberg, R., & Jansen, J. (2018). *A School Where I Belong: Creating Transformed and Inclusive South African schools*. Johannesburg: Bookstorm.

Chapter 2

Adhikari, M. (2006). "God made the white man, God made the black man...": Popular racial stereotyping of coloured people in apartheid South Africa. *South African Historical Journal*, *55*(1), 142-164. http://doi.org/10.1080/02582470609464935

Alvaredo, F., Chancel, L., Piketty, T., Saez, E., & Zucman, G. (2018). *World inequality report: Executive summary*. Retrieved from: https://wir2018.wid.world/files/download/wir2018-summary-english.pdf

Angus, L., & McLeod, J. (2004). Toward an integrative framework for understanding the role of narrative in the psychotherapy process. In L. Angus, & J. McLeod (Eds.). *The handbook of narrative and psychotherapy practice, theory and research* (pp. 367-374). London: Sage.

April, K., & Josias, A. (2017). Diasporic double consciousness, créolite and identity of coloured professionals in South Africa. *Effective Executive*, *20*(4), 31-61.

April, K., & Dharani. B. (2021). *Lived experiences of exclusion: The psychological and behavioural effects*. Bingley: Emerald Publishing Limited.

April, K., & Forster, D. (2020). Religion and diversity management in the Southern African context. In N. Carrim, & L. Moolman (Eds.). Diversity management (pp. 123-142). Pretoria: Van Schaik Publishers.

April, K., & Syed, J. (2020). Belonging: Race, intersectionality and exclusion. In J. Syed, & M. Özbilgin (Eds.). Managing diversity and inclusion: An international perspective (2nd ed) (pp. 142-193). London: Sage.

Balcazar, F. E., Balcazar, Y. S., Ritzler, T. T., & Keys, C. B. (2010). *Race, culture and disability*. London: Jones & Bartlett Publishers.

Bassier, I., & Woolard, I. (2018). *The top 1% of incomes are increasing rapidly even with low economic growth*. Retrieved from: https://www.econ3x3.org/sites/default/files/articles/Bassier%20%26%20Woolard%202018%20Top%20incomes_0.pdf

Biko, S. (1987). *I write what I like*. Oxford: Heinemann, p. 25.

Boxill, B. (Ed.). (2001). *Race and racism*. Oxford: Oxford University Press.

Byrd, M. Y. (2007). The effects of racial conflict on organizational performance: A search for theory. *New Horizons in Adult Education and Human Resource Development*, *21*(1/2), 12-28.

Conley, D. (2003). *What is the difference between race and ethnicity? Race – The power of an illusion*. Retrieved from: http://www.pbs.org/race/000_About/002_04-experts-03-02.htm.

Cox, T. H., & Nkomo, S. M. (1990). Invisible men and women: A status report on race as a variable in organization behavior research. *Journal of Organizational Behavior, 11*(6), 419-431.

Daya, P., & April, K. (2014). The relationship between demographic groups and perception of inclusion in a South African organisation. *The South African Journal of Business Management, 45*(2), 25-34.

Dovidio, J. F., Gaertner, S. L., & Bachman, B. A. (2001). Racial bias in organizations: The role of group processes in its causes and cures. In M. E. Turner (Ed.). *Groups at work: Theory and research* (pp. 415-444). Mahwah, NJ: Erlbaum.

Duncan, N., van Niekerk, A., de la Rey, C., & Seedat, M. (Eds.). (2001). *'Race', racism, knowledge production and psychology in South Africa*. New York: Nova Science Publishers.

Durrheim, K., Mtose, X., & Brown, L. (2011). *Race trouble: Race, identity and inequality in post-apartheid South Africa*. Pietermaritzburg: University of Kwazulu-Natal Press.

Fanon, F. (1952). *Black skin, white masks*. Paris: Éditions du Seuil (translated from the French in Richard Philcox).

Fischer, R. (2007). *Race*. Auckland Park: Jacana Media.

Foner, P. S. (Ed.). (1970). *W.E.B. Du Bois speaks: Speeches and addresses 1890-1919*. New York: Pathfinder Press, p. 275.

Geldenhuys, D. (2015). The weak domestic base of South Africa's good global citizenship. *South African Journal of International Affairs, 22*(4), 411-428.

Gibson, J. L., & Gouws, A. (2003). *Overcoming intolerance in South Africa: Experiments in democratic persuasion*. New York: Cambridge University Press.

Gunew, S. (1997). Postcolonialism and multiculturalism: Between race and ethnicity. *The Yearbook of English Studies, 27*, 22-39. https://doi.org/10.2307/3509130

Heleta, S. (2016). Decolonisation of higher education: Dismantling epistemic violence and Eurocentrism in South Africa. *Transformation in Higher Education* 1(1), a9. http://dx.doi.org/10.4102/the.v1i1.9

Holstein, J. A., & Gubrium, J. F. (2000). *The self we live by: Narrative identity in a postmodern world*. New York: Oxford University Press.

Ibekwe, C. (1987). *Decolonising the African mind*. Novazzano: Pero Press.

Kelley, S. (2000). Race. In A. K. M. Smith (Ed.). *Handbook of Postmodern Biblical Interpretation* (pp. 213-309), St. Louis, MO: Chalice.

Koopman, N. (1998). Racism in the post-apartheid South Africa. In L. Kretzschmar, & L. D. Hulley (Eds.). *Questions About Life and Morality: Christian Ethics in South Africa Today* (pp. 153-167). Sandton: Thorold's Africana Books.

Leech, K. (1996). Ethnicity. In P. B. Clarke, & A. Linzey (Eds.). *Dictionary of ethics, theology and society*. London: Routledge.

Leibbrandt, M., Finn, A., & Woolard, I. (2012). Describing and decomposing post-apartheid income inequality in South Africa. *Development Southern Africa, 29*(1), 19-34.

Lowe, F. (2013). Keeping organizations white. *Journal of Social Work Practice, 27*(2), 149-162.

Mafeje, A. (1998). White liberals and black nationalists: Strange bedfellows. *Southern Africa Political & Economy Monthly, 11*(13), 45-48.

Mashabela, J. K. (2017). Africanisation as an agent of theological education in Africa. *HTS Teologiese Studies/Theological Studies, 73*(3), a4581. https://doi.org/10.4102/hts.v73i3.4581

Mbolo, S., & Mabasa, A. N. (2019). Nativism and narrow nationalism in South African political discourse. *New Agenda: South African Journal of Social and Economic Policy, 2019*(73), 40-43.

McKaiser, E. (30 May 2016). *Epistemic injustices: The dark side of academic freedom.* 2016 DCS Oosthuizen Academic Freedom Memorial Lecture, Rhodes University, Grahamstown. Retrieved from: http://www.iol.co.za/news/epistemic-injustices-the-dark-side-of-academic-freedom-2029747

Mellet, P. T. (2020). *The lie of 1652: A decolonized history of land.* Cape Town: Tafelberg, NB Publishers, p. 314-315.

Mendelek-Theimann, N., April, K., & Blass, E. (2006). Context tension: Cultural influences on leadership and management practice. *Reflections, 7*(4), 38-51.

Millard, A. (Ed.). (1984). *The testimony of Steve Biko.* HarperCollins: New York.

Molefe, T. O. (2016). Oppression must fall: South Africa's revolution in theory. *World Policy Journal, 33*(1), 30-37. http://dx.doi.org/10.1215/07402775-3545858

Montagu, A. (1974). *Man's most dangerous myth: The fallacy of race.* New York: Oxford University Press, p. 62.

Myeza, A., & April, K. (2021). Atypical black leader emergence: South African self-perceptions. *Frontiers in Psychology:* Forthcoming (In Press).

Nicholas, L. J. (Ed.). (1993). *Psychology and oppression: Critiques and proposals.* Cape Town: Skotaville Publishers.

Nkomo, S. M. (2009). The sociology of race: The contributions of W.E.B. Du Bois. In P. S. Adler (Ed.). *The Oxford Handbook of Sociology and Organization Studies: Classical Foundations* (pp. 375-398), Oxford: Oxford University Press.

Nkomo, S. M. (2015). Challenges for management and business education in a "developmental state": The case of South Africa. *Academy of Management & Learning, 14*(2), 242-258. https://doi.org/10.5465/amle.2014.0323

Nyoka, B. (2016). Bernard Magubane's *The Making of a Racist State* revisited: 20 years on. *Journal of Black Studies, 47*(8), 903-927. https://doi.org/10.1177/0021934716658864

Oelofsen, R. (2015). Decolonisation of the African mind and intellectual landscape. *Phronimon, 16*(2), 130-146.

Omer, H., & Alon, N. (1994). The continuity principle: A unified approach to disaster and trauma. *American Journal of Community Psychology, 22*(2), 273-287. https://doi.org/10.1007/BF02506866

Prah, K. K. (2002). Race and culture: Myth and reality. In N. Duncan, P. Gqola, M. Hofmeyr, T. Shefer, F. Malunga, & M. Mashige (Eds.). *Discourses on difference: Discourses on oppression* (Book Series No 24), Cape Town: The Centre for Advanced Studies of African Society.

Prilleltensky, I. (2003). Understanding, resisting, and overcoming oppression: Toward psychopolitical validity. *American Journal of Community Psychology, 31*(1/2), 195-201.

Punt, J. (2009). Post-apartheid racism in South Africa: The bible, social identity and stereotyping. *Religion & Theology, 16*(3/4), 246-272. https://doi.org/10.1163/102308 009X12561890523672

Pyke, K. D. (2010). What is internalized racial oppression and why don't we study it? Acknowledging racism's hidden injuries. *Sociological Perspectives, 53*(4), 551-572.

Richard, O. C., & Johnson, N. (2001). Understanding the impact of human resource diversity practices on firm performance. Journal of Managerial Issues, 13(2), 177-195.

Riessman, C. K., & Speedy, J. (2007). Narrative inquiry in the psychotherapy professions: A critical review. In D. J. Clandinin (Ed.). Handbook of narrative inquiry: Mapping a methodology (pp. 426–456). Thousand Oaks, CA: Sage.

Rose, E. (2004). Discrimination and diversity within the employment relationship. In E. Rose (Ed.). *Employment Relations* (2nd ed) (pp. 555-618). Harlow, UK: Pearson Education.

Rosette, A. S., & Tost, L. (2017). Denying white privilege in organizations: The perception of race-based advantages as socially normative. *Academy of Management Proceedings, 1*, 1-6. https://doi.org/10.5465/ambpp.2007.26508251

Sharma, V., & April, K. (2013). Ethnicity & identity creation: Africa's social work-role lessons from the past. *Effective Executive. 16*(2), 51-61.

Shay, S. (2016). Decolonising the curriculum: It's time for a strategy. *The Conversation.* Retrieved from: https://theconversation.com/decolonising-the-curriculum-its-time-for-a-strategy-60598

Spaull, N. (2013). Poverty and privilege: Primary school inequality in South Africa. *International Journal of Educational Development, 33*(5), 436-447.

Statistics South Africa. (2019). *Inequality trends in South Africa: A multidimensional diagnostic of inequality.* Retrieved from http://www.statssa.gov.za/publications/Report-03-10-19/Report-03-10-192017.pdf

Stevens, G. (2003). Academic representations of 'race' and racism in psychology: Knowledge production, historical context and dialectics in transitional South Africa. *International Journal of Intercultural Relations, 27*(2), 189-207.

Sue, D. W. (2010). *Microaggressions in everyday life: Race, gender, and sexual orientation.* New York: Wiley.

Takaki, R. (1979). *Iron cages: Race and culture in the 19th century*. New York: Alfred Knopf.

Tinsley-Jones, H. (2001). Racism in our midst: Listening to psychologists of color. *Professional Psychology: Research and Practice, 32*(6), 573-580. https://doi.org/10.1037/0735-7028.32.6.573

Valentine, S., Silver, L., & Twigg, N. (1999). Locus of control, job satisfaction, and job complexity: The role of perceived race discrimination. *Psychological Reports, 84*(3), 1267-1273. https://doi.org/10.2466/pr0.1999.84.3c.1267

Chapter 3

Applebaum, B. (2007). White complicity and social justice education: Can one be culpable without being liable? *Educational Theory, 57*(4), 453-467.

Bozalek, V. (2011). Acknowledging privilege through encounters with difference: Participatory Learning and Action techniques for decolonising methodologies in Southern contexts. *International Journal of Social Research Methodology, 14*(6), 469-484.

Collins, P. H. (1998). It's all in the family: Intersections of gender, race, and nation. *Hypatia, 13*(3), 62-82.

Crenshaw, K. (1990). Mapping the margins: Intersectionality, identity politics, and violence against women of color. *Stanford Law Review, 43*(6), 1241-1299.

Desai, A., Maharaj, B., & Bond, P. (2011). *Zuma's Own Goal: Losing South Africa's War on Poverty*. Trenton, NJ: Africa World Press.

Diker, N., & Türkün, A. (2013). Social justice for disabled people. *International Journal of Architectural Research, 7*(2), 221, p. 223.

Diop, B. B. (2000). *Murambi: the book of bones*. Bloomington: Indiana University Press.

Edström, J. (2014). The male order development encounter. *IDS Bulletin, 45*(1), 111-123.

Fanon, F., & de Sousa Santos, B. (2018). What is Racism? In J. Cupples & R. Grosfoguel. (2018). *Zone of being and zone of non-being in the work of Unsettling Eurocentrism in the Westernized University*. London: Routledge.

Fiorenza, E. S. (1995). *Bread Not Stone: The Challenge of Feminist Biblical Interpretation*. Boston: Beacon Press.

Fiorenza, E. S. (2013). *Changing horizons: Explorations in feminist interpretation*. Minneapolis: Fortress Press.

Gordon, L. R. (2004). Critical Reflections on Three Popular Tropes in the Study of Whiteness. In G Yancy. *What White Looks Like: African-American Philosophers on the Whiteness Question* (pp. 189-210). New York & London: Routledge.

Grosfoguel, R. (2011). Decolonizing post-colonial studies and paradigms of political-economy: Transmodernity, decolonial thinking, and global coloniality. file:///C:/Users/cia/Downloads/eScholarship%20UC%20item%2021k6t3fq.pdf

Hanlon, A. R. (2014). Maids, Mistresses, and" Monstrous Doubles": Gender-Class Kyriarchy in The Female Quixote and Female Quixotism. *The Eighteenth Century, 55*(1), 77-96.

Hinson, S., & Bradley, A. (2006). A structural analysis of oppression. Grassroots Policy Project, pp. 1-5. Retrieved from: https://community.thewomensfoundation.org/Document.Doc?id=115

Lamont, M & Molnár, V. (2002). The study of boundaries in the social sciences. *Annual Review of Sociology, 28*(1), 167-195.

Mlilo, S., & Misago, J. P. (2019). Xenophobic Violence in South Africa: 1994-2018: an Overview. Johannesburg: Xenowatch, African Centre for Migration and Society.

Monahan, M. J. (2014). The concept of privilege: a critical appraisal. *South African Journal of Philosophy, 33*(1), 73-83.

Nega, B., & Schneider, G. (2014). Social entrepreneurship, microfinance, and economic development in Africa. *Journal of Economic Issues, 48*(2), 367-376.

Neves, D., Samson, M., van Niekerk, I., Hlatshwayo, S., & Du Toit, A. (2009). The use and effectiveness of social grants in South Africa. Cape Town: *Institute for Poverty, Land and Agrarian Studies (PLAAS)*.

Nkealah, N. (2011). Commodifying the female body: Xenophobic violence in South Africa. *Africa Development, 36*(2), 123-136.

Osborne, N. (2015). Intersectionality and kyriarchy: A framework for approaching power and social justice in planning and climate change adaptation. *Planning Theory, 14*(2), 130-151.

Patel, L. (2012). Poverty, gender and social protection: Child support grants in Soweto, South Africa. *Journal of Policy Practice, 11*(1-2), 106-120.

Rothberg, M. (2019). *The implicated subject: Beyond victims and perpetrators*. Stanford, CA: Stanford University Press.

Santos, B. (2017). The resilience of abyssal exclusions in our societies: toward a post-abyssal law. *Tilburg Law Review, 22*(1-2), 237-258.

Steyn, M. (2012). The ignorance contract: Recollections of apartheid childhoods and the construction of epistemologies of ignorance. *Identities, 19*(1), 8-25.

Steyn, M. (2015). Critical diversity literacy. In S. Vertovec. (2014). *Routledge international handbook of diversity studies*. London: Routledge, pp. 379-389.

Steyn, M., Tsekwa, J., & McEwen, H. (2017). "Whole masses of uncharted territory": Metaphors, Internal Spatiality, and Racialized Relationships in Post-Apartheid South Africa. *Critical Philosophy of Race, 5*(2), 267-295, p. 274.

Stoudt, B. G., Fox, M., & Fine, M. (2012). Contesting privilege with critical participatory action research. *Journal of Social Issues, 68*(1), 178-193.

Sweetman, C. (2011). Introduction: Social protection. *Gender and Development, 19*(2), 169-77.

Tronto, J. C. (1993). *Moral boundaries: A political argument for an ethic of care*. New York: Routledge.

Vanyoro, K. P. (2019). 'When they come, we don't send them back': counter-narratives of 'medical xenophobia' in South Africa's public health care system. *Palgrave Communications, 5*(1), 1-12.

Woolard, I. (2002). *An overview of poverty and inequality in South Africa.* Unpublished briefing paper. Pretoria: HSRC.

Young, I. (1988). 5 Faces of Oppression. *Philosophical Forum, 19*(4), 270-290.

Chapter 4

April, K. A., Ephraim, N., & Peters, K. (2012). Diversity management in South Africa. Inclusion, identity, intention, power and expectations. *African Journal of Business Management, 6*(4), 1749-1759.

Bell, M. P., Özbilgin, M.F., Beauregard, A., & Sürgevil, O. (2011). Voice, silence, and diversity in 21st century organizations: strategies for inclusion of gay, lesbian, bisexual, and transgender employees. *Human Resource Management, 50*(1), 131-146. ISSN 0090-4848

Booysen, L. (2007). A review of challenges facing black and white women managers in South Africa. *Southern African Business Review, 3*(2), 15-26.

Booysen, L., & Nkomo, S.M. (2010). Employment equity and diversity management in South Africa. *International Handbook on Diversity Management at Work: Country Perspectives on Diversity and Equal Treatment,* Cheltenham, UK and Northampton, MA, USA: Edward Elgar Publishing, pp.118–43.

Booysen, L. E., & Nkomo, S. M. (2014). New developments in employment equity and diversity management in South Africa. In A. Klarsfeld, L. A. E. Booysen, & E. Ng (Eds.). *International Handbook on Diversity Management at Work.* Cheltenham: Edward Elgar Publishing.

Bowmaker-Falconer, A., Horwitz, F. M., Jain, H., & Taggar, S. (1998). Employment equality programmes in South Africa: current trends. *Industrial Relations Journal, 29*(3), 222–233.

Brassey, M. (2019). The More Things Change. Multiracialism in Contemporary South Africa. *Constitutional Court Review, 9,* 443-471. doi.org/10.2989/CCR.2019.0017

Commission for Employment Equity (CEE). (2001). *CEE Annual Reports from 1999-2001.* Retrieved from: https://www.yumpu.com/en/document/view/33520324/commission-for-employment-equity-1999-2001-contentpdf

Daya, P. (2014). Diversity and inclusion in an emerging market context. *Equality, Diversity and Inclusion: An International Journal, 33*(3), 293-308.

Department of Labour. (2001). *1st Annual Report- Commission for Employment Equity, 1999-2001.* Retrieved from: https://www.yumpu.com/en/document/read/33520324/commission-for-employment-equity-1999-2001-contentpdf

Department of Labour. (2010). *10th Annual Report- Commission for Employment Equity, 2009-2010.* Pretoria: Government Printers.

Department of Labour. (2015). *Code of Good Practice.* Pretoria: Government Printers.

Department of Labour. (2020). *20th Annual Report- Commission for Employment Equity, 2019-2020*. Pretoria: Government Printers. Retrieved from: http://www.labour.gov.za/DocumentCenter/Reports/Annual%20Reports/Employment%20Equity/2019%20-2020/20thCEE_Report_.pdf

Fredman, S. (2016). Substantive inequality revisited. *International Journal of Constitutional Law, 14*(3), 712-738. doi:10.1093/icon/mow043

Frost, S. (2014). *The Inclusion Imperative*. Philadelphia: Kogan Page.

Human, L. (1996). Managing workforce diversity: a critique and example from South Africa. *International Journal of Manpower, 17*(4/5), 46–64.

Louw, A. M. (2015). The employment equity act, 1998 (and other myths about the pursuit of 'equality', 'equity', and 'dignity' in post-apartheid South Africa). *Potchefstroom Electronic Law Journal, 8*(3), 594-667.

Mbatha, L. (2018). Should race matter in our society? A 'Born Free' perspective. *Transformation: Critical Perspectives on Southern Africa, 96*, 71-94. doi:10.1353/trn.2018.0003.

Mekoa, I. (2019). Towards non-racialism in South Africa: acknowledging the past, changing the present and building the future. *African Renaissance, S1*(1), 85–103.

Oosthuizen, R. M., & Naidoo, V. (2010). Attitudes towards and experience of employment equity. *SA Journal of Industrial Psychology, 36*(1), e1–e9.

Post, C., De Lia, E., DiTomaso, N., Tirpak, T. M., & Borwankar, R. (2009). Capitalizing on thought diversity for innovation. *Research Technology Management, 52*(6),14-25. DOI: 10.1080/08956308.2009.11657596

South African Government. (1998). *Employment Equity Act, No. 55 of 1998*. Cape Town: Government Printers.

South African Government. (2013). *Employment Equity Amendment Act, No.47 of 2013*. Cape Town: Government Printers.

South African Government. (2018). *Employment Equity Amendment Bill, No. 639 of 2018*. Cape Town: Government Printers.

South African Government. (2020). *Employment Equity Amendment Bill, No. 798 of 2020*. Cape Town: Government Printers.

Statistics South Africa. (2014). *Employment, unemployment, skills and economic growth*. Retrieved from: https://www.statssa.gov.za/presentation/Stats%20SA%20presentation%20on%20skills%20and%20unemployment_16%20September.pdf

Statistics South Africa. (2020). *Quarterly Labour Force Survey, Quarter 3*. Retrieved from: http://www.statssa.gov.za/publications/P0211/P02113rdQuarter2020.pdf

The Mapungubwe Institute for Strategy Reflection. (2016). *Nation formation and social cohesion: An enquiry into the hopes and aspirations of South Africans*. Retrieved from: https://mistra.org.za/mistra-publications/nation-formation-and-social-cohesion/

Thomas, A. (2002). Employment Equity in South Africa: Lessons from the Global School. *International Journal of Manpower, 23*(3), 237-55.

Chapter 5

Albertyn, C & Hassim, S, (2004). The Boundaries of Democracy, Gender and HIV/AIDS and Culture. In D.Everrat & V.Maphal (eds.). *The real state of the Nation-South Africa after 1990.* South Africa: Interfund Special Edition, pp.138-164.

Albertyn, C. Goldblatt, B; Hassim, S; Mbatha, L and Meintjes, S, (1999). *Report on Engendering the Political Agenda: A South African Case Study*, Johannesburg, South Africa: University of Witwatersrand, and Centre for Applied Legal Studies.

Adhikari, M. (2005a). Contending approaches to coloured identity and the history of the coloured people of South Africa. *History Compass*, *3*(1): 1-16.

Adhikari, M. (2005b). *Not white enough, not black enough: Racial identity in the South African coloured community.* Ohio University Press.

Adhikari, M. (2006). 'God made the White man, God made the Black man...': Popular racial stereotyping of coloured people in Apartheid South Africa. *South African Historical Journal*, *55*(1), 142-164.

Andrews, P. (1986). The legal underpinnings of gender oppression in Apartheid South Africa. *Austl. JL & Soc'y*, *3*, 92.

B-BBEE Commission. (27 July 2019). Analysis of major B-BBEE transactions report. Johannesburg: B-BBEE Commission. Available at: https://www.bbbeecommission.co.za/registered-major-b-bbee-transactions/

Booysen, L. A., & Nkomo, S. M. (2010). Gender role stereotypes and requisite management characteristics. *Gender in Management: An international journal.*

Bosch, A., Nkomo, S.M., Carrim N.M.H, Haq, R., Syed, J. & Ali, F. (2015). Practices of organizing and managing diversity in emerging countries: Comparisons between India, Pakistan and South Africa. In R. Bendl, I. Bleijenbergy, E. & A. J. Mills (eds.). *The Oxford handbook of diversity in organizations.* Oxford, UK: Oxford University Press, pp. 408-434

Bozzoli, B. (1983). Marxism, feminism and South African studies. *Journal of Southern African Studies*, *9*(2), 139-171.

Butler, J. (1990). *Gender trouble: Feminism and the subversion of identity.* New York and London: Routledge.

Brink, E. (1987). "Only decent girls are employed": the respectability, decency and virtue of the garment workers on the Witwatersrand during the thirties. Johannesburg: University of Witwatersrand: History Workshop.

Carrim, N. M. H. (2012). *"Who am I?"-South African Indian women managers' struggle for identity: escaping the ubiquitous cage.* Doctoral dissertation, Pretoria: South Africa: University of Pretoria.

Carrim, N. M. H., & Nkomo, S. M. (2016). Wedding intersectionality theory and identity work in organizations: South African Indian women negotiating managerial identity. *Gender, Work & Organization*, *23*(3), 261-277.

Cock, J. (1980). *Maids & madams: A study in the politics of exploitation*. Johannesburg, South Africa: Ravan Press.

Department of Labour. (2019). Commission for employment equity. (2019). 19th Commission for Employment Equity Annual Report 2018-2019. Pretoria: Department of Labour.

Crenshaw, K. (1990). Mapping the margins: Intersectionality, identity politics, and violence against women of color. *Stan. L. Rev., 43*, 1241.

Daya, P. (2014). Diversity and inclusion in an emerging market context. *Equality, Diversity and Inclusion: An International Journal, 33*(3), 293-308.

de Lange, N., Mitchell, C., & Bhana, D. (2012). Voices of women teachers about gender inequalities and gender-based violence in rural South Africa. *Gender and Education, 24*(5), 499-514.

Desai, A., & Vahed, G. (2013). Indenture and Indianness in South Africa, 1860–1913. In S. Patel, S. & Uys, T. (eds.). *Contemporary India and South Africa* (pp. 31-44). New Dehli, India: Routledge India.

Destanovic, J. (2016). *Living in and out the closet: An exploration of lesbian identity in the workplace.*(Doctoral dissertation. Johannesburg, South Africa: University of the Witwatersrand.

Dreyer, S., Blass, E., & April, K. (2007). Gender impediments to the South African executive boardroom. *South African Journal of Labour Relations, 31*(2), 51-67.

Dubow, S. (2015). Racial irredentism, ethnogenesis, and white supremacy in high-Apartheid South Africa. *Kronos, 41*(1), 236-264.

Elder, G. S. (2003). *Hostels, sexuality, and the Apartheid legacy: malevolent geographies.* Athens, Ohio: Ohio University Press.

Elder, G. S. (2003). Malevolent traditions: Hostel violence and the procreational geography of Apartheid. *Journal of Southern African Studies, 29*(4), 921-935.

Erlank, N. (2005). ANC positions on gender 1994-2004. *Politikon*, 32(2): 195-215.

Espi, G., Francis, D. & I. Valodia. (2019) Gender inequality in the South African labour market: Insights from the Employment Equity Act data, *Agenda*, 33:4, 44-61

Fredrickson, G. M. (1982). *White supremacy: A comparative study of American and South African history*. Oxford University Press.

Farah, A. A. (1974). South Africa's Apartheid policy: An assessment. In Y. El-Ayouty & H. C. Brooks (eds.). *Africa and International Organization*. Dordrecht: Springer, pp. 71-102.

Freund, B. (1991). Indian women and the changing character of the working class Indian household in Natal 1860-1990. *Journal of Southern African Studies*, 17 (3): 414-29.

Gevisser, M. (1995). A different fight for freedom: A history of South African lesbian and gay organisation from the 1950s to the 1990s. In E. Cameron & Gevisser, M. (eds.). *Defiant desire: Gay and lesbian lives in South Africa.* New York: Routledge. pp. 14-86.

Gold, M. (2018). The ABCs of L.G.B.T.Q.I.A.+. Retrieved from: https://www.nytimes.com/2018/06/21/style/lgbtq-gender-language.html

Gouws, A. (2014) Recognition and redistribution: State of the women's movement in South Africa 20 years after democratic transition, *Agenda*, 28:2, 19-32,

Gouws, A. & Galgut, H. (2016) Twenty years of the constitution: Reflecting on citizenship and gender justice, *Agenda*, 30:1, 3-9.

Hassim, S. (2002). A conspiracy of women: The women's movement in South Africa's transition to democracy. *Social Research: An International Quarterly*, 69(3), 693-732.

Hassim, S. (2005). Terms of engagement: South African challenges. *Feminist Africa*, 4: 10-28.

Hassim, S. (2006). *Women's organisation and democracy in South Africa contesting authority*. United States of America: University of Wisconsin Press.

Hicks, J. (2012). *Opinion piece: gender transformation in the workplace.* Commission for Gender Equality. Available from www.cge.org.za

Hiralal, K. (2010). Docile' Indian women protest – we shall resist: passive resistance in South Africa, 1946–1948. *Journal of Social Science*, 22 (3), 153–162.

Holland-Muter S. (2005). Policy research on the protocol to the African charter on human and people's rights on the rights of women, *South Africa Country Report*.

Hyslop, J. (1995). White working-class women and the invention of Apartheid: 'Purified' Afrikaner nationalist agitation for legislation against 'mixed' marriages, 1934–9. *The Journal of African History*, 36(1), 57-81.

Jaga, A., Arabandi, B., Bagraim, J., & Mdlongwa, S. (2018). Doing the 'gender dance': Black women professionals negotiating gender, race, work and family in post-Apartheid South Africa. *Community, Work & Family*, 21(4), 429-444.

Jones, T. F. (2008). Averting white male (ab) normality: psychiatric representations and treatment of 'homosexuality' in 1960s South Africa. *Journal of Southern African Studies*, 34(2), 397-410.

Kahn, S. (2010). Gender equality in the South African National Defence Force. *Administration Publica*, 18(3), 66-89.

Kiaye, E.R. and Singh, M.A. (2013). The glass ceiling: a perspective of women working in Durban. *Gender in Management,* 28 (1): 28-42

Klausen, S. M. (2010). Reclaiming the white daughter's purity": Afrikaner nationalism, racialized sexuality, and the 1975 abortion and sterilization act in Apartheid South Africa. *Journal of women's history*, 22(3), 39-63.

Kitzinger, C. 2005. Heteronormativity in action: Reproducing the heterosexual nuclear family in after-hours medical calls. *Social Problems* 52 (4): 477-98.

Krikorian, J. (1995). A Different form of Apartheid-the legal status of married women in South Africa. *Queen's LJ*, 21, 221.

Kritzinger, A., & Vorster, J. (1996). Women farm workers on South African deciduous fruit farms: Gender relations and the structuring of work. *Journal of Rural Studies*, 12(4), 339-351.

Lumby, J., & Azaola, M. C. (2014). Women principals in South Africa: Gender, mothering and leadership. *British educational research journal*, 40(1), 30-44.

Maharaj, P. (1995). *The social identities of Indians in a changing South Africa.* M.Soc. Science dissertation, University of Natal, Durban, South Africa.

Mama, A. (2001). Challenging subjects: Gender and power in African contexts. *African Sociological Review/Revue Africaine de Sociologie, 5*(2), 63-73.

Manicom, L. (1992). Ruling relations: rethinking state and gender in South African history. *The Journal of African History, 33*(3), 441-465.

Manion, A. & Morgan, R. (2006). The Gay and Lesbian Archives: documenting same-sexuality in an African context. *Agenda, 20*(67), 29-35.

Moffett, H (2006). These women, they force us to rape them: Rape as narrative of social control in post-apartheid South Africa. *Journal of Southern African Studies 32*(1): 129–144.

Moodie, T. D. with Ndatshe, V. & Sibuyi. G. (1988). Migrancy and male sexuality on the South African Gold Mines,' *Journal of Southern African Studies, 14*(2), 228–56.

Morgan, R. & Wieringa, S. (2005). *Tommy Boys, Lesbian Men, and Ancestral Wives: Female Same-sex Practices in Africa.* Sunnyside, South Africa: Jacana Media.

Morrell, R. (2006). Fathers, fatherhood and masculinity in South Africa. In L. Richter & R. Morrell (eds.). *BABA: men and fatherhood in South Africa,* Pretoria, South Africa: HSRC Press, pp. 13-25.

Morrell, R., Jewkes, R., & Lindegger, G. (2012). Hegemonic masculinity/masculinities in South Africa: Culture, power, and gender politics. *Men and masculinities, 15*(1), 11-30.

Msibi, T., 2012. 'I'm used to it now': experiences of homophobia among queer youth in South African township schools. *Gender and Education, 24*(5), 515-533.

Murray, S.O. & Roscoe, W., 2001. *Boy-wives and female husbands: Studies of African homosexualities.* London: Palgrave Macmillan.

Mvimbi, A. (2009). *The post-Apartheid South African state and the advancement of gender equality: The experience of the National Gender Machinery.* Doctoral dissertation, University of the Witwatersrand.

National Gender Policy Framework. (2008). *Women's empowerment and gender equality, National Gender Policy Framework.* Pretoria: The Office on the status of women.

Nkomo, S. (2011). Moving from the letter of the law to the spirit of the law: the challenges of realising the intent of employment equity and affirmative action. *Transformation: Critical Perspectives on Southern Africa, 77*(1), 122-135.

Nkunzi, N. & Morgan, R. (2006). This has happened since ancient times...it's something that you are born with: ancestral wives among same-sex sangomas in South Africa. *Agenda: Empowering Women for Gender Equity, 67,* 9-19.

Orton, L., Barrientos, S., & Mcclenaghan, S. (2001). Paternalism and gender in South African fruit employment: Change and continuity. *Women's studies international Forum, 24* (3-4), 469-478).

Patel, S., & Uys, T. (Eds.). (2013). *Contemporary India and South Africa: legacies, identities, dilemmas.* New Delhi, India: Routledge.

Pillay, P. (1985). Women in employment in South Africa: some important trends and issues. *Social dynamics, 11*(2), 20-36.

Potgieter, C. A. (1997). *Black, South African, lesbian: Discourses of invisible lives.* Doctoral dissertation, University of the Western Cape.

Potgieter, C. (2006). Masculine Bodies, Feminine Symbols: Challenging Gendered Identities or Compulsory Femininity? *Agenda: Empowering Women for Gender Equity, (67)*, 116-127.

Poinsette, C. L. (1985). Black women under Apartheid: An introduction. *Harv. Women's LJ, 8*, 93.

Ratele, K. (2009). Apartheid, anti-Apartheid and post-Apartheid sexualities. In M.Steyn & M. van Zyl (eds.) *The prize and the price: Shaping sexualities in South Africa*, Cape Town: HSRC, pp. 290-306.

Ratele, K. (2014). Currents against gender transformation of South African men: Relocating marginality to the centre of research and theory of masculinities. *NORMA: International Journal for Masculinity Studies, 9*(1), 30-44.

Ratele, K., & Shefer, T. (2013). Desire, fear and entitlement: Sexualising race and racialising sexuality in (re) membering Apartheid. In *Race, memory and the Apartheid Archive* (pp. 188-207). Palgrave Macmillan, London.

Reddy, V. (2006). Decriminalisation of homosexuality in post-Apartheid South Africa: A brief legal case history review from sodomy to marriage. *Agenda, 20*(67), 146-157.

Radhakrishnan, S. (2005). Time to show our true colors: the gendered politics in post-Apartheid South Africa. *Gender and Society*, 19 (2): 262-281.

Rodriguez, J. K., Holvino, E., Fletcher, J. K., & Nkomo, S. M. (2016). The theory and praxis of intersectionality in work and organisations: Where do we go from here? *Gender, Work and Organization, 23*(3), 201-222.

Rubin, G. (1993). Thinking Sex: Notes for a radical theory of the politics of sexuality.' In H. Abelove, M.A. Barale and D.M. Halperin (eds.). The lesbian and gay studies reader, New York: Routledge, pp. 3–44.

Schaap, R. (2011). State of emergency: An exploration of attitudes towards homosexuality in the SADF, 1969-1994. Unpublished Master of Arts, Stellenbosch University.

South Africa. (1996a). *Commission on Gender Equality Act, No 39 of 1996.* Pretoria: Government Printer.

South Africa. (1996b). *Constitution of the Republic of South Africa, No 108 of 1996.* Available at: www.info.gov.za/documents/constitution/1996/a108-96.pdf –

South Africa. (1998). *Employment Equity Act, No 55 of 1998.* Available at: www.hpcsa.co.za/hpcsa/.../EMPLOYMENT%20EQUITY%20ACT.pdf –

Stats SA. (2014). *Quarterly Labour Force Survey. Quarter 4.* Available at: http://www.statssa.gov.za/?m=2019

Seedat-Khan, M. (2013). Tracing the journey of South African Indian women from 1860. In Patel, S., & Uys, T. (eds.). (2013). *Contemporary India and South Africa.* New Dehli, India: Routledge, pp. 45-57.

Senne, M. Y. (2013). *Individual and organisational barriers to gender equity: A comparative study of two South African universities.* Doctoral dissertation, University of Johannesburg).

Shefer, T., & Ratele, K. (2011). Racist sexualisation and sexualised racism in narratives on Apartheid. *Psychoanalysis, Culture & Society, 16*(1), 27-48.

Steyn, M., & Van Zyl, M. (2009). *The prize and the price: Shaping sexualities in South Africa.* Pretoria: HSRC Books.

Swarr, A. L. Lock. 2009. "'Stabane,' Intersexuality, and Same-Sex Relationships in South Africa." *Feminist Studies* 35(3):524–48.

Swarr, A. L. (2012). *Sex in transition: Remaking gender and race in South Africa.* Albany: Suny Press.

Ulicki, T. (2011). 'Just the way things are': gender equity and sexual harassment in the South African Police Service. *Transformation: Critical Perspectives on Southern Africa, 76*(1), 95-119.

Van Zyl, M., & Steyn, M. E. (Eds.). (2005). *Performing queer: Shaping sexualities, 1994-2004* (Vol. 1). Cape Town, South Africa: Kwela Books.

Van Zyl, M. (2014). Working the margins: Belonging and the workplace for Lgbti in Post-Apartheid South Africa. In *Sexual Orientation at Work* (pp. 151-165). Routledge.

Vincent, L., & Howell, S. (2014). 'Unnatural', 'un-African'and 'ungodly': Homophobic discourse in democratic South Africa. *Sexualities, 17*(4), 472-483.

Walker, C. (Ed.). (1990). *Women and gender in Southern Africa to 1945.* New Africa Books.

Chapter 6

Adam, D. T. & Eghubare, E. F. (2010). The African queen: Queen of Sheba. *Journal for Semitics, 19*(2), 402-420.

Ahmed, S. F., & Carrim, N. M. H. (2016). Indian husbands' support of their wives' upward mobility in corporate South Africa: Wives' perspectives. *SA Journal of Industrial Psychology, 42*(1), 1-13. https://dx.doi.org/10.4102/sajip.v42i1.1354

Blau, F., & Khan, L. (2017). The gender wage gap: Extent, trends, and explanations. *Journal of Economic Literature, 55*(3), 854

Bosch, A., & Barit, S. (2020). Gender pay transparency mechanisms: Future directions for South Africa. *South African Journal of Science, 116*(3/4), page.

Bosch, A. (2016). *Pregnancy is here to stay – or is it?* In A. Bosch (Ed.). *South African Board for People Practices Women's Report 2016* (pp. 3-6). Rosebank, South Africa: SABPP.

Bosch, A. (2020). *The gender pay gap: a guide for the already converted.* Stellenbosch, South Africa: University of Stellenbosch Business School.

Bosch, A., De Bruin, G.P., Kgaladi, B., & De Bruin, K. (2012). Life role salience among black African dual-career couples in the South African context. *The International Journal of Human Resource Management, 23*(14), 2835-2853.

Bosch, A., van der Linde, K., & Barit, S. (2020). *Women on South African boards: facts, fiction and forward thinking.* Stellenbosch, South Africa: University of Stellenbosch Business School.

Broderick, E. (2010). *What does a world of gender equality look like?* Retrieved from: https://humanrights.gov.au/about/news/speeches/what-does-world-gender-equality-look-2010

Brumley, K. (2014). The gendered ideal worker narrative: Professional Women's and Men's Work Experiences in the New Economy at a Mexican Company. *Gender and Society, 28*(6), 799-823.

Butler, J. (1990). *Gender trouble: Feminism and the subversion of identity.* New York: Routledge.

Council on Higher Education. (2018). *VitalStats Public Higher Education 2016.* Retrieved from: https://pdf4pro.com/view/vitalstats-che-ac-za-1ebbc8.html

Crenshaw, K. (1989). *Demarginalizing the intersection of race and sex: A Black feminist critique of antidiscrimination doctrine, feminist theory and antiracist politics.* Chicago: University of Chicago Legal Forum.

Daya, P. (2012). Diversity and inclusion in an emerging market context. *Equality, Diversity and Inclusion: An International Journal, 33*(3), 293-308. DOI: 10.1108/EDI-10-2012-0087

Department of Labour. (2019). *19th Commission for Employment Equity Report 2019.* Retrieved from: https://www.labourguide.co.za/workshop/1692-19th-cee-annual-report/file

Dlamini, J. (2016). *Equal but different: Women leaders' life stories.* Johannesburg: Sifiso Publishers.

Evans, J. (1995). *Feminist theory today: An introduction to second-wave feminism.* London: Sage Publications.

Farré, L. (2013). The role of men in the economic and social development of women: Implications for gender equality. *The World Bank Observer, 28*(1), 22-51.

Geldenhuys, M., Bosch, A., Jeewa, S., & Koutris, I. (2019). Gender traits in relation to work versus career salience. *SA Journal of Industrial Psychology, 45*(0), a1588. https://doi.org/10.4102/ sajip.v45i0.1588

Gouws, A. (2017). Fairness in the family. In A. Bosch (Ed.). *South African Board for People Practices Women's Report 2017* (pp. 8 – 12). Rosebank, South Africa: SABPP.

Griessel, L., & Kotze, M. (2010). The cultural identity of white Afrikaner women: A post Jungian perspective. *Acta Academica, 42*(2), 83.

Hall, K., & Posel, D. (2019). Fragmenting the family? The complexity of household migration strategies in post-apartheid South Africa. *IZA Journal of Development and Migration, 10*(2), 22-48.

Hatch, M., & Posel, D. (2018). Who cares for children? A quantitative study of childcare in South Africa. *Development South Africa, 35*(2), 267-282.

Herrett, M. (May 2010). *Government policy on gender and education in Australia.* Paper to the Alliance of Girls' Schools Australasia Conference, Sydney.

Heywood, L. (2017). *Nijinga of Angola: Africa's Warrior Queen.* Cambridge: Harvard University Press.

Hughes, C. (2002). *Key concepts in feminist theory and research.* London: Sage Publications.

Jacobson, M. (2014). Women's fertility and work. In A. Bosch (Ed.). *South African Board for People Practices Women's Report 2014: Work and women's reproductive health* (pp. 7-13). Parktown, South Africa: SABPP.

Jewkes, R., Morrell, R., Hearn, J., Lundqvist, E., Blackbeard, D., Lindegger, G., Quayle, M., Sikweyiya, Y., & Gottén, L. (2015). Hegemonic masculinity: Combing theory and practices in gender interventions. *Culture, Health and Sexuality, 17*(2), 112-127.

McCollum, S. (2004). *African Queens.* New York: Scholastic Inc.

Mosomi, J. N. (2018). *Distributional changes in the gender wage gap in the post-apartheid South African labour market.* Retrieved from: https://open.uct.ac.za/handle/11427/30000

Mwambene, L. M. (2017). What is the Future of Polygyny (Polygamy) in Africa? *Potchefstroom Electronic Law Journal, (20)*: 1–33. http://dx.doi.org/10.17159/1727-3781/2017/v20i0a1357

Nkomo, S. M. & Rodriguez, J. K. (2018). Joan Acker's influence on Management and Organization Studies: Review, analysis and directions for the future. *Gender, Work and Organization*, (26)12: pp.1730-1748.

Pienaar, H., & Kok, R. (2017). Paternity leave and the archaic gender roles entrenched in employment law. In A. Bosch (Ed.). *South African Board for People Practices Women's Report 2017* (pp. 18-25). Rosebank, South Africa: SABPP.

Powell, G. N. (2011). Gender and the leadership wars. *Organizational Dynamics, 40*, 1-9.

Procher, V., Ritter, N., & Vance, C. (2018). Housework allocation in Germany: The role of income and gender identity. *Social Science Quarterly*, 99(1), 43-61. https://doi.org/10.1111/ssqu.12390

Ratele, K. (2013). Masculinities without Tradition. *Politikon, 40*(1), 133-156, DOI: 10.1080/02589346.2013.765680

Ratele, K. (2014). Gender Equality in the Abstract and Practice. *Men and Masculinities*, 17(5), 510-514.

Rogan, M. (2016). Qualitative perceptions of the meaning of "headship" and female-headed households in post-apartheid South Africa. *Social Dynamics, 42*(1), 175-195.

Rudwick, S., & Posel, D. (2015). Zulu bridewealth (ilobolo) and womanhood in South Africa. *Social Dynamics, 41*(2), 289-306.

SAICA. (2021). *Membership Statistics 2019.* Retrieved from: https://www.saica.co.za/Members/AboutMembers/MembershipStatistics/tabid/502/language/en-ZA/Default.aspx

Sandberg, S. (2013). *Lean In: Women, Work, and the Will to Lead.* New York: Alfred A. Knopf.

Spelman, E. V. (1990). *Inessential woman: Problems of exclusion in feminist thought.* Boston, USA: Beacon Press.

Statistics South Africa. (2015). *Living conditions of households in South Africa: An analysis of household expenditure and income data using the LCS 2014/2015.* Pretoria: Department of Statistics South Africa.

Statistics South Africa. (2016). *Community Survey.* Pretoria: Department of Statistics South Africa.

Statistics South Africa. (2018a). *How do women fare in the South African labour market?* Retrieved from: http://www.statssa.gov.za/?p=11375

Statistics South Africa. (2018b). *Quarterly Labour Force Survey.* Pretoria: Department of Statistics South Africa.

Statistics South Africa. (2018c). *Marriages and Divorces 2018.* Retrieved from: http://www.statssa.gov.za/publications/P0307/P03072018.pdf

Statistics South Africa. (2019). *Quarterly Labour Force Survey.* Pretoria. Department of Statistics South Africa.

Steyn, R., & De Bruin, G. P. (2020). An investigation of gender-based differences in assessment instruments: A test of measurement invariance. *SA Journal of Industrial Psychology, 46*(0), a1699. https://doi. org/10.4102/sajip.v46i0.1699.

World Edonomic Forum (WEF). (2020). *Global Gender Gap Report.* Retrieved from: http://www3.weforum.org/docs/WEF_GGGR_2020.pdf

Chapter 7

Abrahams, N., Jewkes, R., Martin, L., Mathews, S., Vetten, L., & Lombard, C. (2009). Mortality of Women from Intimate Partner Violence in South Africa: A National Epidemiological Study. *Violence and Victims, 24*(4), 546-556.

Abrahams, N., Mathews, S., Martin, L., Lombard, C., & Jewkes, R. (2013). Intimate Partner Femicide in South Africa in 1999 and 2009. *PLoS Med, 10(4), e1001412.*

Adams, J., Mabusela, M., & Dlamini, E. (2013). Sexual harassment: The 'silent killer' of female students at the University of Ayoba in South Africa. *SAJHE 27*(5), 1149–1163.

Bennett, J., Gouws, A., Kritzinger, A., Hames , M., & Tidimane, C. (2007). 'Gender is Over': Researching the Implementation of Sexual Harassment Policies in Southern African Higher Education1. *Feminist Africa, 8,* 83-104.

Chandre, J., & Cervix. (2018). *Rape Culture Pyramid.* Retrieved from: https://www.11thprincipleconsent.org/consent-propaganda/rape-culture-pyramid/

Clowes, L., Shefer, T., Fouten, E., Vergnani, T., & Jacobs, J. (2009). Coercive sexual practices and gender based violence on a university campus. *Agenda, 23*(80), 22-32.

Collins, A., & Gordon, S. (2013). "We face rape. We face all things": Understandings of gender-based violence amongst female students at a South African university. *African Safety Promotion Journal, 11*(2), 93-106.

Crenshaw, K. (1995). Mapping the margins: Internationality, identity, politics and violence against women of colour. In K. Crenshaw, N. Gotanda, G. Peller & K. Thomas. *Critical race theory: The key writings that informed the movement* (pp. 354-383). New York: The New Press.

Dahlberg, L., & Krug, E. (2002). Violence: A Global Public Health Problem. In E. Krug, L. Dahlberg, J. Mercy, A. Zwi & R. Lozano. *World Report on Violence and Health.* Geneva: World Health Organisation.

Davids, N. (2019). Gender-based violence in South African universities: an institutional challenge. *Briefly Speaking: Council on Higher Education, 10,* 1-12.

Department of Higher Education and Training. (2017). *Deputy Minister Mduduzi Manana launches Sexual and Gender-based Violence dialogues at University of Zululand, 24 Feb.* Retrieved from: https://www.gov.za/speeches/sexual-and-gender-based-violence-dialogues-21-feb-2017-0000

Department of Higher Education and Training. (2019). *Minister Naledi Pandor appoints Ministerial Task Team to advise on matters relating to sexual harassment and gender-based violence.* Retrieved from: https://www.gov.za/speeches/minister-naledi-pandor-appoints-ministerial-task-team-advise-matters-relating-sexual

Department of Higher Eduation and Training. (2020). *Policy Framework to Address Gender-Based Violence in the Post-School Education and Training System.* Retrieved from: http://www.dhet.gov.za/Social%20Inclusion/Updated%20GBV%20Policy%20and%20Strategy%20Framework%20for%20the%20PSET.pdf

Department of Planning, Monitoring and Evaluations. (2016). *Diagnostic Review of the State Response to Violence against Womxn and Children.* Pretoria: Department of Planning, Monitoring and Evaluations.

EndRapeCulture Task Team at SU. (2017). *Report: recommendations on addressing EndRapeCulture at SU.* Retrieved from: http://www.sun.ac.za/english/transformation/Documents/Stellenbosch%20University%20EndRapeCulture%20Report%202017.pdf

Finchilescu, G., & Dugard, J. (2018). Experiences of gender-based violence at a SOuth African university: Prevalence and effect of rape myth acceptance. *Journal of Interpersonal Violence.* 088626051876935. 10.1177/0886260518769352.

Gender Links. (2012). *Research: Gender Violence 'A Reality in South Africa'.* Johannesburg: Gender Links.

Gouws, A. (2018). #EndRapeCulture Campaign in South Africa: Resisting Sexual Violence Through Protest and the Politics of Experience. *Politikon, 45*(1), 3-15.

Gouws, A., & Kritzinger, A. (2007). Dealing with sexual harrasment at institutions of higher education: Policy implementation at a South African University. *South African Journal of Higher Education, 21*(1), 68-84.

Gqola, P. (2015). *Rape: A South African Nightmare.* Retrieved from: https://www.amazon.com/Rape-Nightmare-Pumla-Dineo-Gqola-ebook/dp/B0862FL9B6/ref=sr_1_1?d-child=1&keywords=rape+a+south+african+nightmare&qid=1589067303&sr=8-1.

Harvey, R., Brown, K., Miller, B., Williams-Reade, J., Tyndall, L., & Murphy, M. (2016). Theory into Research Practice: Reflections and Recommendations on Collaborative Feminist Research. *Journal of Feminist Family Therapy, 28,* 136-158.

Institute for Security Studies. (2011). *So Why Do the Numbers Keep Rising? A Reflection on Efforts to Prevent and Respond to Domestic Violence and Rape.* Pretoria: Institute for Security Studies.

Interim Steering Committee on Gender-based Violence and Femicide. (2019). *Draft National Gender-Based Violence and Femicide Strategic Plan 2020–2030.* Retrieved from: https://www.gov.za/sites/default/files/gcis_document/201909/nspongbvfdraft.pdf

Kiguwa, P. (2004). Feminist critical psychology in South Africa. In D. Hook, P. Kiguwa, N. Mkhize & A. Collins. *Introduction to critical psychology* (pp. 278 – 315). Cape Town: UCT Press.

Mathews, S., Abrahams, N., Martin, L., Vetten, L., Van der Merwe, L., & Jewkes, R. (2004). *Every Six Hours a Woman is Killed by Her Intimate Partner: A National Study of Female Homicide in South Africa. Medical Research Council Policy Brief. 5.* Cape Town: Gender and Health Research Group & Medical Research Council.

Muller, R., Gahan, L., & Brooks, L. (2014). *Too costly to ignore - Violence against women in South Africa.*

Presidential Summit on Gender-based Violence and Femicide. Retrieved from: https://www.justice.gov.za/vg/201903-GBV-SummitDeclarationBooklet.pdf

Rupiah, R. (2018). #TheTotalShutdown: Memorandum of demands. *Mail and Guardian.* Retrieved from: https://mg.co.za/article/2018-08-02-thetotalshutdown-memorandum-of-demands/

Sexual Violence Task Team. (2018). *'We will not be silenced': A three-pronged justice approach to sexual offences and rape culture at Rhodes University/UCKAR.* Grahamstown, South Africa: Critical Studies in Sexualities and Reproduction.

Shefer, T., Clowes, L., & Vergnani, T. (2012). Narratives of transactional sex on a university campus. *Culture, Health & Sexuality, 14*(4), 435–447.

Slade, B., & Botha, H. (5 September, 2018). Helen Zille in Stellenbosch: A Tale of Three Misreadings. *The Daily Maverick.* Retrieved from: https://www.dailymaverick.co.za/article/2018-09-05-helen-zille-in-stellenbosch-a-tale-of-three-misreadings/

South African Government. (2019). *16 Days of Activism 2019.* Retrieved from: https://www.gov.za/16DaysofActivism2019

Statistics South Africa. (June 2018). *Crime against Women in South Africa: an in-depth analysis of the Victims of Crime Survey data, Report No. 03-40-05.* Pretoria: StatsSA.

Stellenbosch University Anti-GBV Movement. (2019). *SU Anti-GBV Movement Memorandum to the Rectorate of Stellenbosch University.* Retrieved from: http://www.sun.ac.za/english/Documents/2019/GBV%20Memorandum.pdf

Stellenbosch University Rectorate. (2019). *Enough is enough: Stellenbosch University takes a stand against gender-based violence.* Retrieved from: https://www.sun.ac.za/english/Documents/SU-management-response-to-anti-GBV-memo-20190918.pdf

Steyn, M. (2015). Critical diversity literacy: Essentials for the twenty first century. In S. Vertovec. *Routledge International Handbook of Diversity Studies* (pp. 379-389). New York: Routledge.

Stop Gender Violence Campaign. (2017). *Sonke Gender Justice.* Retrieved from: https://genderjustice.org.za/publication/national-strategic-plan-gender-based-violence-shadow-framework/

The Centre for the Study of Violence and Reconciliation. (2016). *Gender-Based Violence (GBV) in South Africa: A Brief Review.* Pretoria: The Centre for the Study of Violence and Reconciliation.

UN Women. (2019). *16 Days of Activism against Gender-Based Violence.* Retrieved from: https://www.unwomen.org/en/what-we-do/ending-violence-against-women/take-action/16-days-of-activism

United Nations General Assembly. (1993). *Declaration on the Elimination of Violence against Women.* Retrieved from: https://www.un.org/ga/search/view_doc.asp?symbol=A/RES/48/104

University of Cape Town. (2020). *Search results 'rape culture'.* Retrieved from: https://www.uct.ac.za/search/?cx=002153019866612815917%3Av6l0orknvrm&cof=-FORID%3A11&query=rape+culture&op=Search&form_build_id=form-QRg9_GjpHr-6r8OASnK-RosZFMFnB2q-zy-hddQbHsfM&form_id=google_cse_results_searchbox_form

University of Stellenbosch. (2018). *SU Vision 2040 and Strategic Framework 2019–2024.* Retrieved from: http://www.sun.ac.za/english/Documents/Strategic_docs/2018/SU_VisieVision_BrondokumentSourcedocument.pdf

University of Stellenbosch. (2020). *Search results 'rape culture'.* Retrieved from: http://www.sun.ac.za/english/search/Pages/results.aspx?k=rape%20culture

University of Stellenbosch Department of Student Affairs. (2020). *Update on Anti-GBV Working Groups.* Retrieved from: http://www.sun.ac.za/english/Lists/news/DispForm.aspx?ID=7062

University of Stellenbosch Transformation Office. (2018). *Talking transformation: A quick reference guide.* Retrieved from: http://www.sun.ac.za/english/transformation/Documents/Talking%20Transformation.pdf

University of the Witwatersrand. (2020). *Search results 'rape culture'.* Retrieved from: https://www.wits.ac.za/search-results/?q=rape+culture

Vetten, L. (2005). "Show Me the Money": A Review of Budgets Allocated towards the Implementation of South Africa's Domestic Violence Act. *Politikon South African Journal of Political Studies, 32*(2), 277-295.

Walby, S. 2009, The cost of domestic violence: up-date 2009, Lancaster University. Retrieved from: http://www.lancs.ac.uk/fass/doc_library/sociology/Cost_of_domestic_violence_update.doc

World Health Organization. (2016). *Global Health Estimates 2015: Deaths by Cause, Age, Sex, by Country and by Region, 2000-2015.* [Retrieved from: http://apps.who.int/violenceinfo/homicide

Zille, H. (27 August, 2018). Two meetings at Stellenbosch University this week gave a rare peek into campus dynamics at many of South Africa's top tertiary institutions. *The Daily Maverick.* Retrieved from: https://www.dailymaverick.co.za/opinionista/2018-08-27-from-the-inside-a-tale-of-two-meetings/

Chapter 8

Beet, P., & Le Grange, L. (2005). 'Africanising' assessment practices: Does the notion of Ubuntu hold any promise? *South African Journal of Higher Education, 19*(S), 1197-1207.

Bencsik, A., Horváth-Csikós, G., & Jubász, T. (2016). Y and Z generations at workplaces. *Journal of Competitiveness, 8*(3), 90-106. https://doi.org/10.7441/joc. 2016. 03.06

Benson, J., & Brown, M. (2011). Generations at work: are there differences and do they matter? *International Journal of Human Resource Management, 22*(9), 1843-1865. doi: 10.1080/09585192.2011.573966

Booysen, L. L. (2007). Societal power shifts and changing social identities in South Africa: Workplace implications. *South African Journal of Economic and Management Sciences, 10*(1), 1-20.

Bornman, D. A. J. (2019). Gender-based leadership perceptions and preferences of Generation Z as future business leaders in South Africa. *Acta Commercii, 19*(1), a708. https://doi.org/ 10.4102/ac.v19i1.708

Breier, M. (2009). Introduction. In J. Erasmus & M. Breier (Eds.). *Skills shortages in South Africa: Case studies of key professions* (pp. 1-21). Cape Town: HSRC Press.

Bussin, M., & Moore, A. (2012). Reward preferences for generations in selected information and communication technology companies. *South African Journal of Human Resource Management, 10*(1), http://dx.doi.org/10.4102/ sajhrm.v10i1.325

Bussin, M., & Van Rooy, D. J. (2014). Total rewards strategy for a multi-generational workforce in a financial institution. *South African Journal of Human Resource Management, 12*(1), 1-11. http://dx.doi.org/10.4102/ sajhrm.v12i1.606

Cameron, A., & Pagnattaro, M. (2017). Beyond millennials: Engaging generation Z in business law classes. *Journal of Legal Studies Education, 34*(2), 317-324.

Chartered Institute of Personnel Development. (2008). *Gen Up: How the four generations work.* Retrieved from: http://www.cipd.co.uk/subjects/dvsequl/general/_genup.htm

Chartered Institute of Personnel Development. (2016). *The Psychological Contract.* Retrieved from: http://www.cipd.co.uk/hr-resources/factsheets/psychological-contract.aspx

Chillakuri, B., & Mahanandia, R. (2018). Generation Z entering the workforce: the need for sustainable strategies in maximizing their talent. *Human Resource Management International Digest, 26*(4), 34- 38.

Cogin, J. (2012). Are generational differences in work values fact or fiction? Multi-country evidence and implications. *International Journal of Human Resource Management, 23*(11), 2268-2294.

Colakoglu, S., & Caligiuri, P. (2010). Cultural influences on Millennial MBA students' career goals: Evidence from 23 countries. In E. Ng, S. Lyons, & L. Schweitzer (Eds.). *Managing the New Workforce* (pp. 262 - 280). Cheltenham: Edward Elgar.

Conway, N., & Briner, R. B. (2005). *Understanding psychological contracts at work: A critical evaluation of theory and research.* London: Oxford University Press.

Cronley, C., & Kim, Y. K. (2017). Intentions to turnover: Testing the moderated effects of organizational culture, as mediated by job satisfaction, within the Salvation Army. *Leadership & Organization Development Journal, 38*(2), 194-209. https://doi.org/10.1108/LODJ-10-2015-0227

Deal, J., Stawiski, S., Graves, L., Gentry W., Ruderman, M., & Weber, T. (2010). Perceptions of authority and leadership: A cross-national, cross-generational investigation. In E. Ng, S. Lyons, & L. Schweitzer (Eds.). *Managing the New Workforce* (pp. 281 - 306). Cheltenham: Edward Elgar Publishing.

Deloitte. (2016). *The Deloitte Millennial survey: Winning over the next generation of leaders.* Retrieved from: http://www2.deloitte.com/content/dam/Deloitte/global/Documents/About-Deloitte/gx-millenial-survey-2016-exec-summary.pdf

Deloitte. (2019). *Deloitte Global Millennial Survey: A "generation disrupted" – South Africa results.* Retrieved from: https://www2.deloitte.com/za/en/pages/about-deloitte/articles/millennialsurvey.html

Department of Labour. (2005). *Code of Good Practice on the integration of employment equity into human   resource policies and practices.* Pretoria: Government Printers.

Dols J., Landrum P., & Weick K. L. (2010). Leading and managing an intergenerational workforce. *Creative Nursing, 16*(2), 1-8.

Edmunds, J., & Turner, B. S. (2005). Global generations: Social change in the twentieth century. *The British Journal of Sociology, 56*(4), 559-577.

Erickson, T. J. (2010). The leaders we need now. *Harvard Business Review, 88*(5), 62-66.

Ferreira, N., & Coetzee, M. (2010). Psychological career resources and organisational commitment: An investigation of high technology employees. *South African Journal of Labour Relations, 34*(2), 25-41.

Glass, A. (2007). Understanding generational differences for competitive success. *Industrial and Commercial Training, 39*(2), 98-103. http://dx.doi.org/10.1108/00197850710732424

Helvey, K. (2016). *Don't underestimate the power of lateral career moves for professional growth.* Retrieved from: https://hbr.org/2016/05/dont-underestimate-the-power-of-lateral-career-moves-for-professional-growth

Hess, N., & Jepsen, D. M. (2009). Career stage and generational differences in the psychological contract. *Career Development International, 14*(3), 261-283.

Hobart, J. W., & Sendek, H. (2014). *Gen Y now: Millennials and the evolution of leadership* (2nd ed). San Francisco, CA: Wiley and Sons.

Hoole, C., & Bonnema, J. (2015). Work engagement and meaningful work across generational cohorts. *SA Journal of Human Resource Management/SA Tydskrif vir Menslikehulpbronbestuur, 13*(1), 1-11. http://dx.doi.org/10.4102/ sajhrm.v13i1.681

Horwitz, F., Heng, C., Quazi, H. A., Nonkwelo, C., Roditi, D., & van Eck, P. (2006). Human resource strategies for managing knowledge workers: an Afro-Asian comparative analysis. *The International Journal of Human Resource Management, 17*(5), 775-811.

Horwitz, F. M. (2013). An analysis of skills development in a transitional economy: the case of the South African labour market. *The International Journal of Human Resource Management, 24*(12), 2435-2451.

Hugo, J., Sauerman, R., Schutte, H., Schutte, D., & Van Eeden, E. (2019). Managing a culturally diverse workforce: A managerial accountant perspective. *International Journal of Management Excellence, 13*(2), 1904-1909.

Joubert, Y. T. (2017). Workplace diversity in South Africa: Its qualities and management. *Journal of Psychology in Africa, 27*(4), 367-371, DOI:10.1080/14330237.2017.1347760

Kupperschmidt, B. (1998). Understanding generation X employees. *Journal of Nursing Association, 28*(12), 36-43.

Kupperschmidt, B. (2000). Multi-generation employees: Strategies for effective management. *Health Care Manager, 19*(1), 65-76.

Lancaster, L., & Stillman, D. (2002). *When generations collide. Who they are. Why they clash. How to solve the generational puzzle at work*. New York: Harper Collins Publishers Inc.

Lappeman, J., Egan, P., & Coppin, V. (2020). Time for an update: Proposing a new age segmentation for South Africa. *Management Dynamics, 29*(1), 2-16.

Lee, M. C. C., Idris, M. A., & Tuckey, M. (2019). Supervisory coaching and performance feedback as mediators of the relationships between leadership styles, work engagement, and turnover intention. *Human Resource Development International, 22*(3), 257-282. doi:10.1080/13678868.2018.1530170

Lloyd, S., Roodt, G., & Odendaal, A. (2011). Critical elements in defining work-based identity in post-Apartheid South Africa. *South African Journal of Industrial Psychology, 37*(1), 1-15.

Lub, X., Nije Bijvank, M., Matthijs Bal, P., Blomme, R., & Schalk, R. (2012). Different or alike? Exploring the psychological contract and commitment of different generations of hospitality workers. *International Journal of Contemporary Hospitality Management, 24*(4), 553-573.

Lyons, S., Duxbury, L., & Higgins, C. (2005). Are gender differences in basic human values a generational phenomenon? *Sex Roles, 53*(9/10), 763-778.

Macky, K., Gardner, D., & Forsyth, S. (2008). Generational differences at work: Introduction and overview. *Journal of Managerial Psychology, 23*(8), 857-861.

Malila, V. (2015). Being a Born Free: The misunderstandings and missed opportunities facing young South Africans. *Rhodes Journalism Review, 35*, 127-135.

Markova, G., & Ford, C. (2011). Is money the panacea? Rewards for knowledge workers. *International Journal of Productivity and Performance Management, 60*(8), 813-823.

Martins, N., & Martins, E. C. (2010). Assessing Millennials in the South African work context. In E. Ng, S. Lyons, & L. Schweitzer (Eds.). *Managing the New Workforce* (pp. 152-177). Cheltenham: Edward Elgar Publishing.

Mattes, R. (2011). *The "Born Frees": The prospects for generational change in post-apartheid South Africa.* Retrieved from: http://afrobarometer.org/sites/default/files/publications/Working%20paper/AfropaperNo131.pdf

Mbigi, L. (2000). *In search of the African business renaissance: An African cultural perspective.* Johannesburg: Knowledge Resources.

McKechnie, I., & Bridgens, S. (2008). Engineering skills – key to effective service delivery in South Africa's electricity distribution sector. In *2008 Electricity Distribution Maintenance Summit* (pp. 1-9). Johannesburg: South African Institute of Electrical Engineers (SAIEE).

Metcalf, O. (2011). *Motivation of technical knowledge workers in a high-tech development environment* (Unpublished Master's thesis). Cape Town: University of Cape Town.

Moroko, L., & Uncles, M. (2008). Characteristics of successful employer brands. *Journal of Brand Management, 16*(4), 160-175.

Mula, A. (2014). *The impact of employment equity legislation on employee engagement within Generation Y* (Unpublished Master's thesis). Pretoria: University of Pretoria.

Nelson, T. D. (2016). The Age of Ageism. *Journal of Social Issues, 72*(1), 191-198. doi:10.1111/josi.12162

Ng, E. S. W., Schweitzer, L., & Lyons, S. T. (2010). New generation, great expectations: A field study of the millennial generation. *Journal of Business and Psychology, 25*, 281-292.

Ng, T. W. H., & Feldman, D. C. (2010). Idiosyncratic deals and organizational commitment. *Journal of Vocational Behavior, 76*(3), 419-427.

Nnambooze, B. E., & Parumasur, S. B. (2016). Understanding the multigenerational workforce: Are the generations significantly different or similar? *Corporate Ownership & Control, 13*(2), 224-237.

Opris, I., & Cenusa, V. (2017). Subject-spotting experimental method for gen Z. *TEM Journal, 6*(4), 83-692.

Ozkan, M., & Solmaz, B. (2015). The changing face of the employees – generation Z and their perceptions of work (a study applied to university students). *Procedia Economics and Finance, 26*, 476-483.

Papavasileioua, E. F., & Lyons, S.T. (2015). A comparative analysis of the work values of Greece's 'Millennial' generation. *The International Journal of Human Resource Management, 26*(17), 2166-2186. doi:10.1080/09585192.2014.985325

Rasch, R., & Kowske, B. (2010). Will Millennials save the world through work? International generational differences in the relative importance of corporate social responsibility and business ethics to turnover intentions. In E. Ng, S. Lyons, & L. Schweitzer (Eds.). *Managing the New Workforce* (pp. 222-241). Cheltenham: Edward Elgar Publishing.

Republic of South Africa. (1998). *Employment Equity Act, No. 55.* Pretoria: Government Printer.

Ronnie, L. (2016). *Age and intention to leave: The case of South African public sector employees.* 10th International Business Conference, Langebaan, Cape Town.

Rousseau, D. M, Hornung, S., & Tai, G. K. (2009). Idiosyncratic deal: testing propositions on timing, content, and the employment relationship [Electronic Version]. *Journal of Vocational Behavior, 74*(3), 338-348.

Rousseau, D. M. (2001). The idiosyncratic deal: flexibility versus fairness? *Organisational Dynamics,* 29(4), 260-273.

Shrivastavaa, S., Selvarajaha, C., Meyerb, D., & Dorasamy, N. (2014). Exploring excellence in leadership perceptions amongst South African managers. *Human Resource Development International, 17*(1), 47-66. http://dx.doi.org/10.1080/13678868.2013.8 57510

Smola, K., & Sutton, C. (2002). Generational differences: Revisiting generational work values for the new millennium. *Journal of Organizational Behavior, 23*(4), 363-382.

South African National Treasury. (2020). *Budget Review 2020.* Retrieved from: http://www. treasury.gov.za/documents/national%20budget/2020/review/FullBR.pdf

Southard, G., & Lewis, J. (2004). Building a workplace that recognizes generational diversity. *Public Management, 86,* 8-12.

Statistics South Africa. (2019). *Quarterly Labour Force Survey: 2019 Quarter 2.* Retrieved from: https://www. statssa.gov.za/publications/P0302/P03022018.pdf.

Tutu, D. (2000). *No future without forgiveness.* Johannesburg: Rider Books.

Van der Walt, S., & Du Plessis, T. (2010). Leveraging multi-generational workforce values in interactive information societies. *South African Journal of Information Management, 12*(1), pp. 1-9. DOI: 10.4102/sajim.v12i1.441

Vetter, A. (2017). Managing Generation Z: These digital natives are surprisingly like Baby Boomers. *Accounting Today, 31*(7), 28.

Weick, K. L. (2003). Faculty for the millennium: Changes needed to attract the emerging workforce into nursing. *Journal of Nursing Education, 42,* 151-160.

Weick, K. L., Prydun, M., & Walsh, T. (2002). What the emerging workforce wants in its leaders. *Journal of Nursing Scholarship, 34*(3), 283-288.

Wilson, B., Squires, M., Widger, K., Cranley, L., & Tourangeau, A. (2008). Job satisfaction among a multigenerational nursing workforce. *Journal of Nursing Management, 16,* 716-723.

Chapter 9

April, K., Ephraim, N., & Peters, K. (2012). Diversity management in South Africa: Inclusion, identity, intention, power and expectations. *African Journal of Business, 6*(2), 1749-1759.

Campbell, C., & MacPhail, C. (2002). Peer education, gender and the development of critical consciousness: participatory HIV prevention by South African youth. *Social Science & Medicine,* 55(2), 331-345.

CCoLAB. (2019). *The Creative Change Laboratory Journey* [Motion Picture].

CDP. (2020). *About us.* Retrieved from: https://www.cdptrust.org/about.html

Freire, P. (2007). *Pedagogy of the Oppressed.* New York: The Continuum International Publishing Group.

Giesler, M. (2017). Teaching Note—Theatre of the Oppressed and Social Work Education: Radicalizing the Practice Classroom. *Journal of Social Work Education, 53*(2), 347-353.

Halberstam, J. (2011). *The Queer Art of Failure.* Durham: Duke University Press.

Hoffman, E. (2004). *After Such Knowledge: Memory, History and the Legacy of the Holocaust.* London: Secker and Warburg.

Johnson-Castle, P. (n.d.). The Group Areas act of 1950. Retrieved from: https://www.sahistory.org.za/article/group-areas-act-1950

Kaminer, D., & Shabalala, N. (2019). Developing a student mental health policy for a South African university: Consultation, contestation and compromise. *South African Journal of Higher Education, 33*(5), 196-209.

Kellerman, N.P.F. (2001). The long-term psychological effects and treatment of holocaust trauma. *Journal of Loss and Trauma, International Perspectives on Stress & Coping, 6*(3), 197-218.

Khan, G. H. (2013). Using drama to (dis)locate queer sexuality. In D. A. Francis. *Sexuality, Society and Pedagogy* (pp. 133-147). Bloemfontein: SUN MeDIA.

Khan, G. H. (2014). Cross-border art and queer incursion: On working with queer youth from southern Africa. *Agenda, 28*(4), 125-137.

Khan, G. H. (2018). The domestic desires of queer youth: narratives of domesticity and dissent of queer students at three South African universities. In T. Morison, I. Lynch, & V. Reddy. *Queer Kinship* (pp. 74-89). Pretoria: Unisa.

Khan, G.H. (2019). The Creative Change Laboratory Journey. Retrieved from: https://www.youtube.com/watch?v=IV1ZAYf0ZUs

Kumashiro, K. K. (2000). Toward a theory of anti-oppressive education. *Review of Educational Research, 70*(1), 25-53. DOI:10.3102/00346543070001025.

Marnell, J., & Khan, G. H. (2016). *Creative Resistance: participatory methods for engaging queer youth.* Johannesburg: Gay and Lesbian Memory in Action.

Mkhize, N. (2004). Psychology: An African perspective. In D. Hook (Ed.). *Critical Psychology* (pp. 24-52). Cape Town: UCT Press.

Mkhize, N. (2008). Ubuntu and Harmony: An African approach to morality and ethics. In R. Nicholson (Ed.). *Persons in community: African ethics in a global culture* (pp. 35-44). Scottsville: University of KwaZulu Natal Press.

Prager, J. (2010). Lost childhood, lost generations: The intergenerational transmission of trauma. *Journal of Human Rights, 2*(2), 173-181.

Runswick Cole, K., & Goodley, D. (2013). Resilience: A Disability and Community Psychology Approach. *Social and Personality Psychology Compass, 7*(2), 67-78.

Seidman, J., & Bonasa, N. (2008). *Tsogang Basadi: Finding women's voice from South Africa's political conflict.* Retrieved from: http://www.judyseidman.com/tsogang%20basadi%20paper.html

Seidman, J., & Schaer, C. (2010). *Art as Advocacy: Breaking the Silence - Raising Women's Voices Through* Visual Media. Johannesburg: Curriculum Development Project Trust.

Seidman, J., & Schaer, C. (2011). *Naledi Yameso: Women Support Women - Claiming Our Lives Through the Visual Arts.* Johannesburg: Curriculum Development Project Trust.

South African History Online. (2020). *Group Areas Act.* Retrieved from: https://www.sahistory.org.za/article/group-areas-act-1950

Wade, A. (1997). Small Acts of Living: Everyday Resistance to Violence and other forms of oppression. *Contemporary Family Therapy ,19*(1), 23–39.

Wright, T. & Wright, K. (2013). Art for women's sake: Understanding feminist art therapy as didactic practice re-orientation. *International Practice Development Journal, 3*(5), 1-8.

Zembylas, M. (2015). 'Pedagogy of discomfort' and its ethical implications: the tensions of ethical violence in social justice education. *Ethics and Education, 10*(2), 163-174.

Chapter 10

Amin, M., MacLachlan, M., Mannan, H., El Tayeb, S., El Khatim, A., ... & Schneider, M. (2011). EquiFrame: A framework for analysis of the inclusion of human rights and vulnerable groups in health policies. *Health and Human Rights, 13*(2), 82-101.

Battle, M. (2010). Ubuntu: The Western World's Contribution. *Sewanee Theological Review, 53*(4), 1-12.

Berghs, M. (2017). Practices and discourses of ubuntu: Implications for an African model of disability? *African Journal of Disability, 6*, 1–8. DOI: 10.4102/ajod.v6.292

Boon, M. (1996). *The African way - The power of interactive leadership.* Johannesburg: Struik Publishers.

Cardinal, L. (2001). What is an Indigenous perspective? *Canadian Journal of Native Education, 25*(2), 180. [Online]. Retrieved from: http://proquest.umi.com/pqdweb?-did=128556851andFmt=7&clientId=8429&RQT=309&VName=PQD.

Chilisa, B. (2012). *Indigenous Research Methodologies.* Thousand Oaks, California: Sage Publications Incorporated.

Cobbah, J. A. M. (1987). African values and the Human Rights Debate: An African perspective. *Human Rights Quarterly, 9*(3), 309-331. [Online]. DOI: 10.2307/761878

Connell, R. (2011). Southern bodies and disability: Re-thinking concepts. *Third World Quarterly, 32*(8), 1369-1381. [Online]. DOI: 10.1080/01436597.2011.614799

Danseco, E. R. (1997). Parental beliefs on childhood disability: Insights on culture, child development and intervention. *International Journal of Phytoremediation, 44*(1), 41-52. [Online]. DOI: 10.1080/0156655970440104

Department of Higher Education and Training. (2019). Annual Report 2018/19. Retrieved from: https://www.dhet.gov.za/Commissions%20Reports/DHET_Annual_Report_201819_WEB.pdf

Devlieger, P. J. (1999). Frames of reference in African proverbs on disability. *International Journal of Disability, Development and Education, 46*(4), 439–451.

Dreyer, J. S. (2015). Ubuntu. *International Journal of Practical Theology, 19*(1), 189-209. [Online]. DOI: 10.1515/ijpt-2015-0022

Dupré, M. (2012). Disability Culture and Cultural Competency in Social Work. *Social Work Education, 31*(2), 168-183. [Online]. DOI: 10.1080/02615479.2012.644945

Durante, C. (2009). Indigenous Pluralism from Human Rights to Bioethics. *Journal of Religious Ethics, 37*(3), 513-529.

Dura-Vila, G. (2010). A gain not a loss: Parental beliefs and family life, Children with Intellectual Disabilities. *Clinical Child Psychiatry, 15*(2), 171-84.

Easby, A. (2016). Indigenous Research Methodologies: Global Thematic Review on Training in

Community-Based Research. Retrieved from: https://unescochair-cbrsr.org/pdf/resource/kp/UVic_IRM.pdf

Edwards, S. D. (2011). A Psychology of Indigenous Healing in Southern Africa. *Journal of Psychology on Africa, 21*(3), 335–348. [Online]. DOI: 10.1080/14330237.2011.10820466

Gade, C. B. N. (2012). What is Ubuntu? Different Interpretations among South Africans of African Descent. *South African Journal of Philosophy, 31*(3), 484-503. [Online]. DOI: 10.1080/02580136.2012.10751789

Garland-Thomson, R. (2005). Disability and Representation. *Publications of the Modern Language Association of America 120*(2):522-527. Retrieved from: www.jstor.org/stable/25486178

Gilbert, J., & Lennox, C. (2019). Towards new development paradigms: The United Nations Declaration on the Rights of Indigenous Peoples as a tool to support self-determined development. *International Journal of Human Rights, 23*(1–2), 104-124. [Online]. DOI: 10.1080/13642987.2018.1562921

Gona, J. K., Newton, C. R., Hartley, S., & Bunning, K. (2018). Persons with disabilities as experts-by experience: Using personal narratives to affect community attitudes in Kilifi, Kenya. *BMC International Health Human Rights, 18*(1), 18. https://doi.org/10.1186/s12914-018-0158-2

Gona, J. K., Mung'ala-Odera, V., Newton, C. R., & Hartley, S. (2010). Caring for children with disabilities in Kilifi, Kenya: what is the carer's experience? *Childcare, health and development, 37*(2), 175-183.

Gouws, A., & Van Zyl, M. (2014). Feminist Ethics of Care through a Southern Lens. In V. Reddy, S. Meye, T. Shefer & T. Meyiwa (Eds.). *Care in Context: Transnational Gender Perspectives* (pp. 99-125). Cape Town: HSRC Press.

Grech, S., & Soldatic, K. (2015). Disability and colonialism: (dis)encounters and anxious intersectionalities. *Social Identities, 21*(1), 1-5. [Online]. DOI: 10.1080/13504630.2014.995394

Grut, L., Mji, G., Braathen, S. H., & Ingstad, B. (2012). Accessing community health services: challenges faced by poor people with disabilities in a rural community in South Africa. *African Journal of Disability, 1*(19), 7. doi:10.4102/ajod.v1i1.19

Guba, E. G., & Lincoln, Y. S. (2005). Paradigmatic controversies, contradictions, and emerging confluences. In N.K. Denzin & Y.S. Lincoln. *The Sage Handbook of Qualitative Research* (3rd ed.). Thousand Oaks, CA: Sage, pp. 191–216.

Hanna, P., & Vanclay, F. (2013). Human rights, Indigenous peoples and the concept of Free, Prior and Informed Consent. *Impact Assessment and Project Appraisal, 31*(2), 146-157. [Online]. DOI: 10.1080/14615517.2013.780373

Harpur, P. (2012). Embracing the new disability rights paradigm: The importance of the convention on the rights of persons with disabilities. *Disability and Society, 27*(1), 1-14. [Online]. DOI: 10.1080/09687599.2012.631794

Healy, K., Hampshire, A., & Ayres, L. (2003). *Engaging communities for sustainable change: Promoting resilience.* Retrieved from: http://www.bensoc.org.au/research/engaging_communities.html.

Hellander, E. (1992). *Prejudice and dignity: An introduction to community – based rehabilitation.* New York: United Nations Development Programme.

Hollinsworth, D. (2013). Decolonizing Indigenous disability in Australia. *Disability and Society, 28*(5), 601-615. [Online]. DOI: 10.1080/09687599.2012.717879

Ingstad, B. (1997). *Community Based Rehabilitation Centre in Botswana: The Myth of the Hidden Disabled.* Lewiston, N.Y: Mellen Press Ltd. pp: 187, 195, 198.

Ingstad, B. (2007). Seeing disability and Human rights in the Local context. Botswana revisited. In B. Ingstad & S. R. Whyte (Eds.). *Disability in Local and Global Worlds.* Los Angeles: University of California Press.

Jansen, G. (1973). *The doctor-patient relationship in an African tribal society.* Assen, Netherlands: Koninklijke Van Gorcum. B.V.

Joan, C. (2010). Creating Caring Institutions: Politics, Plurality, and Purpose. *Ethics and Social Welfare, 4*(2), 158-171.

Keane, M. (2008). *Science Learning and Research in a Framework of Ubuntu.* Retrieved from: https://www.researchgate.net/publication/291485664

King, J. A., Brough, M., & Knox, M. (2014). Negotiating disability and colonisation: The lived experience of Indigenous Australians with a disability. *Disability and Society, 29*(5), 738–750. [Online]. DOI: 10.1080/09687599.2013.864257

MacLachlan, M., Amin, M., Mannan, H., El Tayeb, S., Bedri, N., Swartz, L., Munthali, A., Van Rooy, G., & McVeigh, J. (2012). Inclusion and human rights in health policies: Comparative and benchmarking analysis of 51 policies from Malawi, Sudan, South Africa and Namibia. *PLoS ONE, 7*(5), e35864. [Online]. DOI: 10.1371/journal.pone.0035864

Maistry, M., & Vasi, S. (2010). Social Development, including Social Grants. *The Eastern Cape Basic Services Delivery and SocioEconomic Trends Series: 12.* East London, South Africa: Fort Hare Institute of Social and Economic Research (FHISER).

Martin, K., & Mirraboopa, B. (2003). Ways of knowing, being and doing: A theoretical framework and methods for indigenous and indigenist research. *Journal of Australian Studies, 27*(76), 203-214. [Online]. DOI: 10.1080/14443050309387838

McKenzie, J., & Ohajunwa, C. (2017). Commentary Understanding disability in Nigeria: a commentary on 'Country profile: intellectual and developmental disability in Nigeria'. *Tizard Learning Disability Review, 22*(2), 94-98. [Online]. DOI: 10.1108/TLDR-02-2017-0008

McKenzie, J., Mji, G., & Gcaza, S. (2014). With or without us? An audit of disability research in the southern African region. *African Journal of Disability, 3*(2), 3-8. [Online]. DOI: 10.4102/ajod.v3i2.76

Meekosha, H. (2008). Contextualizing disability: developing southern/global theory. *4th Biennial Disability Studies Conference*. September 2008. Lancaster, UK: Lancaster University.

Meekosha, H. (2011). Decolonising disability: Thinking and acting globally. *Disability and Society, 26*(6), 667-682. [Online]. DOI: 10.1080/09687599.2011.602860

Meekosha, H., & Soldatic, K. (2011). Human rights and the global South: The case of disability. *Third World Quarterly, 32*(8), 1383-1397. [Online]. DOI: 10.1080/01436597.2011.614800

Metz, T. (2007). Toward an African moral theory. *Journal of Political Philosophy, 15*(3), 321–341. [Online]. DOI: 10.1111/j.1467-9760.2007.00280.x

Mji, G., Rhoda, A., Statham, S., & Joseph, C. (2017). A protocol for the methodological steps used to evaluate the alignment of rehabilitation services in the Western Cape, South Africa with the National Rehabilitation Policy. *BMC Health Services Research, 17*(1), 1-11. [Online]. DOI: 10.1186/s12913-017-2141-3

Mpofu, E., & Harley, D. A. (2002). Disability and rehabilitation in Zimbabwe: Lessons and implications for rehabilitation practice in the U.S. *Journal of Rehabilitation, 68*(4), 26-33.

Munsaka, E., & Charnley, H. (2013). We Do not have Chiefs who are Disabled: Disability, Development and Culture in a Continuing Complex Emergency. *Disability & Society, 28*(6), 756-769. [Online]. DOI: 10.1080/09687599.2013.802221

Murugami, M. W. (2009). Disability and Identity. *Disability Studies Quarterly, 29*(4). Retrieved from http://www.dsq-sds.org/article/view/979/1173

National Department of Health (2017). *Annual Report 2016/17*. Retrieved from: https://nationalgovernment.co.za/department_annual/181/2017-department:-health-annual-report.pdf

Ndlovu, H. L. (2016). African beliefs concerning people with disabilities: Implications for theological education. *Journal of Disability and Religion, 20*(1), 29-39. [Online]. DOI: 10.1080/23312521.2016.1152942

Ned, L., Cloete, L., & Mji, G. (2017). The experiences and challenges faced by rehabilitation community service therapist within the South African Primary Healthcare health system. *African Journal of Disability, 6*(0), a311. https://doi.org/10.4102/ajod.v6i0.311

Nielsen, A. M., Stuart, L. A., & Gorman, D. (2014). Confronting the cultural challenge of the whiteness of nursing: Aboriginal registered nurses' perspectives. *Contemporary Nurse, 48*(2), 190-196. [Online]. DOI: 10.1080/10376178.2014.11081940

Nwanze, I., & Sciences, R. (2016). *How can we include Disability Issues in Undergraduate Curricula at the University of Cape Town?* (Doctoral dissertation). Cape Town: University of Cape Town.

Ohajunwa, C. (2019). *Understanding, interpretation and expression of spirituality and its influence on wellbeing: A case study of an indigenous South African community* (Doctoral dissertation). Stellenbosch, South Africa: Stellenbosch University.

Owusu-Ansah, F. E., & Mji, G. (2013). African indigenous knowledge and research. *African Journal of Disability, 2*(1), 1-5. [Online]. DOI: 10.4102/ajod.v2i1.30

Sen, A. (2006). Human Rights and the Limits of Law. *Cardozo Law Review, 27*(6), 2913-2927. [Online]. DOI: 110.1163/22112596-01702018

Series, L. (2015). The development of disability rights under international law: from charity to human rights. *Disability & Society, 30*(10), 1590-1593. [Online]. DOI: 10.1080/09687599.2015.1066975

Setume, S. D. (2016). Myths and beliefs about disabilities: Implications for educators and counsellors. *Journal of Disability and Religion, 20*(1), 62-76. [Online]. DOI: 10.1080/23312521.2016.1152938

Shakespeare, T., & Watson, N. (2002). The social model of disability: An outdated ideology? (2nd ed.). *Research in Social Science and Disability, 2*, 9-28.

Sherry, K. (2016). *Occupations of citizenship: The missing layer in empowered engagement between rural people with disabilities and primary healthcare workers in South Africa.* Cape Town: School of Public Health and Family Medicine, University of Cape Town.

Sherwood, J. (2017). Colonisation – It's bad for your health: The context of Aboriginal health. *Contemporary Nurse, 46*(1):28-40. [Online]. DOI: 10.5172/conu.2013.46.1.28

Soldatic, K. (2015). Postcolonial reproductions: disability, indigeneity and the formation of the white masculine settler state of Australia. *Social Identities, 21*(1), 53-68. [Online]. DOI: 10.1080/13504630.2014.995352

Stammers, N. (1995). A Critique of Social Approaches to Human Rights. *Human Rights Quarterly, 17*(3), 488-508. [Online]. DOI: 10.1353/hrq.1995.0033

Stienstra, D., & Ashcroft T. (2010). Voyaging on the seas of spirit: an ongoing journey towards understanding disability and humanity. *Disability & Society, 25*(2), 191-203. doi: 10.1080/09687590903534411

Stone-MacDonald, A. (2012). Cultural Beliefs about Disability in Practice: Experiences at a Special School in Tanzania. *International Journal of Disability, Development and Education, 59*(4), 393-407. [Online]. DOI: 10.1080/1034912X.2012.723947

Surender, R., Ntshongwana, P., Noble, M., & Wright, G. (2007). *Employment and Social Security: A Qualitative Study of Attitudes towards the Labour Market and Social Grants.* Oxford: Department of Social Policy and Social Work, University of Oxford.

The Constitutional Assembly. (1996). *The Constitution of the Republic of South Africa.* Cape Town: CTP Web printers.

Toebes, B. (1999). Towards an Improved Understanding of the International Human Right to Health. *Human Rights Quarterly, 21*(3), 661-679.

United Nations. (2006). *Convention on the rights of persons with disabilities.* Retrieved from: http://www.un.org/disabilities/.

Van Rooy, G., Amadhila, E.M., Mufune, P., Swartz, L., Mannan, H., & MacLachlan, M. (2012). Perceived barriers to accessing health services among people with disabilities in rural northern Namibia. *Disability and Society*, *27*(6), 761-775. [Online]. DOI: 10.1080/09687599.2012.686877

Vergunst R., Swartz L, Hem K-G., Eide AH., Mannan H., MacLachlan M., Mji, G., Braathen, SH., & Schneider, M. (2017). Access to health care for persons with disabilities in rural South Africa. *BMC Health Services Research*, *17*, 741. https://doi.org/10.1186/s12913-017-2674-5

Wanless, D. (2007). Ubuntu - we all belong to each other. *International Congregational Journal*, *7*(1), 117-119. [Online]. Retrieved from: http://search.ebscohost.com/login.aspx?direct=true&db=aph&AN=28086416&site=ehost-live%5Cnhttp://0-content.ebscohost.com.libraries.colorado.edu/ContentServer.asp?T=P&P=AN&K=28086416&S=R&D=aph&EbscoContent=dGJyMMTo50Sep644v+bwOLCmr02ep7JSsqu4TLaWxWXS&Content.

World Health Organization. (2010). *CBR guidelines*. Retrieved from: http://www.who.int/disabilities/cbr/guideline/en/

World Health Organization. (2011). World report on disability 2011. *American Journal of Physical Medicine Rehabilitation*, *91*, 549. [Online]. DOI: 10.1136/ip.2007.018143

Chapter 11

African Union. (2015). *Agenda 2063: The Africa we want*. Retrieved from: https://au.int/en/Agenda2063/popular_version.

Agang, S.B., Hendriks, H.J., & Forster, D.A. (Eds.). *African Public Theology*. Carlisle: Langham Partnership: Hippo Books.

Allport, G. W. (1954). *The Nature of Prejudice*. Boston, MA: Addison-Wesley.

April, K. A., Makgoba, T., & Forster, D. A. (2018). Spirituality and Workplace Diversity Practices in Africa. In J. Syed, A. Klarsfeld, F.W. Ngunjiri, & C.E.J. Härtel (Eds.). *Religious Diversity in the Workplace* (pp. 223–263). Cambridge: Cambridge University Press.

Aronson, E. (1978). *The jigsaw classroom*. Thousand Oaks, CA: Sage.

Booysen, L. (2013). Societal power shifts and changing social identities in South Africa: workplace implications. *South African Journal of Economic and Management Sciences*, *10*(1), 1-20. DOI: 10.4102/sajems.v10i1.533

Brewer, M. B., & Kramer, R. M. (1985). The Psychology of Intergroup Attitudes and Behavior. *Annual Review of Psychology*, *36*(1), 219-243. DOI: 10.1146/annurev.ps.36.020185.001251.

Carrim, N. M. H. (2015). Managing religious diversity in the South African workplace. In S. Groschl & R. Bendl (Eds.). *Religious Diversity in the Workplace* (pp. 113-136). Farnham, UK: Gower.

Carrim, N. M. H. (2017). To be or not to be: Muslim identities in South Africa. In J. Mahadevan & J.C. Mayer (Eds.). *Islam, workplace diversity and reflexive HRM* (pp. 77–94). New York, NY: Routledge.

Dixon, J., Durrheim, K., & Tredoux, C. (2005). Beyond the Optimal Contact Strategy: A Reality Check for the Contact Hypothesis. *American Psychologist, 60*(7), 697–711. DOI: 10.1037/0003-066X.60.7.697

Dovidio, J. F., Glick, P., & Rudman, L. (2008). *On the Nature of Prejudice.* Hoboken, NJ: John Wiley & Sons.

Du Toit, C. W. (Ed.). (2004). *The Integrity of the Human Person in an African Context: Perspectives from Science and Religion.* Pretoria: Research Institute for Theology and Religion.

Forster, D. A., Gunner, G., & Gerle, E. (Eds.). (2019). *Freedom of Religion at Stake: Competing claims among Faith Traditions, States and Persons.* Church of Sweden Research Series no. 18. Eugene, OR: Wipf & Stock Publishers.

Forster, D. A. (2018). Translation and a politics of forgiveness in South Africa? What black Christians believe, and white Christians do not seem to understand. *Stellenbosch Theological Journal.* 14(2):77–94. DOI: http://dx.doi.org/10.17570/stj.2018.v4n2.a04.

Forster, D. A. (2019a). *The (Im)possibility of Forgiveness: An Empirical Intercultural Bible Reading of Matthew 18.15-35.* Eugene, OR: Wipf and Stock Publishers.

Forster, D. A. (2019b). From "prophetic witness" to "prophets of Doom"? The contested role of religion in the South African public sphere. In D.A. Forster, E. Gerle & G. Gunner (Eds.). *Freedom of Religion at Stake: Competing claims among Faith Traditions, States and Persons* (pp.18-39). (Church of Sweden Research Series). Eugene, OR: Pickwick Publications.

Forster, D. A. (2019c). A Social Imagination of Forgiveness. *Journal of Empirical Theology,* 1(32), 70-88. DOI: doi:10.1163/15709256-12341387

Forster, D. A. & April, K. A. (2020). Religion and diversity management in the southern African context. In N. M. H. Carrim & L. Moolman (Eds.). *Managing diversity in the South African Workplace* (pp. 94-114). Cape Town: Van Schaik.

Gane, N. (2002). *Max Weber and Postmodern Theory: Rationalization versus Re-enchantment.* New Jersey, NJ: Springer.

Gesthuizen, M. J. W., Scheepers, P. L. H. & Savelkoul, M. J. (2011). Explaining relationships between ethnic diversity and informal social capital across European countries and regions: Tests of constrict, conflict and contact theory. *Social Science Research, 40*(4), 1091-1107.

Gledhill, R. (8 May, 2009). Churchgoing on its knees as Christianity falls out of favour. *The Times.* Retrieved from: https://www.thetimes.co.uk/article/churchgoing-on-its-knees-as-christianity-falls-out-of-favour-vrcl8gvnmqz

Hendriks, J., & Erasmus, J. (2005). Religion in South Africa: 2001 population census data. *Journal of Theology for Southern Africa, 121,* 88-111.

Hewstone, M., & Swart, H. (2011). Fifty-odd years of inter-group contact: From hypothesis to integrated theory. *British Journal of Social Psychology, 50*(3), 374-386.

Inglehart, R. (2015). *The Silent Revolution: Changing Values and Political Styles Among Western Publics.* Princeton, NJ: Princeton University Press.

Kotzé, H. (2016). Shared values in South Africa? A selection of value orientations in the field of personal ethics. *Scriptura*, *75*, 437-448.

Kotze, H. (2019). Religiosity in South Africa and Sweden: A comparison. In D. A. Forster, E. Gerle & G. Gunner (Eds.). *Freedom of Religion at Stake: Competing claims among Faith Traditions, States and Persons* (pp. 3-17). (Church of Sweden Research Series no. 18). Eugene, OR: Pickwick Publications.

Kotzé, H., & Garcia-Rivero, C. (2017). Institutions, crises, and political confidence in seven contemporary democracies. An elite-mass analysis. *Journal of Public Affairs*, *17*(1–2), 1-17.

Lugo, L., & Cooperman, A. (2010). *Tolerance and tension: Islam and Christianity in sub-Saharan Africa*. Washington, DC: Pew Research Center, pp. 1-147.

Matthee, K. (2019). Freedom of Religion: Individual? Collective? As perceived by the South African state. In D. A. Forster, E. Gerle & G. Gunner (Eds.). *Freedom of Religion at Stake: Competing claims among faith traditions, states, and persons,* (pp. 117-134). Eugene, OR: Wipf & Stock Publishers.

Mbiti, J. S. (1970). *Concepts of God in Africa*. Santa Barbara, CA: Praeger Publishers.

Mbiti, J. S. (1990). *African Religions & Philosophy*. London: Heinemann.

Mndende, N. (2019). African Traditional Religion and Freedom of Religion in South Africa. In D. A. Forster, G. Gunner & E. Gerle (Eds.). *Freedom of Religion at Stake: Competing claims among Faith Traditions, States and Persons,* (pp. 157-174). Eugene, OR: Wipf & Stock Publishers.

Norris, P., & Inglehart, R. (2011). *Sacred and Secular: Religion and Politics Worldwide*. Cambridge: Cambridge University Press.

Palm, S. (2019). Building Bridges or Walls? Human Rights and Religious Freedom. A South African History. In D. A. Forster, G. Gunner & E. Gerle (Eds.). *Freedom of Religion at Stake: Competing claims among Faith Traditions, States and Persons,* (pp. 175-198). Eugene, OR: Wipf & Stock Publishers.

Parker, J. E. (1968). The interaction of negroes and whites in an integrated church setting. *Social Forces*, *46*(3), 359-366.

Pettigrew, T. F. (1998). Intergroup contact theory. *Annual Review of Psychology*, *49*(1), 65-85.

Pettigrew, T. F., & Tropp, L. R. (2006). A meta-analytic test of intergroup contact theory. *Journal of Personality and Social Psychology*, *90*(5), 751-755.

Prozesky, M. (2013). Corruption as the new treason? Global ethics, Africa's moral wisdom and the corrupting of the future. *Ubuntu: Journal of Conflict Transformation. Special issue: corruption and public venality in Africa*, *2*(1 & 2), 7-19.

Schoeman, W.J. (2017). South African religious demography: The 2013 General Household Survey. *HTS Teologiese Studies / Theological Studies*, *73*(2), 1-7. DOI: 10.4102/hts. v73i2.3837

Sherif, M. & University of Oklahoma. Institute of Group Relations (1961). *Intergroup conflict and cooperation: The Robbers Cave experiment*. Norman, OK: University Book Exchange.

Sherif, M., Harvey, B., White, J., Hood, W. R., & Sherif, C. W. (1961). *Intergroup Conflict and Cooperation: The Robbers Cave Experiment.* Retrieved from: http://psychclassics. yorku.ca/Sherif/chap7.htm?wptouch_preview_theme=enabled

Statistics South Africa. (2014). *General Household Survey 2013.* Pretoria, South Africa: Statistics South Africa. Retrieved from: http://www.statssa.gov.za/publications/ P0318/P03182013.pdf

Swart, H., Hewstone, M., Christ, O., & Voci, A. (2010). The impact of crossgroup friendships in South Africa: Affective mediators and multigroup comparisons. *Journal of Social Issues.* 66(2):309–333.

Swart, H., Turner, R., Hewstone, M. & Voci, A. (2011). Achieving forgiveness and trust in post-conflict societies. In L. R. Tropp & R. K. Mallet (Eds.). The importance of self-disclosure and empathy. *Moving beyond prejudice reduction: Pathways to positive intergroup relations* (pp. 181-200). Washington, DC: American Psychological Association.

Taylor, C. (2004). *Modern Social Imaginaries.* Durham, NC: Duke University Press.

Taylor, C. (2009). *A Secular Age.* Cambridge, MA: Harvard University Press.

Van Der Meer, T. W., Te Grotenhuis, M. & Scheepers, P. L. (2009). Three types of voluntary associations in comparative perspective: The importance of studying associational involvement through a typology of associations in 21 European countries. *Journal of Civil Society, 5*(3), 227-241.

Ward, G. (2018). *Unimaginable: What we imagine and what we can't.* London: I.B.Tauris.

Wilcox, C. (2011). *Bias: The Unconscious Deceiver.* Bloomington, IN: Xlibris Corporation.

Williams Jr R. M. (1947). The reduction of intergroup tensions: a survey of research on problems of ethnic, racial, and religious group relations. *Social Science Research Council Bulletin, 57*(xi), 153.

Winter, S. & Burchert, L. T. (2015). *Value change in post-apartheid South Africa.* Retrieved from: http://www.kas.de/wf/doc/kas_41566-1522-2-30.pdf?150609093459

Zuma, B. (2014). Contact theory and the concept of prejudice: Metaphysical and moral explorations and an epistemological question. *Theory & Psychology, 24*(1), 40-57. DOI: 10.1177/0959354313517023.

INDEX

M

Manpower Survey, 73
microaggressions, 5, 24–25, 30, 196
multi-generational mix, 141, 148, 200

N

narratives of racism, 5, 11, 15
neoliberalism, 6, 33–34, 36, 45
new age cohorts, 134
Noluthando Home for Children with
    Disabilities, 166–168, 170
nuances of privilege, 6, 33, 41, 43, 45
numerical progress, 49, 62

O

occupational distribution by gender, 73
organisation level, 61

P

passive privilege and education, 58
pay gap, 7, 95, 97–98, 103
perceived marginalisation, 168–169
poor reporting, 61, 115
poorly distilled, 61
post-Apartheid era, 81
power systems, 6, 33, 38, 44
prevention, intervention, and research,
    114
privilege, 3, 5–6, 9, 14, 33, 36–45, 58,
    60–61, 63, 152, 154, 156, 197
privilege and exacerbates poverty, 33
privilege scale, 6, 33, 43–44
professionally qualified, 6, 48, 53–56, 62,
    93, 96
progress by gender, 56
protest, 18, 122, 124–125, 129, 133, 199
psychology of racism, 5, 26

public life, 116, 175, 177–180, 184, 186,
    192–193, 201

Q

qualified women, 7, 96
qualitative input, 60
quantitative analysis, 55

R

race and gender group, 49
race reconciliation, 5, 16
race reparations, 5, 16
racism, 5–6, 9, 11–17, 19, 22–24, 26–31,
    36, 38–39, 63, 65, 86, 89, 195–196,
    198
rape culture, 7, 116–119, 121, 124–125,
    129, 199
rape culture pyramid, 117, 124
recruitment and retention across
    generations, 136
rehabilitation, 8, 159–161, 163–164,
    166–176, 201
rehabilitation service model, 174
religion, 3, 5, 8, 19, 48, 93, 109, 163, 177–
    186, 192–193, 201
religion and existential security, 180
religion and social identity, 185
religious affiliation, 183
religious diversity and inclusion, 184–186
resistance to oppression, 154–155
role of religion, 179

S

senior management, 6, 52–53, 55–56,
    62–64, 75, 85, 95–96, 145, 184, 197
sexualities, 67, 69, 78, 88
sexualities under apartheid, 78
social change, 156